HOME IN AN

G000144093

Roy Nash's buccaneering life and times
eral different homes in Andalusia over
age of 29, with an income of £10 a week from property, he decided to quit England and find a place 'where the livin' is easy'.

Southern Spain fitted the bill perfectly. Exploring the coastline, he eventually came to the horseshoe-shaped bay known from its conformation as La Herradura, due south from Granada. It proved to be love at first sight. The climate was perfect and the cost of living suited his pocket. A glass of wine or beer cost only one and a half pesetas and a three-course meal only thirty. He found it a struggle to spend half his income, and when the thousand-peseta note came into circulation, nobody local could offer change. Not much had altered in the forty years since Gerald Brenan had settled in the nearby village of Yegen.

Roy Nash's first house was built on a small hill for 300,000 pesetas, then worth £1,800. Some years later, he bought two adjoining houses near the beach at a cost of 100,000 (£600). When development started nearby he sold these and moved to a property a short distance inland. He now lives in a small village house, his fifth home in Andalusia.

The characters he meets and introduces in this captivating environment include a handful of foreign residents, colourful groups of hippies, and a smattering of American draft-dodgers. He describes how they brought the 'Swinging Sixties', with their pop music culture, drugs and 'free-love', to a part of the world where people's morals had hitherto been rigidly controlled by Franco's church and state.

His story will fascinate anyone who has ever dreamed of living in Spain, and those who have already taken the plunge.

North from Granada has evoked the following glowing praise from reviewers. "Roy Nash's engaging account of his walk from La Herradura to Madrid makes you want to pack your knapsack and hit the road. The honesty of Nash's account, the dialogue, his willingness to engage with people, and his delight in what he finds make for an entertaining and informative read" — Rob Stokes, *Spain Magazine*. "An impressive read, for walkers and armchair travellers alike ... packed with fascinating historical facts and literary references from both Spanish and English travel writers, along with humorous personal anecdotes... Nash comes across as an old-time romantic adventurer, absorbed in the timelessness of La Mancha – a modern Don Quijote" — *The Broadsheet*, Madrid.

HOME in ANDALUSIA

Roy Nash

The Oleander Press

The Oleander Press
16 Orchard Street
Cambridge CB1 1JT
England

The Oleander Press
1133 Broadway, Suite 706
New York, N.Y. 10010
U.S.A.

ISBN 0-906672-45-7

"Oleander Travel Books" series

Typeset in Great Britain and printed and bound in India

CONTENTS

v

    In which I ask:

        Where have all the old times gone, when me and my
        mates could share
        A drink or two without no fuss and still have time to
        spare?
        Nobody had white marks on their wrists, for watches
        were obsolete.
        We didn't live to a schedule or have appointments to
        keep.

List of Illustrations

Acknowledgements

I should like to thank those who have allowed me to publish their photographs in this book: Lars Bordorgesson, Antonio de Haro Muñéz, Francisco Alaminos Rodrigo, Jan Henshall, Anna di Gesù and María del Mar Alvarez Cienfuegos.

This book would never have been completed without the aid of three people: my son, Oliver, who has regularly supplemented his pocket money by helping me unravel the mysteries of the computer; our IT guru, John Tarry, who came to the rescue when all was thought lost; and my wife, Zenda, whose patience has been severely tested at times. I am very grateful to them all.

I am also greatly indebted to Philip Ward, my editor, whose advice has, as ever, been invaluable.

1

1966

*In which I set off for Spain accompanied by the
Bloch-Watsons.*

There they are! Driving through Victoria Station's car park gates
I spot them at once, standing together at a pre-arranged meeting place with the early morning hustle and bustle going on all
around them and three large suitcases and a hold-all by their
side. The larger of the two, Mrs Cynthia Bloch-Watson, resplendent in light-grey fur coat with matching Cossack-style hat,
looks as though she's waiting for a coach and horses to take
her to the Kremlin Ball. She looms head and shoulders above
the dapper man at her side. He stands bolt upright, shoulders
back to attention, both hands held in front of him to grasp a
shiny leather briefcase. As I pull up in my battered old ex-army
Land Rover, their anxious expressions seem to change from
expectation to disbelief. John Bloch-Watson quickly recovers
from his initial shock and makes an attempt to smile a greeting,
but his wide-eyed, statuesque wife continues to stare. It looks
for a moment as though they might decide to call the whole
thing off so, before they have a chance to consider this option, I
jump out, stow the luggage, help them aboard and make straight
off.

This elderly couple had been the first to answer my newspaper advertisement offering a lift to southern Spain to anyone
willing to help out with expenses. During our little chat on the
telephone I tried to describe the sort of vehicle they would be
sharing but, as I later learned, the Bloch-Watsons had envis-

aged something quite different. The word 'Rover' had brought to Cynthia's mind the luxurious Rover P5 saloon, the model chosen by the Queen!

On the drive south to Dover, nobody says very much. I warn Cynthia, who sits on the far end of the bench seat, to keep her elbow well away from the door handle: it has a loose catch. On hearing this, she glowers, then slides more towards me, squashing her poor husband into my side. When I glance down, all I can see of him are two beady eyes peeping out from the folds of a fur coat. He reminds me of a baby seal pup.

The Land Rover, bought from a scrap-metal merchant for £90, has two major faults. With broken suspension springs over the rear wheels and a defunct heater, the 1200 kilometre (750 mile) drive through France that late November proves both bitterly cold and most uncomfortable. From Calais we take the N 1 to Abbeville, then the N 28 to Rouen, the N 154 to Chartres and, finally, the N 10, passing through Tours, Poitiers, Angoulême, Bordeaux and Biarritz to cross the border into Spain at Hendaye. Little John braves the freezing temperatures to stay with me up front but his poor wife, in an effort to keep warm, lies on the floor at the back, wrapped in my sleeping bag and her coat, by now not-so-light-grey. The furry hat, I notice, has become her foot muffler.

On the other side of the frontier, we bump our way along the badly-surfaced N 1, via Vitoria, Burgos, Aranda de Duero and Puerto de Somosierra to arrive, 600 kilometres further south, in Madrid. We are half-way through Spain. After this, road conditions become worse still. The state of the N 4, which passes through Aranjuez, Puerto Lápice, Manzanares, Bailén, Jaén and on to Granada, deteriorates so much that each time we pass over a particularly deep pothole, four distinct noises can be heard coming from behind. First, a hard, metallic 'clank!' as the Land Rover body crunches down on its chassis, almost instantly followed by the combined 'thud!' of the three suitcases. The coinciding duller, heavier 'plump!' of padded flesh is accompanied by a low 'aaah.'

Road conditions become worse still

Before long, further effects of this constant jolting become apparent. Among other things, the bolts holding our bench seat in place rattle loose and have to be tightened from time to time; one side mirror, the rear-view mirror and both rear-light covers fall off; and the exhaust pipe shakes free from its bracket. Once retrieved, this has to be tied back in place with shoelaces removed from John's spare shoes. At one stage, Cynthia's discomfort is heightened by a sudden fierce wind which rips holes in our canvas awning, making it flap about, threatening to disintegrate completely.

The man at my side may be short in stature, but he is certainly not short of breath. He makes up for his earlier smothered silence, between London and the Channel port, by blowing his own trumpet almost non-stop for the rest of our journey south. His discourse, for the most part, comes in the form of lectures.

John Bloch-Watson turns out to be a cantankerous, though intriguing, character who has spent much of his life in South America. Disillusioned at the age of 65, when what he calls the 'gangsters' took over from the *Peronistas* in Argentina, John sold his cattle ranch, returned to the UK, promptly married Cynthia and tried to settle in London. Now, at 73, English weather has finally defeated him. City dampness has brought on chronic rheumatism and doctors advocate moving to a warmer climate. He speaks fluent Spanish, of course, and this fact, combined with his attitude towards the country's present regime, leads him to believe that the sunny south of Spain may well be the answer. With proceeds from the sale of his house, he intends to buy a property there. This will be a reconnaissance trip. He starts off by telling me more about himself.

In 1915, at the age of 22, Lord Kitchener's pointing finger shamed him into joining the British Army, but he doesn't dwell too much on the horrors of World War I for, like many other old soldiers, including my father, he considers that terrible conflict best forgotten. In 1920, he quit England to try his luck at cattle farming in Argentina and there he stayed for the next forty years. The best times, he reckons, were between 1943 and 1955, when his good friend, General Juan Domingo Perón, assisted by his wife, the legendary Eva, brought stability and economic recovery to a country that previously had known nothing but poverty and chaos.

"If you kept your nose clean and steered clear of politics in those days, my young friend, you had nothing to worry about. I make no bones about the matter. From personal experience, I've found nothing wrong with nationalists or military dictators so long as they are honest and work for the people."

I fear that whenever John addresses me as his 'young friend', another ear-bashing is in the offing. I'm right. Imprisoned together as we are in the cab of the Land Rover, I have no choice but to bite the bullet and listen. He goes on to tell me that Spanish people should consider themselves very fortunate to have a man like General Franco running things at the moment for, in the past, their country, too, has been through the grindstone. The constant changes of government had resulted in bedlam.

"Do you know, Roy, how many *coups d'état* took place in Spain between 1814 and 1923?"

I shrug my shoulders. How would I know a thing like that? I am soon enlightened. "Forty-three, that's how many! What chance did the poor country have? Why, it's no surprise to me that one of the finest times for the Spanish people happened to be the seven-year period when another dictator, Primo de Rivera, took control of things in 1923. His *Movimiento Nacional* introduced a programme of public works that kept everybody happy by giving them work. In point of fact, Juan (he always refers to General Perón by his first name) took a leaf out of Primo de Rivera's book."

(I find this to be true with regard to education. In 1900, 80% of the rural population had been illiterate. By 1930, thanks to Rivera's school-building projects, this figure had fallen to 66%.)

"But then, my young friend, you know what those bastard Republicans did at the start of the Civil War?"

I do not, but before I have a chance to admit to it, he continues.

"They shot Juan's son, José Antonio, that's what! The one man who might have been able to prevent hostilities! Ah, well, maybe things are on the mend again now that a man like Franco's ruling the roost."

I try putting my oar in. I felt I had sat silent long enough.

"But didn't his lot overthrow a democratically elected government?"

This really seems to wind him up. How dare I interrupt!

"Democratic fiddle, you mean!" he cries, with a dismissive wave of his hand. "Let me tell you, my young friend, the same thing happened in Argentina in 1955. 'Fixed' elections voted a gang of bloody, double-dealing crooks into power and that's when things started to go from bad to worse. You wouldn't believe the blatant corruption I witnessed taking place. Perhaps

I should have buried my head in the sand and waited for the whole thing to blow over. But I couldn't. Neither could I bring myself to grease the right palms or lick arses so, in the end, like Juan, I came to the end of my tether and called it a day. If I'd stayed I'd have found myself in trouble.

I nearly burst out laughing at what he says next. He is quite serious.

"For," he adds, "I am not a man to hold my tongue. How much do you know about the Spanish Civil War, Roy?"

I tell him that I've read George Orwell's *Homage to Catalonia* (1938).

"I see," he says, prolonging the 'ee' in a patronising sort of way. "And I suppose you've seen the film of Hemingway's *For Whom the Bell Tolls* as well, with handsome Gary Cooper helping poor partisans in their fight against those wicked Fascists?"

"Well, I –"

I'm too slow. He's off again. "You realise, I hope, that the book and Mr. Hemingway's story behind the film were written by those who fought on the Republican side." He gives a little sigh. "But then, that's the case with media coverage and nearly all literature published in English. Franco's lot are always made out to be the 'baddies' of the piece, with the glorious International Brigade rushing from all parts of the globe to rescue the luckless, downtrodden, working class of Spain. There are a few exceptions, of course. In A *Stranger in Spain* (1955), the author, H.V. Morton, tells of a meeting with a Spanish friend in Madrid who says that the average Spaniard considers Franco an honest, God-fearing man who is respected for ending the Civil War and steering the country through the hard times that follow.

He shakes his head. " I tell you, Roy, my friend, dictatorship is confused with manipulation and tyranny. People think too much in terms of the 'Big Brother'."

I jump in, quickly.

"Well, from what I heard tell, the Nationalist forces were a bit heavy-handed, weren't they? And don't forget, they got help from Fascist Germany. What about Guernica? Hitler's Condor

Legion was responsible for the bombing, was it not? We in England didn't like the sound of that at all!"

Hearing this from me really seems to wind him up. Am I not paying attention? His voice becomes soft and steely and I sense a calm before a storm.

"Heavy-handed, you say? You accuse Franco's forces of being heavy-handed, my young friend?"

Here it comes, I think to myself.

"Let's face it, Roy. Wars – civil wars in particular – are messy affairs, with atrocities committed by both sides. There's no getting away from that. But do you know what these so-called Republicans did before the conflict itself had even started? No? Well, let me tell you. Firstly, they knocked off anyone they think might have more than their fair share of grey matter or too many pesetas jangling in their pockets. Artists, musicians, writers, poets, landowners, government officials – thrown into prison, tried by kangaroo courts, found guilty of nothing at all – and shot. Why, it's said that they even arrested anyone caught wearing a tie!"

Much to his annoyance, I butt in once again.

"What about Lorca, though? He ended up being executed by the other side – the Nationalists – didn't he?"

My question stops him in his tracks.

"Lorca? Lorca?" He pauses for a moment, perhaps for breath.

"Yes, yes. It's true enough. You're right, I suppose. You see, Roy, Lorca and quite a few other rich kids of his generation did throw their lot in with the Republic at the start of it all – and some paid the penalty. The country's so-called intellectuals thought it the 'in' thing, in those days, to support the working class. They believed strict left-wing Socialism to be the answer to anything and everything – as did many of their contemporaries in other countries. Take Burgess and Maclean in England, for example. Poor souls! In Spain, these types couldn't win. In truth, the people they supported saw them as members of the ruling class – well-heeled, privileged, highbrow eggheads, born with silver spoons in their mouths. For the first two or three years after the election in 1931, all went fairly smoothly. A sort of liberal, middle-of-the-road, bourgeois government took charge. But then, in 1933, with Alejandro Lerroux as Prime Minister, politics gradually moved to the right and when the newly formed ultra-right Falange started to gain support, the 'Lefties' got worried. The final six months leading up to 1936 saw the workers' parties flex their muscles – and that's when all the back-street violence began, leading to open war, with the Nationalists coming down hard on anyone they considered reactionary, or 'Red'. Many, including Picasso and Dalí, saw how things were shaping up and fled abroad. Lorca wasn't so lucky. Imagine if you will, Roy, the French Revolution's reign of terror all over again. Citizens lived in fear of being rounded up by Republican bully-boys and taken for what they called a 'car ride' – one way. Even your mate Orwell, who was supposed to be on the Republican side, remarks on the sudden, mysterious disappearance of some of his International Brigade comrades – for his lot weren't exempt. He said there existed at the time a 'horrible atmosphere of suspicion and hatred'. At the same time, these Republican 'goody-goodies' you seem to stick up for turned against another institution they blamed for past and present difficulties: religion. They imagined collusion between church and authority simply because men of the cloth were often seen standing alongside the rich and powerful at official functions. Indiscriminate killings resulted in the deaths of nearly seven thousand priests. Why, in the first six months of the war, angry workers' parties wrecked 250 churches and forbade all religious instruction. Nuns, too, had a hard time of it. Many ended up raped and murdered, while even their mummified corpses were taken from tombs, defiled and left on display."

At this, he sees me look round at him in disbelief.

"Don't just take my word for it, my friend. I'm quoting from a book called *Spain: A Tragic Journey*. These attestations are backed by photographs. The American author, F. Theo Rogers, witnessed the barbarities himself. Perhaps you should take it on board. His first-hand account might give you a different perspective on the Civil War."

I tell him he makes the Republicans sound like a lot of Communists.

"Aha! There you have it, my young friend! Now you've hit the nail on the head! That's exactly what they were! One lot, the POUM (*Partido Obrero de Unificación Marxista)* didn't pretend to be anything else. They went around singing the Internationale and shouting '*Viva el Soviet!*' Why, the leader of the Popular Front, as they called themselves, a character named Francisco Largo Caballero, became known as the Spanish Lenin. [State Councillor in Primo de Rivera's time, the man became Minister of Labour in the new 1931 Republic. From 1936 to 1937 he was President of the Council of Ministers, then, at the end of the Civil War, went into exile. Taken prisoner and locked in a concentration camp by the Germans, he was freed by the Allies in 1945 and died a year later]. Just about all the other workers' parties may have given themselves fancy titles, like CNT (*Confederación Nacional del Trabajo*), UGT (*Unión General de Trabajadores*), PSOE (*Partido Socialista Obrero Español*), but they were all Reds."

Phew! The man may have stayed out of politics in Argentina, I think to myself, but he certainly seems to know plenty about Spain's affairs.

(Some years later, I find his remark about 'Reds' to be absolutely correct. During my long-distance walks around Spain (see my *North from Granada*) I come upon many monuments marking the spot where Nationalist fighters were ambushed. In every case their assassins are referred to as *los Rojos* or 'the Reds'.)

John adds that a number of those who fled Spain ended up in Argentina. Once there, they supported Franco from afar and, along with them, he had celebrated the Nationalist victory in 1939.

"We were over the moon! Oh, yes, my friend, we cracked open a few bottles at the news, I can tell you!"

He believes that the Spain of today, 1966, with its military dictatorship, will provide a similar setting to that of his loved and lost *Peronista* days.

"If Franco proves to be anything like Juan, things won't be so bad," he affirms.

At the end of the Civil War, he says, the starving populace of Spain would have suffered much more if it had not been for the financial support given by Argentina.

As well as continually harping on about how hunky-dory my future state of affairs will be under a Fascist regime, my talkative companion goes on to give a fuller account of his days on the pampas. I have no way of telling how tall his stories are but, if half were true, he would surely have been able to teach Indiana Jones a thing or two.

His wife, too, has a tale to tell. At the end of the first day, after a hot meal, followed by a brandy or two, she warms and loosens up enough to inform me that, many years ago, she danced in a chorus line. I eye the woman sitting opposite more closely. Under the two or three layers of sweaters I can just make out a hefty bulge of bosom. Stretching my imagination, I conjure up a picture of a long-legged Cynthia doing the can-can at the *Folies Bergères*.

John's knowledge of the language proves invaluable, especially when trying to find our way. In 1966, the main route, the N 4, runs through the centre of villages and towns alike. There are few by-passes and signs are rare. (On subsequent trips I find that a compass comes in handy, particularly in some of the larger towns like Vitoria, Burgos and Madrid. By steering north or south, as the case may be, I nearly always manage to come out the other side on more or less the right track.)

Road improvements seem to be on Spain's agenda. We pass teams of men wielding picks, shovels and heavy wooden mallets, straightening out corners here and there or filling in some of the larger holes. It appears that the country has plenty of manpower to spare, but is lacking in heavy machinery. Only rarely do we come across huge, antiquated steam engines being used to roll surfaces flat. Belching out steam and moving at a snail's pace, these old 'Puffing Billies' look to have been commandeered from some museum.

Three days after leaving England, we arrive in Granada. Although the evening shadows are beginning to lengthen, we nonetheless consider carrying on to our intended destination: Almuñécar. However, when we stop for our final fill of petrol, the man handling the pump warns us that to attempt the passage over the Sierras de Tejeda, Almijara and Alhama in the dark will be asking for trouble. Many of those that have tried it, he declares cheerily, have subsequently been dragged up from one of the many deep ravines. So, with this alarming news in mind, we decide to stay put for the night and complete the last 70 kms on the morrow.

Cynthia, partly due to her prolonged pummelling, finds it difficult to make an early start, so the sun has plenty of time to be well up and shining on the glistening snow-capped Sierra Nevada before we set out. After a ten-kilometre drive along the N 323, heading towards the port of Motril, we turn off right along a minor road which, according to a wooden signpost, leads to the villages of Otívar, Jete and Almuñécar.

At this mournful spot, in 1492, Boabdil, the last of the Moorish kings, is supposed to have paused to take one last look back at his beloved Granada – the city that he has just handed over to the Christians. As he stands there lamenting his loss, his mother Fatima, just to make him feel a little better, nags, "You do well, my son, to weep as a woman for what you could not defend as a man."

No wonder he sighed. For this reason the site is known as *El Último Suspiro del Moro*, providing Salman Rushdie with the title for his celebrated novel, *The Moor's Last Sigh* (1996). Today, a hotel marks the spot.

After cutting its way through five kilometres of flat, open countryside, with blood-red earth standing out against a landscape of sombre browns and greens, the deserted road starts to climb upward, past Venta del Fraile, to a high point near Herrero. Here we pause for a moment to take in the magnificent, sweeping panorama spreading across pine-covered hills, down to the sparkling Mediterranean some fifteen hundred metres below. The sight takes my breath away! As we look down to the twisting, tunnelling stretch of narrow road snaking its way through a precipitous descent, we agree that it was a good move to have heeded the petrol attendant's warning the day before, or we might well have provided extra work for cranes. Keeping the Land Rover in first gear, with its engine whining, we slowly make our way downhill. With flat, perpendicular rock-face jutting skywards on one side of the road and sheer, plummeting drops on the other, the drive is certainly not for the faint-hearted. Out of the corner of my eye I catch a glimpse of a tense, tight-lipped John gripping the dashboard so firmly that his knuckles show white. At least, for the moment, he's stopped talking.

Hairpin bends

By concentrating so much on steering round hairpin bends, I completely forget my poor passenger behind me, lying cocooned, with arms trapped inside my sleeping bag. Before long, the unfortunate lady's plight is brought home by the sound of her slithering about. A shrill squeak accompanies each 'clump!' as she strikes the sides of the Land Rover and, to make matters worse, as we go down the really steep bits, the hapless woman slides forwards as well, hitting the back of our seat with her head, 'smack!' But I dare not stop. With restricted space, any other vehicle chancing to round a corner ahead would quite likely push us, or itself, over the edge. In fact, this very nearly happens. Because we have seen no other traffic since turning off the N 323 an hour ago, I begin to think that I have the road to myself and foolishly drive in the middle instead of keeping over to the far right. Suddenly, a loud blast of motor horn makes me jump in my seat! The sound is almost immediately followed by something large and red appearing round the bend in front, blocking my path completely. I brake hard, and, to the smell of burning rubber, finish up inches away from a large, red bus. A very close shave! I put the Land Rover into reverse gear and carefully back up. With hearts in mouths, John and I watch as the bus, which, by now, has half its front wheels hanging over the edge of the precipice, follows suit. Then it slowly moves forward – turning the corner and continuing on its precarious way. Those sitting in the first two rows of seats, I notice, who must have had a bird's eye view of the rocks a thousand feet below, look a little concerned!

Eventually, our path becomes straighter and the gradient less severe. From here on, with the Sierra del Chaparral to our right, the terrain bordering each side of the road becomes more cultivated and greener. John recognises and identifies some of the trees: oranges, lemons, figs, bananas. As the names of these fruits roll off his tongue, I feel, for the first time, an estrangement from England. We are now in a foreign land, more akin to Africa than to Europe. The exotic crops he mentions were indeed brought across the Mediterranean and introduced to the Spanish mainland by the Moors. The Arabs also pioneered the growth of sugar cane, which later led to numerous plantations and refineries springing up along the coast – an industry still active today, in 1966.

An hour and a half after leaving Granada we arrive at a village called Otívar. Pulling up at the nearest bar, a bruised and shaken Cynthia is gently helped down from the Land Rover and led inside. We are all in need of a drink. A short, fat, bald man pours our order of two beers and a cognac, then disappears through a door at the back without saying a word. He returns a few moments later carrying a large plate of sliced, purple-coloured sausage, which he places on the table in front of us and then scurries off again. The room we are in is quite spacious, with a cluster of hams hanging from a beam above our heads and a collection of tatty, curling photos pinned to its whitewashed walls. I can see no other customers and no other furniture other than the pieces we are using. The bar has a 'no-nonsense' air about it. It looks to me as though people come here to drink – and not much else.

A few minutes later, though, one or two scruffy-looking individuals do come in. They slouch past, lean against the wooden counter, light up cigarettes and stare at us with undisguised curiosity. Before long, they are joined by a rag, tag and bobtail crew, while, at the same time, a group of short, tubby women, with a flock of small ragged children at their feet, stand goggling from the doorway. When the little ones see me looking in their direction, they turn shyly away and bury their faces in their mothers' skirts. Strangely, from what I have seen of other Spanish bars, all is very quiet. John makes the first move. He nods at the line of standing men and wishes one and all *Buenos días*. This seems to break the ice and, with his greeting echoed back at him, a barrage of question comes from everybody, all at once. Which country are we from? England. England, eh? Why, we are told, English foreigners are nothing new. Only last year, two others of that nationality passed this way. John listens patiently and answers as best he can. He fascinates the crowd.

How is it, they ask, that someone not of their country can speak their language so well? His explanation leaves them looking perplexed until one young man, who has relatives in South America, explains that Argentina is part of Mexico.

We remain sitting there, being ogled, for quite some time, while a few more drinks go down the hatch. The bartender is now very busy. With each fresh order he serves up different plates of side-dishes. A hard, salty cheese, known as *manchego*, wedges of tomato skewered onto pieces of onion, and cuts of ham, which take a lot of chewing. By now, I know these little tit-bits go by the name of *tapas,* having already made their acquaintance earlier in the day at one of our roadside stops. There, John had lost no opportunity in telling me more about their history. It seems that it is customary, especially in the south of Spain, to give some sort of appetiser with each drink. Over a century ago, he said, some publican or other found that by placing a thin slice of bread on top of a glass he could prevent insects from toppling inside. The bar owner noticed that customers not only ate the bread but also tended to drink more. Other innkeepers followed suit and enlarged the menu to include just about anything edible. Salty things, they found, induced ever greater thirst. The word *tapa* came into common use because it translates as 'lid' or 'top'.

For much of the time, one of the chairs at our table remains empty, for John spends his time rubbing shoulders and chatting with those up at the counter. The 'rubbing shoulders' is literal. Perhaps, I think to myself, he fancies the idea of mixing with people of his height for a change for, when standing with Cynthia and me, he has had to stretch his neck quite a bit in order to look us in the eye. Before long, he is lost in conversation with one particular person – an old man who, to my surprise, appears to do most of the talking. Later, back in the Land Rover, John passes on an interesting story.

In the early 1900s, the fourth husband of the Marquesa de Cazulas 'violates' a young woman of Otívar. (A nearby property bears the name 'Cazulas'.) An act such as this cannot go unpunished. Her immediate family seek revenge. Three pieces of folded paper (one marked with a cross) are put into a hat and one apiece removed by husband, father and brother. The one marked with a cross falls to the father, so it is he that must kill

Cazulas

the villainous rapist. The Marqués is shot from his horse, the bullet striking him in the head and killing him instantly. Although the act is considered justified by many, the perpetrator wisely flees the country. Police enquiries are made but questions are answered with the words, *"Fuenteovejuna lo hizo"* – ("Fuenteovejuna did it.") Let me explain.

On 23 April 1476, in the village of Fuente Ovejuna, the local inhabitants had risen up against another tyrannical landlord, Fernán Gómez, Comendador of the Order of Calatrava. Having stormed his palace, the villagers toss his person out of the window, then stab him with a lance and swords and, just to make sure, finish him off by hacking his body to pieces. As in Otívar, collective responsibility gave rise to the saying, *"Fuenteovejuna lo hizo".* And it is the subject of one of Lope de Vega's greatest Golden Age plays.

On my way out from the bar I take a look at the photographs on the wall and discover that one of them shows a bus, similar to the one we passed on the road earlier, lying on its side at the bottom of a steep incline. We are told that it recently crashed over the edge of a bridge a few yards from where we are standing.

In later years, the same bar-restaurant, called '*El Capricho*' ('Whim' or 'Fancy'), becomes well-known for its flavoursome chicken meals. *Pollo al ajillo* (garlic chicken) with thinly cut fried potatoes is a speciality. At first, only those 'in the know' ate there and tried to keep the location a secret but, before long, the word spread and coachloads of people from nearby resorts started to arrive. The whole place smartened up and added an extension with a roof-terrace. Today, reservations are needed.

For the rest of the journey Cynthia sits with John and me on the front bench seat. No need of her furs now for three or four cognacs have warmed her up and we have, at last, left the cold weather behind. On then, down through the village of Jete, to the fertile valley of Río Verde, where, just past a hamlet known as San Sebastián, we turn the final bend in the road. Through my dusty, insect-splattered windscreen, across lush, green

'El Capricho'

fields of sugar-cane, I get my first glimpse of Almuñécar – a craggy mound, topped by a ruined building overlooking a jumble of white, interlocking, oblong shapes.

2

1966

In which I meet some of the foreign contingent, see the last of the Bloch-Watsons and begin an intimate relationship with Anthea.

In 1934, Laurie Lee arrived in Almuñécar by the coastal route from Málaga. His thousand-kilometre hike from Vigo, in the northwest of the country, took him six months. In *As I Walked Out One Midsummer Morning* (1969), he described the village as being 'gloomily Welsh', inhabited by poor peasants who made their living by fishing, farming or a combination of the two. Not wanting to risk incriminating anyone he met there who voiced Republican sympathies, he changes the name Almuñécar to El Castillo, otherwise Franco's *Brigada de Investigación Social* (Secret Police) would have found his book an interesting read. His disguised appellation proves fitting enough, for just about every one of the steep, narrow, cobbled street leads up to the remains of a large Moorish castle, El Castillo de San Miguel.

Deemed by Laurie Lee, in his book *A Rose for Winter*, to have once been a pirate stronghold, San Miguel has served as a protective fort to the town of Almuñécar for many centuries. Established in Phoenician times, it was later occupied by the Romans and the Moors. Its fortifications may have been able to withstand attacks by slings and arrows but the stone and mud ramparts proved no match for the salvoes from British gunboats which blasted them to rubble in 1812 during their occipation by Napoleon's troops. Another shelling took place at the start of the Civil War when a Republican destroyer accidentally fired on the town – mistaking it for the Nationalist stronghold of Altofaro, farther along the coast!

Palacete de la Najarra

Aerial view of Almuñécar, 1966

The thirty-one-year interval between Laurie Lee's first visit in 1935 (he returned sixteen years later) and mine in 1966 does not appear, initially, to have brought about many changes. As we drive down the Carretera Suspiro del Moro, past a petrol station and into a shabby square, an air of neglect and poverty still hangs about the place. The buildings are ramshackle: crumbling walls, splintered doors and untidy roofs with tufts of dry grass sprouting between loose tiles. Not many people come out on the street. These few wave as we drive past. I am struck by the shabbiness of their dress. However, at the end of the long Avenida de Europa, where the road meets with Paseo de las Flores, things start to improve. On our right we find a splendid, pink-painted structure, complete with arched windows and multi-coloured tile surrounds, looking, in all its splendour, like a miniature Alhambra. This flamboyant residence, the Palacete de la Najarra, completed in 1850, was originally built as a home for the owners of the sugar factory, which stands nearby. In front of us, on the other side of the Playa San Cristóbal, lies a shimmering expanse of sea. The Mediterranean at last. Journey's end!

Turning left, we drive along the Paseo Prieto Moreno and continue on past a large semicircular building. I have to do a double take at the sign above the entrance, which proclaims it to be the Hotel Sexi! The hotel's colourful appellation may account for its popularity for quite a few famous people are known to have stayed there, including the film actor David Niven.

From this point on, road surfaces begin to improve and so does the state of the buildings. New apartments have been built into the rockface on our left and farther on still, at Playa Puerta del Mar, we come across another hotel, this time standing on the beach itself, called the Hotel Mediterráneo. Its shabby, weatherbeaten, rather Art Deco appearance leads me to think that it has been there for quite some time and wonder if this might be where Laurie Lee worked in 1934.

Hotel Mediterráneo

In this locality things look much healthier. At the end of a shady, tree-lined *paseo* an attractive-looking property has tables and chairs laid out invitingly on a sunny, terrace. Judging the number of people sitting about, it looks prosperous. The two levels above have large windows opening onto intricately fashioned, wrought-iron balconies and, at first sight, I take it to be another hotel. As we get nearer, though, I see the ground floor at least, is a Cafetería, the Al Quirós. (It was, in fact, originally a hotel, one of the first to open in Almuñécar. At the turn of the century, it went by the name of Hotel Marina.)

Not wanting to pull up directly in front, I park alongside a nearby building which has a tattered red and yellow flag hanging limply from an upstairs window. Parking has never been a problem, for the number of vehicles seen on the road since leaving Granada, apart from a few belonging to the *Guardia Civil* or *Policía*, could be counted on the fingers of one hand.

We climb down from the Land Rover, make our way to the Cafetería and wearily sit down at one of the tables. Almost immediately, a young boy, who looks as though he should be at school, comes over, takes our order and promptly returns with two very welcome cold beers, a cognac, a glass of red wine and *tapas* of fried fish.

We sit back and enjoy our drinks, but, as we do so, I cannot help but notice that just about all other customers spread about the terrace are watching us intently. They follow our every movement and I sense we must be the topic of their whispering. It's like Otívar all over again – but with one major difference. Mostly fairhaired and dressed in typical 'hippie' fashion, these colourful characters are not Spanish.

Eventually, one of them, who can contain himself no longer, calls across to us. He must have seen the Land Rover's numberplate for he speaks in English.

"Just arrived in town?"

I turn towards the questioner and switch on one of my friendliest smiles.

"That's right. Made our way down from England, through

France. It's been a long, hard drive."

This simple statement is enough for just about everyone on the terrace to start speaking at once. One squeaky voice cuts through all the rest. It comes from a lanky, bearded individual whose funny accent makes him difficult to understand.

"Haf you bring books wit you?"

"Books?"

He raises his voice.

"Books, sí, books! You know, zose tings zat haf pages wit werts!"

What's all this? I don't like being bellowed at and might well have responded differently another time but, as it is, I simply turn my back on him and sip my beer. I have been in the place only a few minutes and am not looking for trouble. Besides I know that nothing is more discouraging than unappreciated sarcasm.

A few moments later, a pretty young girl appears in front of us. With a charming smile, she places the palms of her hands on our table and leans forward. As she does so, her loose, baggy shirt falls open at the neck and I can't help but notice that she has an all-over suntan. Tight denim jeans, straining at the seams where they cover her rounded buttocks, look as though they've been sprayed onto her body.

"Forgive Felix," she pleads, apologetically. "It was very rude of him. He probably hasn't recovered from last night."

Whatever Felix the Rude may have been up to the night before I neither know nor care. I could have forgiven her any-thing. Something about her juicy, puppy-like freshness brings to mind a ripe plum, waiting to be plucked. I wave to an empty chair and invite her to sit down and join us, but she nods towards a gathering of gawks at another table.

'Thanks, but I'm with friends over there."

"What's all this about books?"

The young lady tells me that books, at least books written in English, are in very short supply. Those living hereabout are starved of reading material and, in an attempt to get hold of something fresh, make a point of asking any newcomer whether they happen to have anything of that nature with them.

I jerk my thumb towards the thin man with the beard who apparently is still recovering from something or other.

"You won't get far if you let him do the asking."

She grins.

"Oh, he's not normally like that. You have to get to know Felix. He lets himself down sometimes by becoming over-excited," and adds, as if it excuses his bad behaviour, "He plays good guitar."

My two companions have nothing in the way of books on offer but I give her the titles of a couple of tatty paperbacks I've brought with me from England. She turns and shouts the titles to her friends.

Like a shot, one of them raises his hand. "Me first!"

Then someone else. "After you!"

This animated 'booking' goes on for quite some time.

With refilled glasses, the Bloch-Watsons and I stay where we are a while longer, basking in the warmth of a brilliant sun beaming down from a clear blue cloudless sky: our first taste of Costa del Sol weather. Slowly, we begin to defrost. The autumn of that year had delivered an exceptionally icy spell to Europe, making the French part of our trip decidedly chilly. Northern Spain, too, had been very cold. Only once through the Despeñaperros Pass, and into Andalusia, had the temperature risen a little, but then it fell again when we reached Granada. An uncommon north-easterly wind, sweeping across the snow-capped Sierra Nevada, had blown freezing cold air into the city. Just about everyone we saw on its streets had been wrapped in overcoats and scarves.

But this is more like it. John, flopping back in his chair, eyes closed, presents a picture of cat-like contentment. Had he been able, I am sure he would have purred. Cynthia, perhaps comforted by the two glasses of wine and cognac also looks much more at ease. She has not only removed her heavy woollen cardigan, but has gone so far as to unfasten the top two buttons of her blouse, exposing an inch or two of cleavage. I try to guess her age. Fifty? Her former haughty expression has melted away and, as her features soften, I begin to espy Mrs. Bloch-Watson in a new light. Not an unattractive face. Long legs. Full hips. Large breasts. My mind starts to wander.

All at once, the sounds of scraping chairs and rattling glasses wake me from my reverie. Those seated roundabout have suddenly risen *en masse* and started to make their way in the direction of my Land Rover. Their number includes the charming creature I spoke to earlier. As she passes by, I place my hand on the soft, fleshy part of her upper arm, and ask, "What's going on? Why the exodus?"

I rather hope that she might bend forward again and present me with another display of suntan, but have no such luck. Instead, she gives me another of her lovely smiles and points across to the building flying the red and yellow flag, where a door now stands open.

"The post's arrived."

Looking more closely, I see a faded *Poste Restante* painted on the wall.

In 1966 many such signs are written in French. This is the language that has been taught in Spanish schools for generations. Besides being physically and historically closer to Spain than any other European country, France has involved itself in Spanish affairs often in the past. French monks were responsible for instigating the famous pilgrimage to Santiago de Compostela. Known as 'the French route', the Spanish section of this *Camino de los Peregrinos* (Pilgrims' Way) starts at Roncesvalles in the northeast of the country and runs 800 kilometres (500 miles) in a westerly direction, passing through Pamplona, Burgos, León and Puerto Marín, to Santiago de Compostela itself. I have walked it on four occasions. A Frenchman became the first Archbishop of Toledo and, at the time of the Crusades, France sent no fewer than 34 expeditions to help the Christians in their fight against the Muslims. More recently, in 1808, Napoleon marched his armies into Spain, and put on the throne his eldest brother, who ruled the country as José I for three years. (He departed after his defeat by the Duke of Wellington at the battle of Vitoria on 21 June 1813, to be replaced by Fernando VII, victim of a forced abdication five years earlier.)

The Post Office with the Spanish flag hanging from its window deals with all incoming and outgoing mail for people living in Almuñécar and La Herradura. It opens at round about midday and closes again at 2 p.m. With the number of foreigners increasing all the time, the poor postmaster has his work cut out in sorting through the envelopes and then doing his best to hand over the right ones to the right persons. Recipients are required to identify themselves by showing their passports and it helps if their name is clearly printed, in capitals. Usually, but not invariably, the letter ends up in the right hands.

As in France, postage stamps can be obtained not at the Post Office, but only at an *estanco* – a tobacconist's. The one in Almuñécar that has stamps for sale also does a brisk trade in a cheap, black type of cigarettes, smoked all day and every day by just about every man in town. It amuses me to watch the girl behind the counter painstakingly wrap a postage stamp in brown paper and then seal the tiny parcel with a piece of string or sticky tape before handing it over to the customer, even though she might see that someone waiting behind is desperate for a fag. She will not be hurried.

Gradually, the colourful bunch drifts back to the Cafetería again. Most wait until they are seated before opening their correspondence but some, more impatient, rip it open straight away where they stand. One hopeful pulls out the sheets of paper, shuffles them through frenziedly and then desperately shakes the upturned envelope. The expression on his face, when nothing falls out, is one of a person just given the death sentence. It also reminded me of the dejection of Billy Bunter when his long-awaited postal order fails to arrive.

My two travelling companions are anxious to find lodgings for the night so, after one more round, I help them carry their belongings to a place recommended by the young waiter: the nearby Hostal Victoria. Cynthia approves the name. She reckons it to be a good omen. We part company with a 'See you later' for, we suppose, in a village the size of Almuñécar, that we are bound to meet again. I deliberately do not use the expression 'bump into' – for Cynthia's sake. But we do not meet each other later or at any other time. I have no idea how long my travelling companions stay in town or why they leave so soon, but the Bloch-Watsons disappear from my life forever.

Back at the Land Rover I delve into my bag, retrieve the two coveted books, then cross, once again, to the Cafetería Al Quirós. Most customers are gone by now, but five remain, settled at a table in a shaded part of the terrace. Their number includes the girl with the loose-fitting shirt and my old pal, the live wire, Felix the Rude.

To my surprise, as I approach, it is he who pulls up another chair and waves a thin, bony hand in its direction. His nails, I notice, are well manicured, unlike the rest of him.

"Hey, man! Please to seet wit us. Sorry I am not *correcto* before. Much of ze booze last night, you know."

I do as instructed and sit. He calls through the open window and a glass of beer is instantly brought out and placed before me.

"Iss beer you drink, yes?" I can see they do not miss much. Felix then proceeds to do the honours.

Judy I have already met. At her side is Donald, a short, blond, rather elegant man who leans back in his chair, looking me up and down in a self-assured manner. For a moment he makes me think of a younger version of little John. Without waiting to be introduced, the tall, broad-shouldered man next to him raises his glass and announces, in a deep, throaty voice,

"Antonio."

This man might well have stepped from a film set. Star material, for sure. With thick black hair, big brown eyes and slightly cruel mouth, he possesses the sort of animal magnetism that would bring a flutter to the heart of any young lady. Both he and Donald, cool and calm, look as though they have just stepped out from the office for a coffee break. Their outfit of shirt,

Antonio

trousers, shiny shoes and socks, rather sets them apart from others seen on the terrace earlier, for their uniform of the day appears to be blue jeans, a variety of tops, and open-toed sandals. It surprises me that nobody wears shorts. I subsequently learn that, rather as in Victorian England, authorities regard the sight of a woman's bare ankles – or worse still a thigh – as sexually stimulating and frown upon such display in public places. At this time, 1966, women in trousers still bring wolf whistles and men have only just started taking off their jackets in restaurants and cinemas – even in the heat of the summer months.

Attitudes to such matters are rapidly becoming more liberal though, especially in some of the larger resorts like Torremolinos and Marbella. Franco faces a dilemma. On one hand, he does not want to upset the church authorities but, at the same time, realises that if he wants visitors to Spain – with sunny beaches being the main attraction – he will have to relax his strict censorship laws. Attempting to safeguard foreigners' morals is a lost cause anyway. Rules regarding people's dress may continue to apply to the Spanish, but tolerance must be shown to tourists for the currency they spend is extremely important to the country's economy.

Not so long ago, the religious powers-that-be in Spain decreed that women must not wear dresses that were too tight in places that might 'provoke the evil passions of men'. Neither should the dresses be too short, too low cut or have short sleeves. At the age of twelve, girls had to wear dresses that reached the knee and boys were not to be seen on the streets with upper legs bare. Also, women were not allowed to ride bicycles, wear trousers or indulge in what is known as 'modern dancing'. Up until 1964 censors did not allow a bikini-clad woman to appear on the cinema screen, while not many years earlier, the state employed *retocadores* or 'retouchers' to paint vests onto bare torsos of boxers and diminish the size of women's breasts (if considered too large) when their picture appeared in a newspaper or magazine. (I reckon Judy's bosom would have been quite a challenge). By 1978, by contrast, topless bathing would become quite commonplace on the Costas and today, 2003, two nudist beaches can be found within ten kilometres of Almuñécar.

Lastly, Felix acquaints me with the young lady sitting directly opposite. Anthea. With a slim, boyish figure, high cheek-boned brown face and dark, close-cut hair, she resembles a little pixie. Her figure contrasts completely with that of Judy. Although pretty much bosomless, she has large, hard nipples pushing out from her tight T-shirt, looking like a pair of bell-pushes. (It seems no rules govern the wearing of bras.) Her nervous, jittery attention is divided between the literature on the table and myself. I apparently win the battle for, in the end, she turns her big, brown eyes on me like searchlights, and asks, "Are you staying in town long?"

I reply that I have no definite plans but intend to look around with the idea of perhaps staying a while. Questions then follow thick and fast, from everybody, all at once. Again, I am reminded of the bar in Otívar, only this time I understand the language. It only wants a bright light to be shone in my face to complete the picture of a 'third degree'. Name? Where from? Why here? Who are my two friends? At first I answer politely but after a while the tedious, non-stop probing begins to get on my nerves. Do they want to know the colour of my underpants? Fortunately, at this point, Felix steps in. Perhaps he sees I've had enough. He changes the subject and starts to complain, in his high-pitched voice, about the price of drinks.

Apparently, the cost of a glass of wine or beer has recently increased from two to three pesetas and he lets it be known that he considers this rise outrageous. In 1966 one pound sterling, or 240 'old' pence, buys 166 pesetas, so the drinks have gone up from 4 'old' pence to 6. Today, in the early 21st century, with decimal curency at 100 'new' pence to the pound, these sums would equate to 1.8 and 2.3 'new' pence. (I shall henceforth refer to prices in 'new' pence). Holding forth in a jumble of Spanish and English he demonstrates his indignation by wildly gesticulating.

I can tell that the others have been subjected to this sort of thing before. Donald ostentatiously holds up his arm to look at his wristwatch, then stifles a pretend yawn. Antonio glances in my direction and raises his thick eyebrows. Judy picks up one of the books, a science fiction novel by John Wyndham called *The Day of the Triffids* (1951) and starts to leaf through its pages. Felix either doesn't notice or doesn't care. He turns to me and holds three long fingers under my nose, shrieking,

"*Tres pesetas*! Before, it iss two! Fifty *porcentaje* more iss *mucho*, yes? Is bloody *turistas* make it so! I drink at home only. I no drink in bars."

I wonder if his reference to tourists is directed at me. From what I have seen of him so far, though, his resolve to drink only at home has not yet started. He's been the first to order a fresh round of drinks but when it comes time to share the bill, disappears to the toilet.

The nerve-wracking drive down from Granada, combined with the beers, had made me sleepy and, although, initially, the delightful *tapas* took the edge off my appetite, I now begin to feel peckish again. Can anyone suggest somewhere to eat? Anthea says she is hungry too and offers to guide me to a restaurant, which, she promises, serves good food. So, with *hasta luego* all round, we leave the others to Felix's animated ranting and raving and head towards the centre of town.

La Posada serves a three-course meal-of-the-day, which includes bread and beverage of choice – all for the princely sum of thirty pesetas (18 pence).

By law, all restaurants in Spain are obliged to provide this lunchtime *menú del día* and the price they can charge depends on their number of *estrellas* or stars they can display. This is determined by government inspectors who assess the establishment on its overall appearance, quality of food and, more importantly, the sort of comments customers have written in the mandatory *libro de reclamaciones,* or complaints book.

Between 1959 and 1973, the number of visitors to Spain increases from 3 to 34 million and the authorities do their utmost to ensure that nothing upsets the much-needed source of revenue they bring with them. If valued patrons are not completely satisfied with food or lodging, they are at liberty to register their grievance in the provided *libro*. Too many entries result in the loss of a star, which in turn means a drop in status and consequent loss of profit, for all charges must fall in line with their new rating.

I don't know which category La Posada falls into but whatever it is does not seem to affect its popularity. At 4 p.m., plenty of people are still sitting down to a meal. People in this part of Spain eat late. It is not uncommon to find customers taking their lunchtime *comida* or *almuerzo* at this hour and an evening meal, *la cena*, can be ordered at any time, even after midnight. Mealtimes vary in other parts of the country but it is still impossible to lunch in a Spanish restaurant much before 2 p.m. or to dine earlier than 9 p.m. However, just across the border in France, 2 p.m. is too late for lunch and by 9 p.m. they have sometimes stopped serving evening meals! This disparity is hard on the appetite clock. My stomach has not yet adjusted to this new regime and I know that but for those *tapas* I would be starving by now.

Anthea helps me with the mysteries of the menu. For starters I choose *paella*, which turns out to be a mound of yellow saffron rice burying cuts of sweet red pepper, peas, onions and a variety of little sea creatures, including shrimps, mussels and (a first for me) octopus. I wolf the lot.

On this occasion the plate of food comes up as an hors d'oeuvres, but *paella valenciana*, considered by many to be Spain's national dish, can also come as a main course. On the coast, the ingredients consist mainly of fish, but further inland where seafood is harder to come by, meats such as chicken, pork and rabbit take its place. Some say the word *paella* stems from *para ella* or 'for her' because a love-sick chef concocted the dish for the woman he loved. Alas! The truth (involving French influence once again) is more likely to be less romantic. Most people believe that *paella* takes its name from the old

French word for a frying-pan, *la poêle*. The Spanish adopted the word and call the cooking utensil *paellera*.

For the next course, I play it safe and order *pollo al ajillo con patatas fritas* (garlic chicken and chips). The pieces of chicken, still on the bone, come wallowing in a pool of olive oil in which swims a flotilla of garlic knobs. It all looks pretty greasy but I soon learn that bread dunked into this mixture tastes yummy. To finish off, for *postre* (afters), I try the speciality of the house – a dish known as *flan*, the French *crème caramel*. I fall in love with this little delicacy at once.

Flan is probably the most popular of all Spanish desserts and can be found listed on nearly all Spanish menus. In the '60s, before the introduction of frozen foodstuffs, most restaurants made the dish to their own recipe. The amount of milk, eggs or egg-yolk, sugar and vanilla extract varies from place to place, with the end result delivering different tastes and textures. Some have a hard toffee-like surface which has to broken open to get at the creamy mixture underneath, while others are soft right through but come covered in a nectareous caramel sauce. Connoisseurs are known to patronise establishments purely for the sake of their *flan*. Nowadays, most restaurants find it too much trouble to make it themselves and stock only the standard little tubs of *flan* which are simply torn open at the top and tipped on to the plate.

Each time dishes are brought to the table, I notice that I am served before Anthea. The same thing happened in the restaurants we stopped at on the drive down through Spain. Cynthia had to wait until her husband and I had a plate of food in front of us before she received hers and John and I were always first to have wine poured into our glasses or soup ladled into our bowls. Here in La Posada, I find the three-way conversation quite amusing when it comes to ordering the meal. A young man, pencil and notepad at the ready, comes to stand by our table and asks me, in Spanish, what I would like to eat. Anthea interprets and I answer, in English. She forwards my request to the waiter who writes down the order and hurries away. Not once does he look in her direction.

It doesn't take me long to realise that a woman's lot in '60s Spain is very different from that of her counterpart in the UK. Article 57 of the Spanish Civil Code states that 'The husband must protect his wife and she must obey her husband'. Without her spouse's permission a woman cannot take a job, start a business, open a bank account, be involved with legal proceedings, enter into contracts, buy or sell goods or even travel far from home. Although adultery is officially illegal, punishable by between six months and six years in prison, there is a different set of rules for men and women. Sexual misconduct by a woman is a crime whatever the circumstances but only considered serious for the man if he commits the offence in the family home. Not until 1976, a year after Franco's death, does the first feminist demonstration take place. I remember asking a Spanish friend, at that time, what he thought of the new Women's Liberation Movement. He gave a dismissive wave of his hand.

"Oh, it gives the ladies something to do in their spare time."

When I've finished the splendid meal, I lean back contentedly in my chair with a small black coffee and a glass of Spanish *Magno* brandy on the table, smoking a rock-hard *Farios* cigar. At my request, Anthea tells me more about the other characters sharing her table at Al Quirós. Donald and Antonio, she says, in cahoots with another man called Juan, recently combined their money and energies to develop an estate of houses just outside town, on the road to Motril. The venture paid off and, with most of the properties now sold, they have started another enterprise in a little village to the west of Almuñécar, called La Herradura.

Felix she describes as a Belgian layabout. He arrived from Morocco some years earlier, accompanied by an Algerian woman and two young children. She and the infants did not stay long but Felix somehow manages to remain in town and keep his head above water. His fluency in Spanish, French, German and knowledge of English, combined with his talents for painting and guitar-playing, earns him a few pesetas and – at this point, Anthea hesitates.

"Be careful, Roy. A word to the wise. He might act the fool and seem like he's got a screw loose, but I advise you not to be seen too much in the company of Mister Felix. He's being watched."

"Watched? By whom?"

She holds her finger to her lips.

"Shush! Keep your voice down. By the authorities."

I'm intrigued.

"What for? What authorities? What's he done?"

Anthea glances around the room.

"Drugs," she whispers, and goes on to tell me more.

Spain's proximity to North Africa, apparently, leads many hard-up young people to take the ferry from Málaga to Tangier, buy the readily-available marijuana on sale there, bring it back into this country and sell it for a good profit. Easy – so they imagine. Anthea keeps her voice low.

"I don't know how you're fixed for money, Roy, but please don't be tempted to try this sort of thing yourself. I guarantee you'll end up in prison. It's happened to a good friend of mine. There's not much goes on around here that the powers-that-be don't know about."

By 'powers-that-be' she means the *Guardia Civil*. This band of shiny-hatted, strong-arm men, over 50,000 in number, was formed in 1844 to replace the politically unstable militia. Originally, they were active in trying to combat banditry, but these days their duties include not only keeping a close watch on activities taking place in sparsely populated areas of rural Spain but also, and especially, along the Mediterranean coastline. Posted to regions far away from their hometown, neither they nor their families are permitted to mix socially with locals for fear of bias when it comes to meting out punishment. Their unlimited power and toughness make them none too popular. In 1936, when civil unrest boiled over into insurrection, many of their number ended up being massacred by resentful villagers and workers belonging to the Popular Front. During the ensuing war the *Guardia Civil* sided with General Franco and, when the conflict ended in victory for his Nationalist Party, they took a terrible revenge on those that slaughtered their brothers. Federico García Lorca calls them 'patent-leather men with patent-leather souls'.

I thank Anthea for her warning, saying that I intend to toe the line and keep my nose clean.

"How come you know so much about all this?"

She seems to sag a little and, with a little sigh, she replies, "I've learned the hard way. Listen, Roy, this might give you some idea of what things are like out here. I'll tell you a true story. I arrived from England six months ago with my boyfriend, Mike. We were both pretty green. Almuñécar had it all. Everything about the place suited us down to the ground. We were in seventh heaven. You know – lots of fellow hippies, cheap booze, easy-going life-style – that sort of thing. Anyway, although we didn't exactly live it up, the little cash we'd brought with us gradually ran out and eventually we found ourselves stony broke. But the thought of returning home didn't exactly turn us on. Back to what? Boring old England? No thanks! Mike decided we should look for work so, stupidly, we sold our return air tickets in order to stay put. Of course, we soon found there was nothing doing on the employment front and, although our friends helped us out a little, they didn't have too many pesetas to spare themselves. Then Mike meets this guy who offers him a job driving across to Morocco to pick up a few boxes of those little neck beads – you know, like the ones everybody's wearing. Well, of course we're suspicious, but this guy, Danny, says it's all above board. The boxes would be left open, he said, and Mike could check them out before bringing them back to Spain. I still didn't like the idea but we were in a spot. So, we thought, what could they do to us, anyway? We weren't criminals. We had British passports. So Mike meets up with this Danny in Torremolinos, crosses to Tangier in a Dutch registered van, checks first, then picks up the beads – and is stopped by the Guardia as he drives ashore in Málaga. They find the 'chocolate' (marijuana) inside the van's door panels. Mike gets six years."

I listen to what she says as best I can, but it's not easy for, once again, my attention is distracted by the tantalising sight of two dark-brown buds, stretching, almost to breaking point, the covering of her thin cotton shirt. Maybe the display is intentional, for Anthea sits with her arms thrust straight down behind her chair forcing her shoulders back and chest out.

By 6 p.m. the restaurant is almost empty. A weary waiter starts to clear away the dishes and pile chairs on tables while a plump young girl, delicately singing flamenco, meticulously sweeps the tiled floor with a broom made from a combination of long twigs and leaves. The débris consists mainly of cigarette-ends, for ashtrays do not seem to have found their way this far south.

The bill comes to sixty pesetas (36 pence). This includes my three-course meal, Anthea's salad, cognacs and a cigar. I feel like asking for the *libro* and writing some sort of accolade. On the other hand, I reckon, too much praise from a foreigner might boost the establishment's classification and lead to an increase in prices.

From La Posada, I make my way back to the Land Rover, accompanied by Anthea, who appears to have nothing better to do than keep me company. I ask her if she knows somewhere called Velilla. The way I say it makes the word sound like the flavouring 'vanilla'.

She doesn't. I try again, showing her the name printed on a piece of paper. Giving a little laugh, she cries,

"Oh, Belleeya! The spelling's right but your pronunciation isn't. In Spanish, the letter 'v' comes out as 'b' and double 'l' sounds like a 'y' – as in 'you'. Yes, I know the place. It's a development a few kilometres out of town, on the Motril road. Why do you ask?"

I tell her that my reason for ending up in this part of the world is to view a property for sale which, I've been led to believe, will provide both 'home and income'. It consists of two apartments, one of which can be lived in and the other let. The owner, back in England, has given me the name of someone living near the building who, he assured me, will be happy to show me over the premises.

"What's the name of this someone?"

Philip Ashby. Does she know him?

"Philip! Of course I do! Everybody knows everybody around here. I'll show you where he lives."

We drive east along the coast a few kilometres until we come to a small cluster of properties lying huddled close together on the seaward side of the road, leaning into each other for support, like a gang of drunken sailors ashore for the night. I have the immediate impression that if any part of any one of them were removed, the whole lot would fall down in a heap. Anthea leads me along a broken path to a house on the far side of the estate where we rouse a sleepy-eyed Philip from his siesta and explain our mission. Somewhat grudgingly, he leads us through a maze of crumbling bricks and cement blocks to a building that looks to have been thrown together in a hurry by a blind, unskilled, do-it-yourself handyman. Everything about the place is out of line. The flat roof isn't. Rusting, metal-framed windows, set into badly-rendered walls, are levelled at peculiar angles and the floors have a definite list. I feel it could serve at a fun fair as the 'crazy house'. Contrary to the owner's expectations, Mr. Ashby does not seem at all happy to be showing us round and shows no surprise when I give the thumbs down. I have a distinct hunch the man has been through this many times before.

Back in Almuñécar, Anthea wants to know where I intend to stay the night. When I reply that it will probably mean joining my friends at the Hostal Victoria, she places a small, brown hand on my arm, gazes up at me with her puppy-like, soft brown eyes and whispers quietly,

"You can stay with me if you like."

I like. Rucksack on shoulder, I follow her into the centre of town and along one of the narrow streets that leads up to the castle. After a short climb, we turn into an opening by the side of a carpenter's workshop and go up a steep flight of stairs.

At the top, a heavy door opens into an area about 3 metres by 4 metres, almost completely filled by a magnificently carved wooden bed. Inside, it is very murky, the only illumination coming from a shuttered window in the adjoining, curtained-off area. The cramped space does not allow for such luxuries as a wardrobe or a chest-of-drawers. Clothes are hanging from wooden pegs fixed to the wall. Unlike my property back in Twickenham, the accommodation could not even be thought of as a bed-sitting room for, apart from the bed, I found no sign of anywhere to sit. The door has to be closed before I am able to squeeze past the footboard and reach a corner that provides enough elbow-room for Anthea to remove the pack from my shoulders. Once she has placed it on the floor, she folds her thin arms around my waist and rests her bristly head on my chest.

"It's not too late to take a siesta, Roy."

Without answering, I pull the 'T' shirt over her closely-cropped head, and, bending over, gently caress with my tongue those two titillating points that have been taunting me all afternoon. She lets me carry on for a minute or two, all the while pulling at my hair and making little whimpering sounds, then, hurriedly, we pull off our clothes. It's her turn to crouch down – but not for long. With unexpected strength in someone so petite, she springs up and pushes me back onto the mattress.

3

1966

In which I make the acquaintance of Pepe and Paco, learn something of Almuñécar's past and give Anthea an account of my own.

I stay with Anthea for the next three weeks. The rent she pays for the two small rooms is only 330 pesetas (less than £2) a month, which is cheap, even by Spanish standards. I soon come to realise why.

Each morning, bright and early, a combined pandemonium of doors banging, pans clattering, babies crying and men and women bellowing, rouses us from our slumbers. After a short respite, hammering, sawing and out-of-tune singing drifts up from the workshop underneath, making any chance of further sleep impossible. Noise is not the only thing that disturbs us. We might have been able to put up with the hullabaloo and stay in bed a while longer had it not been for the stink that comes wafting into our room soon after the carpenter's arrival. Glue. A pot of this evil, glutinous mixture sits bubbling away atop a small charcoal grill directly under us and, as the sticky stuff is concocted by boiling the bones of fish, pig or chicken, the smell can be imagined. One whiff is enough for Anthea. She tries to be up and out before the pong starts. If too late, the sickening stench puts paid to any chance of her being able to face breakfast, she says.

Accompanying the noise and the glue bouquet, a layer of fine wood-dust also manages to filter its way into our room – even though we keep the door and window firmly closed. Sometimes, when waking up from one of our little afternoon lie-downs, I glance down at Anthea by my side to find that her dark hair has turned completely white.

Of course, there's no bathroom. Instead, we make do with a stone trough that stands on the flat roof above. Each morning, before going out, we fill this washing tub, known as a *pila*, or *lavadero*, with cold water and by mid-afternoon the sun has heated the liquid enough for us to strip naked and bathe ourselves. Sometimes, this sensuous session of soaping and rubbing our hands over each other's body leads to a hasty trip downstairs for an early siesta. For a short while, glue odours are ignored.

The *pila* is built into the corner of a stairwell, which means, we hope, that it cannot be overlooked. If nosy neighbours do complain at our antics, Anthea reckons, the *Guardia* will soon let us know. Still, with all the lodging's faults, every cloud (of dust?) has a silver lining, I suppose. With no temptation to remain in bed in the mornings, we have plenty of time for other things. It doesn't take long for me to become acquainted with the two men responsible for creating the racket each morning. On my way out I make a point of stepping into the cold, cement-grey, sunless room on the ground floor and, trying not to breathe in too deeply, shout, "*¡Buenos días!*"

On hearing my greeting, Paco and Pepe immediately stop whatever they are doing, appear from within the befogged interior, shake me by the hand and, inevitably, offer up a cigarette. Each time, I shake my head – but it does not seem to matter. Although I refuse at least a dozen times, the packet is always proffered. It seems to be some sort of ritual. Although we cannot communicate verbally, we make do quite well with sign language. I quickly learn that Paco, a boat-builder by trade, has married carpenter Pepe's sister and, as there seem to be more opportunities in furniture than boats, has joined his brother-in-law's line of business. With an abundance of construction-work taking place all along the coast, building materials and allied tradesmen are in great demand. Fishermen swap oars for shovels and those in possession of screwdrivers or spanners pass themselves off as electricians or plumbers.

Paco and Pepe are chain smokers. They puff away on cigarettes all day and every day and, I must admit, the fact that they smoke in an area littered with highly flammable material gives me some concern, especially as I live above!

The space in which these two men work may be dusty, untidy and scruffy but their tools of trade are kept meticulously clean. With no power points and therefore no mechanical gadgets, everything is made by hand. Slotted into a rack on the wall above one of the workbenches, polished and neat as Guardsmen on parade, stands a row of shiny chisels with handles of almond or olive-wood. They, along with planes and saws, have been inherited from Pepe's father, killed in the Civil War, and will more than likely be passed down the line to Pepe's sons in later years. Considered family heirlooms, they are treated as such. Each morning starts with a ceremonial sharpening and oiling of these treasured items, an act repeated at intervals throughout the day. I sometimes wonder if the two carpenters do not spend more time honing and cleaning these tools than actually using them.

Paco's boat-building experience has made him master of adze and axe. He can hack a rough piece of timber into a pile of furniture components in a very short space of time, enabling his brother-in-law, by the dextrous use of hand drill, saw and mallet, to assemble the pieces into splendid tables, chairs, stools, windows, doors and shelves. No nails or screws are needed, for all joints are glued, then wood-pegged. Most of the chairs have short legs. They are popular with many of the older folk of the village who seem to find it more comfortable to sit crouched, with knees raised in a pose that comes across as something between the traditional Muslim squat and the more upright, Christian, sitting position.

Once a week, a tired-looking mule, led by a shrivelled, ragged old man, clip-clops its way up the cobbled street to collect the chair frames which are taken away to have rush seats fitted.

These seem to be the only items for which there is no pressing need for, although the two men appear to be continually busy, they never seem to be able to complete other orders on time. Nearly every day, some hot-under-the-collar person arrives to collect something or other, only to be casually informed that it will be ready *mañana*.

I intuit that this old-fashioned method of carpentry, with its complete disregard for urgency, won't allow Paco and Pepe to stay in business much longer. Already, many of the items they make are being churned out by new, modern factories equipped with up-to-date machinery. The ever-increasing demand from developers, anxious to take advantage of the unprecedented building boom, means that quantity takes precedence over quality. However, my fears have proved wrong. Today, in the early 21st century, discriminating people still prefer to buy furniture assembled in the old-fashioned way. In fact, early examples of traditional handiwork, made from locally grown hardwoods, now fetch quite high prices in antique shops.

Amid the wood shavings that litter the workshop floor lies a mound of flotsam, from which glitters a pair of brilliant green eyes: the studio cat. It keeps very still, staring intently at a wire birdcage hanging on the wall by the door. The object of the cat's attention does not seem at all perturbed at being ogled from the heap of sawdust and warbles away all day long, oblivious to its turbulent, and possibly dangerous, environment. Every time the bird shakes its little feathered body, the poor thing evaporates in a powdery cloud. The constant veil of dust makes it impossible to determine either the breed of bird or the original colour of cat.

As well as spending time with my carpenter friends, I do my best to find out more about the history of this part of Spain. Between the Romans' departure in the 4th century and the arrival of the Moors in the 8th, Vandals overran much of Southern Spain and some say this brought about the term 'Vandalucia.' But the origin of the word Andalucía remains uncertain for Al-Andalus, in the mediaeval world of Islam, denoted the whole of Spain and Portugal. As well as this, when the Vandals quit Roman Baetica (a province they had occupied for 20 years) to invade North Africa in 533, the Arabs called the area 'al-Andalish'. Then again, cut off from the rest of the country by the Sierra Morena in the North and the Cordillera Bética in the East and South, the region also became known to the Arabs as the 'Jazira Andalus' – the Island of Andalucía. The Vandals may or may not have contributed to the name Andalucía but their reputation for wanton destruction added a word to the dictionary: vandalism.

Before leaving England, I made some attempt to learn the meaning and origin of the word Almuñécar. According to my Spanish dictionary, the word *muñeca* translates as 'wrist' or 'doll' so I initially guess that the town gets its name from some wrist-shaped contour of rock on the nearby stretch of coastline. Once here, though, I discover that the name comes from the Arabic *Al-Munakkab*.

Yaqut, the Arab geographer, mentions Almuñécar or al-Munakkab briefly, deriving the origin of its name from the Arabic root 'n-k-b', meaning in this context something protected. Its anchorage was indeed well sheltered, and al-Idrisi describes its wealth of fish and fruit, with a water-tower and water-wheel. Its Islamic history begins in 755 A.D., when the Umayyad prince 'Abd ar-Rahman bin Mu'awiya al-Dakhil set foot on the soil of al-Andalus before setting out to defeat the governor Yusuf bin 'Abd ar-Rahman al-Fihr.

Almuñécar formed part of the province of Granada and, situated only forty miles away from the capital, necessarily suffered the joys and sorrows of the city. So, for example, when Sulayman bin 'Umar bin Hafsun rebelled against Granada, he seized Almuñécar in 923, slaughtering all the males and taking the females into captivity. The small town also served as the last bastion of the Zirids of Granada in the following century. Besieged in the fortifications of Almuñécar, the Zirid ruler 'Abdullah had to surrender and suffer exile in 1090. The town and port finally fell to the Catholic Monarchs in December 1489.

The story goes that, when he saw the net closing in on his city of Granada, 'Abd al-Hassan summoned his wise men around him, placed a gold dish in the middle of a large carpet and offered:

"Whosoever can grasp the dish without treading on the carpet, can keep it." The wise men were not wise enough to solve the problem. The Prince simply rolled up the carpet from its edge and, walking behind it as he did so, retrieved the prize, saying, "So shall fall our beloved city."

Hassan's prophecy proved correct for, three years after the fall of Almuñécar, the Catholic armies of Fernando and Isabela triumphantly marched into Granada, forcing Hassan's son and successor, Boabdil, to leave the city and reluctantly make his way south across the Sierras into exile in North Africa. Standing high on a rock, opposite the Hotel Sexi, a stark, stone cross looks out over the Mediterranean, marking the point of his departure.

I find it interesting to learn that among the crowd witnessing the ceremonial deliverance of Granada stood one Christopher Columbus who, later that year, would set sail for the New World.

Long before the Arabs' arrival, the presence of copper and silver in the hills behind, combined with good anchorage and friendly local tribes, prompted the Phoenicians to settle in Almuñécar. They called the town *Ex* or *Sexi*. (Hence the Hotel Sexi, the semi-circular hotel we saw on our first day.) The Romans supplemented the name by calling it *Sexi Firmum Julium* and continued to expand their predecessors' fish industry. They built a seven-kilometre long aqueduct, still in use, to bring water from the Río Verde at Jete to feed into *salazoneras* (salting-pits) in Almuñécar. Therein, little *boquerón* fish were prepared and treated in much the same way as today. Once filleted, soaked in a mixture of salt, olive-oil, garlic, lemon and bay leaves, they became anchovies and, as such, were exported from *Sexi Firmum Julium* in large quantities. Today, menus list them as *boquerones en vinagre* or *anchoas*. They are undoubtedly tasty, especially when served as *tapas,* but I prefer to eat

Cross marking the point of Boabdil's departure

my *boquerones* fried or grilled. Simply pull off their heads and crunch up the rest, bones and all.

For many centuries, the town of Almuñécar, along with the rest of southern Spain, slipped quietly out of the history books and remained much as I find it in 1966 – a small, unassuming farming and fishing community. But changes are taking place very rapidly.

Further west, nearer the airport at Málaga, they have already taken place. It is said that an Englishman, Sir George Langworthy, contributed greatly to the development in this southwest corner of Spain. At the turn of the century, he started the ball rolling by buying an 18th-century fortress in Torremolinos and transforming it into a splendid mansion – the Castillo Santa Clara. He then opened part of the building as a residence for foreigners and introduced charter flights to and from the nearby aerodrome, 'El Rompedizo'. In 1932, the National Tourist Board, seeing money-making potential for the region, invited international journalists, along with several VIPs, to view and make known the delights on offer. Reports were favourable and, benefitting from regular flights from Málaga airport, the tourist industry started to take off. In 1942, another hotel, La Roca, started business at La Carihuela, offering full board for 32 pesetas a day. 1950 saw the launch of the Marbella Club, instigated by a Dutch engineer, Alfons zu Hohenlohe and then, gradually, year by year, the 'jet-set' started to move into the area. By the mid-'50s, celebrities such as Ava Gardner, Marlon Brando, and Prince Rainier of Monaco, accompanied by his new wife Grace Kelly, are seen locally. By the '60s the list includes James Stewart, Rock Hudson, Sean Connery and Frank Sinatra. Between 1960 and 1965 the worldwide number of people coming to Spain jumps from 4 to 14 million and the '80s see the sum total surpasses the nation's population of 54 million. Thanks to all this wealth flowing into the country, Spain becomes Europe's star performer with regards to annual growth. (By the early 21st century it has overtaken France as destination of choice for the British. According to the Office of National Statistics, 14 million Britons visit each year).

By the time of my arrival, Spain has been delivered from its *años de hambre*, hunger years, suffered during and after the Civil War, and moved into its *años de desarrollo*, years of development. Although by European standards local people are still pretty poor, the country is undergoing a dramatic transformation, developing faster than any other in the non-communist world, except Japan. From 1961 to 1973, the economy grows at a rate of 7% and, although imports exceed exports, invisible earnings from tourism more than make up the deficit. Because of this, the government goes out of its way to increase tourist potential. As well as relaxing censorship laws, the authorities encourage any sort of building that might attract more visitors. Although strictly necessary, nobody seems to concern themselves with things like planning permissions or licences. A plot of land is simply purchased and built upon. If, at a later date, the authorities decide to take action and penalise the builder or house-owner, a fine of between one and five per cent of the cost of construction equals less than buying an official permit. Afterwards, when the fine is settled, the property can be registered and be given a proper title-deed or *escritura*. Stretches of land near the coast are being bought by far-sighted investors for something like 100 pesetas per square metre. Ten years later this figure has risen to 4,000 pesetas per square metre and today, in the early 21st century, the same plot fetches 12,000 pesetas.

The uncontrolled, chaotic promotion taking place farther west has not yet started in Almuñécar, for developers prefer to exploit the less-undulating terrain near the airport, which they find easier to build on. Besides, visitors flying to Málaga will have a shorter distance to travel. Torremolinos, Marbella, Fuengirola, Benalmádena – all are rapidly changing beyond recognition, with high-rise apartment blocks sprouting up all over the place and quickly selling to those eager for their slice of Spanish sunshine. Olive and almond plantations are bulldozed from the fields to make way for new housing estates, which start to creep over the landscape like some spreading white fungus.

Fortunately, at the time of my arrival in 1966, this promotion has travelled along the coast only as far as the town of Nerja. Between this point and Almuñécar, the 20-kilometre stretch of dangerous, narrow road discourages entrepreneurs from risking capital in developments further east, for they fear the treacherous drive will deter people from buying. After all, most of the new retirement and holiday homes are selling to older, less adventurous folk.

(Later, tunnelling, bridging and straightening of the N 340 makes this territory more accessible, bringing about its transformation. One guidebook, published in 1990, describes Almuñécar as 'an uninviting agglomeration of apartment blocks').

Anthea and I normally meet up at the Cafetería Al Quirós at around midday to join others waiting for the daily mail delivery. I do not expect anything in the way of correspondence myself, but the rendezvous gives me a chance to meet some of the colourful bunch from many countries. At first, being a new boy in town makes me an object of curiosity. Although I have already told them a bit about myself, they want to know more.

Felix inevitably seems to be the front man. On my second day in Almuñécar, he walks straight across to where Anthea and I are sitting and, without being asked, plonks himself down in a vacant chair.

"Vot you do 'ere, Roy? You come to zis pless and swip my fren Anthea from 'er foot?"

In an attempt to be funny, I answer, "I'm a policeman on a secret mission."

Felix is not amused. The grin leaves his face and he looks questioningly at Anthea, who scowls in my direction.

This woman, by now, knows all my hang-ups. On that first evening, after the session in the carved bed, we had made our way to a nearby bar and, assisted by a couple of bottles of tongue-loosening wine, learned more about each other. The first thing she wanted to know is how a person of my age could think of buying a house and living in this part of the world without working.

"Did you rob a bank or something? Are you on the run?"

Her question makes me think for a moment before answering, "I didn't rob any bank, but perhaps you're right about being on the run."

Gerald Brenan informs us, in *South from Granada*, that he left England to live in a remote part of Spain because he wanted to escape the English class system, which he found 'stifling'. Although we come from different backgrounds – I from a working class family in the East End of London, and he from a much posher set (public school and all that) – perhaps, in a way, we share the same point of view.

In 1957, at the age of twenty, I too had the desire to get away and find somewhere, as Brenan puts it, 'with a more breathable atmosphere', for my involvement with class had left me with bitter feelings.

Four years earlier, I had dropped out of school to join a crew of seven aboard a seventy-four foot yawl, *Celia*, that set sail from England on a seven-year voyage around the world. The disastrous trip ended when the battered, sinking yacht dropped anchor in Las Palmas. Once ashore, I ended up being questioned by the local police and arrested for not having the necessary papers. (In 1953, visitors to Spain or her territories needed a visa). The offence resulted in spending Christmas and my seventeenth birthday 'in custody' at the local Guardia Civil barracks. After a while, someone from the British Consulate managed to persuade the authorities to set me free and then found me a job as deckboy aboard a British tanker, the *British Holly*. This way, I worked my passage back to England.

So far, so good. Adventure all the way. My next move turned out to be a tragic mistake. In 1954, I signed on, for a period of three years, in the Royal Horse Guards. The satirical magazine *Punch*, from an article in the *Evening News*, put it like this:

It seemed like every boy's dream of adventure when sixteen-year old Roy Nash set out on a world tour as cabin-boy in the 74-ft yawl Celia. *But…the trip ended…after a month of hardship. The old boat, battered by storms, was leaking. Food was short…Now Roy, six foot and fair-haired, is safely home…and looking forward to new adventure as a Regular soldier in the Royal Horse Guards. And he is writing his story of 'the worst month of my life'.*
Better hang on a few weeks

The advice given by the caption in bold letters proved perfectly correct. Those next three years turned out to be far worse than anything I'd known in the past. Ridiculous disciplines and inane punishments were bad enough to take, but what got under my skin most were the tremendous advantages I witnessed being accorded the officer class. Nearly all these 'toffs', for want of a better word, had some title to their name, like Lord so-and-so, or Sir something-or-other and, with two of us to act as 'slaves' – a batman to care for their equipment, military and personal; and a groom, who saw to their horse and saddlery (both, incidentally, provided by the army at taxpayers' expense) – these people lived in a world far removed from us common troopers. We slept twenty to a room, in cold, miserable barracks dating from the time of the Crimean War, while the officers had their own separate, comfortable quarters. Yes, it did not take me long to see that there are those who have it easy, and the other sort – my kind.

I realised a class structure existed, of course, but lived in the belief that the upheavals of World War II, along with a programme of Labour Government, might have changed the status quo. Not so. It soon became clear that the birthright advantages offered to these aristocratic Guards officers gave them access to political power, educational opportunity and a cushy lifestyle. This inherited privilege filled me with a sense of outrage.

In 1957, having finished my nightmare three years of square bashing, ear bashing and mind bashing, I returned to 'Civvy Street' bearing a large chip on my shoulder. Matters were not made any better by the Prime Minister of the day, Harold Macmillan, informing me that 'I had never had it so good!'

In 1951, a play by John Osborne, *Look Back in Anger,* provoked the expression, 'angry young man', and I suppose this title fitted me pretty well at that time. Being an accomplished spit-and-polisher, proficient horseman and expert whitewasher of coal did not stand me in very good stead when looking for work in West Ham. The local Labour Exchange had nothing on its books for the likes of me. Besides, my resolve never to call anyone 'Sir', combined with a reluctance to acknowledge authority, made it virtually impossible to hold down a job. My 'touchy' moods and short fuse caused all sorts of bother, for anything I considered a personal affront prompted me to act first and worry about the consequences later. Some of the skirmishes involved the police, who must have had me down in their little black books as a 'nasty bit of work'.

Laurie Lee, in *As I Walked Out One Midsummer Morning*, tells us that when he forsook his Gloucestershire home, aged 19, he was still 'soft at the edges'. Well, at 20, any soft edges of mine had been forged into hard edges. What to do? A psychiatrist might have helped. If an opportunity to join some nefarious enterprise had presented itself in those mixed-up days – well, who knows? With criminal activity on the increase, I might well have been tempted in that direction. Between 1955 and 1960 the number of violent crimes doubled, with gangs like the notorious Krays and Richardsons just starting to flex their muscles. Fortunately, probably because I stayed away from pubs and clubs, the invitation to enlist did not come my way.

For a while, I spent my time hanging around coffee bars in Soho, wearing baggy sweaters, tight trousers, shoes without socks and carrying a copy of Jean-Paul Sartre's *Age of Reason* under my arm, doing my best to appear 'bohemian'. This way, I met plenty of long-haired, bra-less, green-lipsticked young ladies who seemed ready and willing enough to share the existentialist's liberal attitude towards sex. However, I did not really make the grade as a bohemian. My robust looks and short hair put paid to any chance of looking the part. (The film *The Rebel* (1960), starring Tony Hancock, portrays these stereotypical characters to perfection.)

Anyway, nobody looking even slightly 'alternative' dared show themselves on the streets where I lived in the East End of London. They would have been an immediate target for those who had already decided what could, and what could not, be worn: the 'Teddy Boys'. A vicious lot, these. Decked out in Edwardian costume of black, velvet-collared jacket, very narrow 'drainpipe' trousers, white shirt, 'bootlace' tie, they padded about in thick crêpe-soled shoes, looking for 'bother'. Their top pockets held cut-throat razors which were used to slash rival gang's faces – or anyone else's whom they considered needed 'doin' over'. When these filthy weapons became outlawed, an ordinary razor-blade pushed into a raw potato performed the same act. Being caught in possession of these two items could not be an offence, could it?

Trying to sort my life out, I spent long hours at the public library, catching up on my reading, for I had not opened a book in three years.

Sartre's works made sense, but I preferred the ideology of two nineteenth century Americans: Ralph Waldo Emerson and Henry David Thoreau.

'A rich man is he who needs little – a man who needs much will forever be poor'.

I liked that. Or, 'If a man does not keep pace with his companions, perhaps it is because he hears a different drummer. Let him keep in step to the music he hears, however measured or far away'.

I heard a different drummer all right!

Jack Kerouac, a poet of the time, described his quest for spiritual renewal in his *On the Road* (1957) although, to me, it read like a beat version of a book written a hundred years before – Thoreau's *Walden* (1854).

Thoreau's and Kerouac's philosophy, I am sure, meant something to those happy-go-lucky types who wanted simply to 'bum around', but I wanted more than that, reasoning that words like 'little' and 'freedom' depended on the individual. In my case, 'freedom' had to include enough to eat, a roof over my head and an environment in which I could feel free to say what I liked, to whomever I liked, when I liked, without fearing the consequences.

So, with this in mind, I made it my primary objective to find some way of getting enough capital together, preferably legally, to buy my desired independence.

For the next nine years I toiled away at whatever paid most. Back to sea for a while, working in hotels, on building sites, as a club bouncer, film extra, male model, entertainer – and so on. Eventually, in 1960, I struck it lucky as a door-to-door salesman. Working on a commission-only basis I suddenly found myself making more money in one evening than most salaried people earned in a week! Before long, the company promoted me to team leader and then area manager – which meant I received a percentage from all sales. How the money rolled in! My associates considered me a tight-fisted Scrooge – and they were right. While they roistered on a spree, I stayed behind in my cheap bed-sitting room, practising my guitar, reading and diligently stashing away every penny possible, with my goal approaching as my bank balance grew.

With no need of cigarettes, drugs, nor much in the way of alcohol, and my only weakness being sex, which cost me nothing, saving came easy. The 'Swinging '60s' yielded plenty of young ladies just awaiting the chance to burn their bras and meet someone who would help them become 'liberated', so, unselfishly, I did my best to oblige. I may have 'needed little' but, after all, there were limits.

1966 found me with enough cash to put down a deposit on a house in Twickenham, Middlesex, which had been divided into ten bed-sitting rooms. At that time, many such properties were on the market for a Rent Act, recently introduced by Harold Wilson's Housing Minister, Richard Crossman, gave all tenants security of tenure, at a fixed rent, known as a 'fair rent'. If people complained to the council that, in their opinion, they were being overcharged for accommodation, a government inspector, sent to the address, decided what the greedy landlord could rightly charge. This adjudicated 'fair rent', in nearly all cases, turned out to be extremely 'fair' to the tenant, but often did not allow the house owner to cover running expenses, and so forced him to sell up. I knew nothing of this at the time and bought in all innocence. As it happened, probably because my rents were pretty low anyway, none of the tenants groused at what they were paying for their room, so I had no problems with officialdom. Just as well. I hate to think how I might have behaved if some nosy snooper had shown up on the doorstep.

After living at the house and administering things for a while, I calculated that, after bills such as mortgage and rates, I cleared £30 per month. Next, I arranged for one of the tenants, a retired accountant, to take over the management of the property. His tasks included emptying gas and electricity meters, collecting rents and paying all monies into my bank account. For this, along with a bit of gardening and extras, he lived rent-free. The arrangement suited us both. He delighted in having something to occupy his time and the small amount of residual cash offered me a way out.

A newspaper advertisement caught my eye, offering 'home and income for sale in Andalusia'. Spain, I'd heard, was friendly, hot and cheap, and the name Andalusia had a nice ring to it, so I decided to follow things up. Two books, in particular, influenced my decision. *The Presence of Spain* (1964), by James (now Jan) Morris states that 'Spaniards of all classes treat each other with casual courtesy, almost a familiarity'. It goes on to say that 'grandees, belles, grooms, lackeys and all, seem to converse with a dashing kind of fellowship, so that you are hard put to tell which is master'. That sounded my cup of tea. Then, as a final clincher, a work by R.A.N. Dixon, entitled *A House in Spain* (1964) reckoned that one of the disadvantages with moving to Spain involves 'loss of status'. Just the job! Having no status to lose, I rather fancied the idea of moving to a place where people are statusless.

Anthea sits quietly while I gabble away. She listens patiently and attentively, re-filling my glass when empty, tut-tutting here and there and occasionally shaking her pretty head. At the end of it all, I feel much clearer in my mind. This late-night disclosure has done me a power of good. Catholic confessionals make sense.

"So you were a bit of a naughty boy back in England, eh?"

"A long time ago, Anthea. It's all out of my system now. Thanks for being so tolerant and putting up with my tales of woe. You asked why I came here and I suppose one thing led to another."

"Oh, I didn't mind lending an ear. In fact, I found your story fascinating. In a way, I feel a lot closer to you now."

She leans across and places both her hands on my arm.

"But if you'll take my advice, Roy, I wouldn't tell too many people around here about your brushes with the law back in England. The shiny-hatted brigade might prick up their ears and, believe me, they'll have you across the border into France as quick as a flash if they consider you might be troublesome."

"Don't worry. Like I say, I'm a good boy now."

It is now her turn to hold forth. I already know how long she has been in town and of her involvement with the unfortunate Mike, but Anthea seems determined to tell me more about herself. Brought up in a little village near Brighton, Sussex, divorced, no children, part-time teacher, she met with poet/folk-singer, Mike, a few years before coming to Almuñécar, and broke away from her insipid, conventional life-style to join the more colourful, happy-go-lucky culture of the early '60s. Like me, she and Mike had heard good things about this part of Spain and decided to investigate. The rest of the sad saga I already know.

For no reason in particular, I ask about her parents.

"My father is a chief inspector of police," she answers, with a smile.

4

1966

In which I seek out the best bars in town and witness the demise of certain monetary pieces of the day.

We didn't have much in common, I suppose. Anthea liked to hang around bars all day, drinking and chatting with friends, while I preferred to spend my time either on the beach or tramping about the countryside. Nightlife attracted her but I turned in quite early (well, early by Spanish standards – about midnight). We must have made an odd-looking couple, with my muscular, six-foot three-inch build alongside her slight-bodied frame only five-feet tall. Nevertheless, despite our differences, I shall never forget my skinny little friend and lover.

Pint-sized she may have been, but her vigour, at times, left me shattered. Up early and out until late, Anthea would steal quietly back into our room in the small hours, slip into bed where I lay sleeping and, snuggling up close, wake me up by gently running her petite hands over various parts of my anatomy. When ready, I would be rolled over on to my back and, with her tight little buttocks held apart, her taut body lowered itself onto my erect penis. Then, after squatting still for a moment or two, she began bouncing up and down like a yo-yo. Holding back until I had ejaculated, she would make a final deep, hard thrust downwards, hold still for a moment or two, then fall forward onto my chest. This way, we managed to climax at the same time, and there we would lie, in each other's arms, our bodies covered in sweat and sawdust.

The two establishments known as 'foreign bars' in Almuñécar

remain open nearly all night. With dim lighting, soft, cushioned seating and atmospheric music, they cater primarily for the non-Spanish. Occasionally, though, especially if a girl is seen sitting alone, a few of the local lads invest in a drink with hopes of making contact. The more popular of the two bars, La Ventura, which is there to this day, stands to the left of Plaza de la Rosa, in Alta del Mar. Its large, heavy wooden doors, which open at 11 p.m., lead into a cavernous, beam-ceilinged room. On the rough, whitewashed walls are paintings by local artists. The two Swedes running the place have, with the minimum of decoration, made the interior most inviting. Tommy, with his long, lanky frame, shoulder-length hair and thin, bearded face, looks the spitting image of a blond Don Quixote, while his short, rotund partner, Joss, fits the bill as a female version of Sancho Panza. With loose-fitting, Moroccan shirts, old, faded, patched blue jeans, bangles dangling at the wrist and a few rows of beads encircling their necks, they consider themselves, and certainly look, veritable 'hippies'. Trendy footwear to match the costume consists of either open-toed sandals, or locally made canvas shoes, soled from old car tyres.

At this stage of the town's development, Scandinavians seem to have cornered the market in providing something more exotic than the somewhat featureless Spanish bars, for La Ventura has competition from Los Vikingos: a bar run by a per-manently cheerful Dane named Leif. It faces the sea a little dis-tance from the centre of town, in the Paseo Prieto Moreno. Drinks there cost slightly less than in La Ventura, but, maybe because of its position, it lacks the wherewithal to entice enough customers to become a going concern and closes down a few months after I arrive. From time to time I keep company with Anthea in both of these places, but usually I opt to patro-nise one of the many neighbourhood bars dotted about town. Admittedly not so comfortable as their foreign competitors, the little places have a 'Spanishness' which appeals to me more. Besides, drinks cost less there. As Felix so noisily pointed out that first day at Al Quirós, a glass of beer or wine has recently risen in price from two to three pesetas. The same beverage in both La Ventura and Los Vikingos costs at least twice as much, without *tapas*.

Although each of the Spanish bars in Almuñécar serves some sort of *tapas* with each drink, the amount and quality vary. The tastiness of these little side dishes usually decides which gains most custom. One little bar, known as 'The Bicycle Place' (so called because of a rusty old bike tied to the wall) is very popular. With fine mountain wine, or *vino de terreno*, poured from a large earthenware jug and served up with a variety of free fodder that includes egg and chips, fish and chips or *chorizo* and chips, it stands out from the rest. Another favourite, 'The Bird Place', has numerous cages of songbirds hanging from its walls and ceilings. This small unkempt room, with rough, cobbled floor and bamboo ceiling, also comes up trumps with *tapas*. Juicy *albóndigas* (meatballs), *mejillones* (mussels), *pulpo* (octopus), *calamares* (squid) – a saucerful of one or the other comes with every fresh order. On my first visit, it strikes me as peculiar that everybody in the place appears to be holding a hand over the top of his glass. It doesn't take me long to discover the reason. My first sip of wine leads to a bout of choking and spluttering, while spitting out seed husk that has fallen into my drink from above, where the birds are busy scratching and pecking.

On one occasion, in this same bar, something looking like a tiny chicken is placed on the bar counter alongside my glass of wine. I stare at it for a moment and then glance upwards, anxiously. To my relief, none of the cages seems to be empty. The number of peckers and scratchers has not diminished. My *tapa* proves to be nothing other than a *gorrión*, or sparrow. Children go out at night with torch and airgun and shoot these poor creatures from their perch as they roost on overhead wires. The tiny roasted thing on the dish in front of me represents one of their dwindling number.

These little drinking establishments, tucked away down side streets, are not always easy to find, for many have no signs on the walls outside. As their entrances look no different from the doorways next to them, it's better to know which is which or it might lead to walking straight into someone's house. In fact, I hear an account of this actually happening. A thirsty foreigner walks boldly into a person's sitting room, sits down with others at the table and promptly orders a glass of wine. The startled occupants, thinking that perhaps a madman has burst in upon them, oblige. Apparently, when the mistake is discovered, they all have a good laugh. Nobody minds in the least!

At first, I find the standard loud clamour and thick fug of cigarette smoke a bit aggravating but, after a while, I take no notice. To sample the cheap booze and mouth-watering titbits on offer, you need toleration and adaptation. Women, at this time, are never seen in Spanish bars – unless introduced by a foreigner. The only part of a woman I've ever seen in these strictly male preserves are the arms of a barkeeper's wife who, from time to time, slides steaming dishes of tasty morsels through a hole in the wall.

Once I escorted a somewhat well-developed Australian girl into a neighbourhood bar known to us foreigners as 'The Hole in the Wall'. As we pushed our way through the door, the loud chatter inside stopped dead, as if suddenly turned off at a switch. At the same time, the sharp intake of breath seemed, for a moment, to clear the air of cigarette smoke. As my buxom, short-skirted companion made her way towards the bar, large buttocks wobbling seductively from side to side, those standing in her path stumbled over each other in an effort to give passage. Others stood rooted to the spot, staring open-mouthed with fag-ends dangling from their lips. Some, feeling perhaps that this unique occasion justified further action on their part, silently removed their hats. Neither she nor I understood the mutterings being whispered behind our backs, which is probably just as well.

It is not often that a bar falls silent. With no soft furnishings to speak of, and tiled walls and floors, perfect acoustics augment the decibel level. It takes only a few vociferous people, speaking at their normal pitch (i.e. loud), to create quite a commotion. Powerful vocal chords are cultivated at an early age. At the tender age of two or three a child is able to shatter eardrums with its piercing cry of '¡Mamá!'

Fireworks are great noise-makers and particularly applauded, especially those that shoot up into the sky to explode at full pitch. Boom! On the coast, this blast of sound, as it echoes across sea and through valley, sets all the dogs a-barking to the accompaniment of the seagulls a-squawking. When no firework displays or noisy fiestas are in the offing, young folk do their best to prevent things becoming too dull by roaring through narrow streets on motorbikes with silencers deliberately removed. The two most popular games played in bars – dominoes and cards – are also performed with great zeal. A domino piece, cracked down onto a hard, wooden surface, can, with practice, be made to sound like a rifle-shot, and I am certain, if ever a competition were to take place to discover who can produce the loudest 'splat!' by slapping down a playing card, I know a couple of Spaniards who would win every time! All this fracas is infuriating at first but, after a while, becomes acceptable and eventually, particularly when drinking, totally ignored.

I find that not all places charge three pesetas for a red wine or beer. With a two-and-a-half peseta coin in circulation, many bar owners stick to this price for a glass of something or other. It makes life easier, especially as, next up the scale, the duro, or five-peseta coin, will cover the cost of two measures. Small-change currency includes coins to the value of ten céntimos (one tenth of a peseta), a real (twenty-five céntimos or a quarter of a peseta), fifty céntimos (half a peseta) and the peseta itself. The real continues to be used as a monetary term for a short while after my arrival in 1966, but the word duro lasts much longer. Local folk nearly always refer to a twenty-five-peseta coin as cinco duros and the fifty-peseta piece as diez duros. To this day, I am pretty sure, most of the older inhabitants will immediately understand the price if quoted in duros – even though we now speak in euros.

But times change. I witness the demise of many of these monetary pieces. Rampant inflation means that the humble, lightweight, ten céntimos and then the real, are rapidly losing worthwhile purchasing power and so are on the point of extinction. Before long, the shiny, newly minted peseta will be the coin of lowest denomination.

It makes sense, I suppose, for it means that, while they are in use, drinks are sometimes paid for with a pile of little pieces. It takes twenty-five of the ten-céntimos to pay for one wine or beer! Barkeepers, not bothering to count, sweep the whole lot into a container, where they remain until they have a chance to pass the coins on to someone else. Unwary customers, not used to the ropes, who don't offer the correct amount when paying, can sometimes find themselves leaving a bar with heavy, bulging pockets full of small change.

As these battered, often out-of-shape, low-value bits of aluminium are worth hardly anything at all, many people, considering them to be simply a bit of a nuisance, end up tossing them into the sea. Perhaps because of compassion for the underdog, I feel rather sorry for these ill-used bits of currency. They've been around for some twenty-five years and not so long ago would have been treated very differently.

After the Spanish Civil War, the rest of Europe, represented by the newly-formed United Nations, decided to give Spain the cold shoulder, for the country was governed by a Fascist right-wing dictator. Besides, unlike Italy and Germany, there would be no danger from Communist encroachment with a man like Franco in charge.

The ensuing *años del hambre* or 'hunger years' saw the people of Spain experience hard times. Dogs and cats disappeared from city streets, and peasants, in an effort to ease hunger pains, boiled and ate grass and weeds. Many perished. At the beginning of the 20th century, a day-labourer earned one and a half pesetas a day in Andalusia, if he was lucky enough to find work. Farther north, the rate stood at four pesetas a day. In the 1920s the amount, locally, rose to two pesetas while the corresponding national average rose to ten. This meant that the poor in the south suffered more than before. I imagine that a handful of these now unwanted coins might well have made the difference between life and death to some starving family. (Not during periods of the Civil War, though, for in many parts of the country there was nothing in the shops to buy! People were issued with vouchers by the occupying force to exchange for food, household supplies and clothing). Even by the late '40s, wages do not seem to have increased by much. Norman Lewis, in his book *Voices of the Old Sea* (1984), writes that when he went to live in Farol, a small fishing village on the Costa Brava, in 1948 he found the wages for a carpenter-mason to be fixed by the state at 21 pesetas a day.

Coinage of a similar denomination, in the late 19th and early 20th centuries, during the reign of Alfonso XIII, had a much more elevated status. Half, one, two and five peseta coins were minted in silver and those to the value of ten, twenty and one hundred pesetas, in gold. No watery grave for those! An example of how the same currency can remain in circulation for a long period is illustrated in *South from Granada*. In the village of Yegen, a local shopkeeper hands Gerald Brenan some odd-looking pieces in his change. When he looks more closely at the coins he sees that some were minted in Roman times. How long, he wonders, have these, and others he buys from villagers at a peseta apiece, been in use as local currency?

Grubby, much-handled one and five peseta banknotes are also due for retirement, for in December 1965, a crisp new brown coloured one hundred-peseta note is put into circulation. One side has the picture of the handsome, bearded young Spanish poet Gustavo Adolfo Bécquer, while, in contrast, the other shows the pinched, bespectacled head of the Spanish composer Manuel de Falla. I think it rather strange that this man's face should appear on a banknote in Franco's time, for he is known to have been one of the intellectuals closely associated with the Popular Front at the outbreak of the Civil War. He narrowly escaped being shot when, in 1936, he tried to prevent the execution of his friend, Federico García Lorca. The fact that he was a devout Catholic may have saved his life.

A blue five hundred-peseta note makes a brief appearance; then, in the '70s, banks issue a new green one thousand-peseta note. This represents a great deal of money to most folk and causes all sorts of headaches when presented as payment.

I remember a film, *The Million Pound Note* (1954), based on the classic tale by Mark Twain, in which the penniless character played by Gregory Peck is given a million-pound note to spend. The donors want to prove that a man of such obvious wealth can live off the fat of the land for a whole month without having to break into it. Of course, they are proved correct. Nobody can give change. Much the same happens when the thousand-peseta note is introduced.

When proffered as payment for something or other, the barkeeper or shopkeeper would inevitably shake his head and say,

"Pague mañana." "Pay tomorrow."

It strikes me as bizarre that whereas, for a while, money of too little value is hard to get rid of, at the other end of the scale, too great an amount, in one lump, finds itself in the same situation. Before long, though, as costs rose all the time, the thousand-peseta note becomes commonplace.

5

1966

In which I part from Anthea, search the coastline, fall in love with La Herradura and seek help from John the Plumber.

It is the end of my third week in Almuñécar. Anthea slowly makes her way back to the Cafetería Al Quíros with a light blue envelope in her hand. As she gets closer, I see it has blue and red striped edges. Air mail. She sits herself down, carefully tears along one edge, pulls out a single sheet of thin paper, unfolds it and starts to read. After a moment or two, her body stiffens and, under the table, I see her toes poking out from her sandals curl tightly together. By this time I know Anthea to be a cool, composed, 'laid back' sort of person. Except for our sex sessions, nothing much else seems to turn her on. The contents of the letter must be important. She glances at me, opens her mouth as if to say something, shuts it again and then looks down once more. I sip my drink and keep quiet. When, after a couple more false starts, she eventually speaks, she doesn't look up but keeps her eyes lowered.

"It's from my father. Through his contacts, he's found out where Mike is. A prison up near Madrid."

So, that's it. I make no comment. What can I say? She raises her head. With wet streaks running down her screwed up face, she blurts out,

"Oh, Roy, I don't know what to do! He might need me. If I don't go, I'll feel rotten and never forgive myself!"

After a moment or two more of silence, with Anthea biting her lower lip, I take another swig of beer and say,

"Of course you wouldn't. You have to go. You couldn't relax if you stayed here."

Moving round to her side of the table, I pull up a chair and put my arm around her narrow, quivering shoulders. This brings on a fresh burst of loud sobbing. Giving her a peck on her salty-wet cheek, I whisper in her ear, "You go to him. He needs you."

The crying eases off a little. Anthea turns her face towards me. Her voice has a hard edge to it.

"Don't you need me, Roy?"

Without thinking, I reply, "Oh, don't you worry about me. I'll be all right. I'm sure Mike needs you more than I do."

She pushes my arm away and stands up. Those at the other tables have, by now, stopped whatever they are doing and are staring in our direction. Our little drama interests them. I sense that, before long, one or more of them will be coming over to join us. We are in no mood for company. Anthea has noticed their unabashed curiosity as well.

"Let's go."

We slouch back through the streets with Anthea squeezing my hand tightly all the way. The carpenter's workshop has ceased activities for a siesta break so, without saying a word, we climb the dusty stairs, onto the dusty bed and stir up a cloud of granulated sawdust for the last time. Afterwards, a sniffling Anthea turns to me.

"Don't you care at all that I might be going, Roy?"

The dampness around her eyes has caked with powder making it look as though she's wearing glasses.

"Of course I care. It won't be the same without you." Then, leaning up on one elbow and looking down at her, I ask, half jokingly, "By the way, will you be taking Mike's guitar with you?"

The instrument is in her safekeeping and I've been using it. Anthea doesn't see the funny side. "You keep the bloody guitar! I'm leaving on the bus first thing tomorrow morning!"

Trying to be helpful, but making matters worse, I point out, "I think there's one tonight." Tact has never been my strong point.

Anthea does take the Madrid bus the following morning. I think that if I'd switched on the charm a bit – used a bit of the old 'gift of the gab' picked up during my door-to-door selling days – I might have been able to sweet-talk her into staying but, as things stand, I don't want her to get the impression that our relationship is anything more than casual or short-term. Having only recently gained my long awaited freedom, being tied to anything or anyone is not what I'm after.

A song, *Four Strong Winds*, going around at the time, has the lines:

> '*But the good times are all gone*
> *And we must be movin' on*'.

Accompanying myself on Mike's guitar, I gently sing this song to Anthea in La Ventura that night before she leaves. It really seems to switch on the waterworks.

It doesn't take long for word of her imminent departure to spread around town. Her friends seem truly sorry to see her go. I've come to understand that the close-knit foreign community in and around Almuñécar comprises one large family and anything happening to one affects us all. Throughout the evening, more and more people crowd into the bar to make sad, sometimes emotional, farewells. Believing that I have a need to drown my sorrows, consolation comes my way in the form of a never-ending supply of alcohol. Felix, in particular, demonstrates his distress at the parting of the ways by sitting beside me for much of the time. His glass, I note, placed on the table very close to mine, often becomes refilled by mistake.

For once, I manage to stay awake long enough to spend the whole night in Anthea's company and then escort her back to our lodgings to collect her rucksack. From there we make our sad way to the petrol station, where the Málaga bus will pick her up and drop her at the airport. Just before stepping inside the bus, Anthea puts down her bag, circles her thin arms about my waist and pushes her stubbly head into my chest.

"Don't forget me, Roy, will you? Things were working out, weren't they? As soon as I've sorted things, I'll be back, I promise."

As I lean forward to kiss her hair, I glance up to see the driver watching us impatiently. He wants to be on his way. Anthea keeps him waiting a moment longer. Lifting up her face towards mine, her face streaked with wet lines, she adds, "I hate leaving this place. It's wonderful here. Look after yourself, Roy." Then, with a wave of the hand she turns and climbs the step. Just as the doors are swinging shut I hear her call out, "See you. *Hasta pronto.*"

But she doesn't see me *pronto*, or at any other time. News reaches Almuñécar a year later that Mike committed suicide while in prison and Anthea returned to England. I must admit, I missed her. For a while, I half-expected, and hoped, to see her sitting among the crowd at Al Quirós or feel her wiry little body slide in beside mine during siesta.

The next week sees me taking long hikes in the range of hills behind Almuñécar and La Herradura or along the Río Seco as far as Jete and Otívar. On the way, I sing love songs to my absent Anthea. One of my favourite excursions is to walk up the dirt track that crosses the Cerro del Gorbal and Cerro de la Capellanía. Passing two small clusters of houses called El Cerval and El Rescate, I eventually arrive at an area known as Peñón de los Castillejos, wherein stand the ruins of a Moorish castle. At 1000 metres above sea level, the views alone make the steep climb worthwhile, but an added delight is the wonderfully fragrant mountain air, scented by sea lavender, sage and honeysuckle. The local wild life includes mountain goat or ibex; lizards, large and small; various types of snake; a selection of birds, including eagles; and hundreds of different sorts of insects. Several species of butterfly are not only unique to this part of Spain, but are found nowhere else in the world. I've heard rumours that a few wild cat, or lynx (those that have managed to escape the hunter's bullet, that is) can occasionally be seen as well, but I haven't come across any myself.

Inevitably, I end up with scratched legs, but I do my best to avoid too much contact with strange plants for, in his book *History of the Reign of Ferdinand and Isabella* (1854), William H. Prescott records that the Moors poisoned the tips of their arrows with the juice of a plant called wolf's bane 'which grew rife in the Sierra Nevada'. One wound, however trivial, 'was sure to be mortal'.

I love to watch the people at work once the wheat is cut. First they lay the sheaves on a circle of stones, known as an *era,* then give the whole lot a severe bashing with a jointed stick (flailing or threshing). Then, when the stalks are broken up enough, they are tossed up in the air so that the chaff flies away in the wind and the grain falls back onto the ground (winnowing). After the corn has been collected and bagged, it is taken away to be crushed into flour.

Although by now well into December, the weather in Almuñécar remains warm and sunny. The mountain ranges to the north provide enough shelter for winter temperatures to

Winnowing

average 20 degrees Centigrade in this part of Spain and, because of its unique, sub-tropical climate, the whole 60-kilometre stretch of coastline between Málaga to the west and Almería to the east, is known as the Costa Tropical.

I remain living in Anthea's rooms above the workshop for only a few days more. I could have stayed longer, for the rent has been paid until the end of the month, but somehow, it doesn't feel the same without her, particularly when I lie alone in the big bed: it holds too many memories.

Several of my new friends offer me accommodation, but I decide to rent a room in the Hostal Victoria and live on my own for a while. I need to think things over. Everything about Almuñécar leads me to believe that it would be an ideal place to hunt around for a property. The happy-go-lucky lifestyle, the weather, the people, the cost of living: all suit me down to the ground. What more could I want? But, nevertheless, in the back of my mind I sense there might be somewhere even more idyllic just around the corner. After all, Almuñécar has been my first port of call. Those I speak to assure me that this stretch of coastline can't be bettered, but, for my peace of mind, I decide to check things out for myself.

I start my search by heading eastward, towards Almería. After twisting and turning along the N 340 for about fifteen kilometres, I come upon a cubist conglomeration of white houses on the seaward side of the road, tumbling, one on top of the other, down the side of a steep hill. This is the village of Salobreña. One part looks to have been chopped off with a giant Saracenic scimitar, exposing sheer rock face.

Turning right off the main highway, I drive up a steep incline along a bumpy narrow track, past an ugly, brick-built, smoke-belching sugar factory to park at the summit alongside a large, 10th-century Moorish fortress. Stepping down from my vehicle, I look about me. What a view! There, to the north, across a flat, green landscape of waving sugar cane I take in a series of rugged, corrugated mountain foothills sweeping up to the Sierras Chaparral and Guajaras. A little to the east lies the long

Salobreña

line of Alpujarras, dwarfed by the stunning, glistening, snow-capped Sierra Nevada behind.

As I stand there, spellbound, a shrunken, stooped old man comes out from one of the nearby terrace of houses. After staring in my direction for a moment or two, he slowly makes his way towards me. The jacket he wears is at least two or three sizes too large for him, with its bottom almost reaching his knees and sleeves rolled back six inches or more. The sight reminds me of a frightened little fledgling bird peeping out from its nest. Dangling from his hand I see a large, rusty key. On reaching me, he removes his beret and peers up into my face, as if expecting something from me.

I point over the rooftops towards the wonderful, distant panorama, at the same time trying out one of the few Spanish words I've learned.

"Bonita".

He doesn't have to look. He's seen it before.

"Ah, sí. Sí, señor, gracias a Diós."

Then the muddle starts. The man starts by holding up his key in front of my face. Not quite knowing what to think, I reach out my hand to take it from him. Could it be for sale or is he just showing it to me, I wonder? The poor fellow stands there for a moment or two in a state of utter confusion and then hands the key over. To keep him happy, I think it only polite to ask the price, so try another scrap of vocabulary I've picked up.

"*¿Cuánto?*"

This really sparks things off. He lets loose in a broadside of fast, angry-sounding Spanish and jumps up and down inside his cavernous, flapping coat, trying to snatch the key back again. What have I done? Why is he getting so hot under the collar? Have I mispronounced the word and insulted him in some way? Does he think I want to hire or buy his daughter – or granddaughter? I become more and more flummoxed. Only towards the end of his outburst does he point towards a large, arched portico built into the castle wall. That's it! It suddenly dawns on me that the excited one wishes to know whether I want to go inside and look around. If so, he will unlock the gate. He's the custodian of the key – or will be, if he ever gets it back! After returning his cherished key, I raise my eyebrows, shrug my shoulders and hold my hands, palms uppermost, in the air. He understands my sign language.

"*Ah! Entiendo. No hablas español.*"

Shaking his head, he gives a broad toothless smile. All is forgiven.

I suppose, after that mix-up, I should at least take up his offer and make a token inspection of the mediaeval building, but, as I want to get on, I tap my watch and point to the Land Rover. My wrinkled friend gets the message and, looking a little let down, trudges back towards the row of houses, swinging the precious key in his hand. Viewed from the back, he reminds me of a tortoise.

By this time, others, mostly women with young children, have shown themselves in doorways. Some, who must have been watching our little pantomime, are laughing. As I drive off, they all wave goodbye. It looks to me as though this place has not seen many foreigners – yet.

Salobreña, I think to myself, certainly has a lot going for it, especially with such wonderful views to the north, but, looking in the other direction, I see that the very long stretch of coastline below the village runs in one unbroken line. Fine for swimming and sunbathing, I suppose, but since nothing offers shelter from the wind, I can see that it will be difficult to launch or beach a boat from the shore. The few I have seen are pulled up on the shingle close to one solitary rock which might offer some shelter, but not much.

Back down the hill again, past a large Guardia Civil barracks, I turn again onto the N 340 and continue in the direction of Motril. Here, the landscape changes. Instead of the craggy, rocky terrain I had driven through earlier, the next five kilometres pass through flat, fertile land watered by the river Guadalfeo. In every direction stretch abundant fields of sugar cane, a crop brought to Spain in the 8th century by the Moors. I guess that cultivating and processing the crop provides plenty of work for those living locally. Today, in 2004, the sugar factory in Salobreña is the only one in Europe still operating.

I don't stay long in Motril. Its hustle and bustle does not impress me and, anyway, large towns are not on my itinerary. Later, however, when I get to know the place better, I discover Motril's hidden charms. Good, inexpensive fish restaurants are dotted around the dock area and, in one or two working boatyards, large wooden fishing boats are put together. Later on, I spend quite a bit of time in this honest, unpretentious port. Boatyards may not be everyone's hobby, I know, but I find them fascinating. The tools employed in boat-building are similar to those used by Paco and Pepe and, once again, I love to watch the way an adze, in the right hands, can chop away at a rough piece of timber and, with slivers of wood flying in all directions, give it shape. Later, of course, when power gadgets take over, the old hand-implements used in boat-building become obsolete and end up decorating some bar or restaurant wall.

On the other side of Motril I make my way through many little hamlets that hug the coast until, just past La Rábita, I arrive at the provincial borders of Granada and Almería. At this point I reckon I've seen enough. None of the villages compares favourably with Almuñécar. Perhaps if I'd checked them out more thoroughly or stayed longer, one or two might have proved more appealing but, as things stand, I simply turn around and drive back to my starting point.

Next day I try looking in the other direction – westwards along the coast towards Málaga. Nine kilometres out of Almuñécar, after zig-zagging around at least twenty bends, I get my first sighting of La Herradura. Wow!

Pulling off to the left of the N 340, I park a hundred metres or so along a tree-lined promontory (Punta de la Mona or Monkey Point), and step out from my Land Rover. There spreads out below me an exquisite, glistening, horseshoe-shaped bay. I close my eyes, then open them again to make sure I'm not hallucinating. Never in my wildest dreams could I have imagined anything

The bay of La Herradura from Punta de la Mona

The bay of La Herradura from Cerro Gordo

like this! My eyes wander along the kilometre-long stretch of beach to a cape called Cerro Gordo or Fat Pig on the other side, jutting far out into the blue Mediterranean. Turning to look inland, I take in a splendid, sweeping backdrop of furrowed hills meandering their way down, almost to the shoreline itself. I know at once. This is it! La Herradura is my idea of paradise.

A stiff breeze is blowing that day, so the waves rise as white foam, but, even so, I catch sight of a few small boats out on the sea sheltering in the lee of the far point, where it's calmer. I recognise, at once, that while the cliffs offer safe haven from westerly winds at that end of the bay, the headland on which I now stand would offer a protective shield from easterly winds at this end. In other words, from whichever wind direction, one or other promontory will provide safe harbour. A fisherman's paradise! I picture myself sitting out there in a little dinghy, basking in the hot sun, trying my luck with hook and line. I feel sure that a property in this locality would suit me down to the ground. My reveries keep me transfixed a while longer but then, in order to completely satisfy myself, once and for all, that even this most charming spot cannot be bettered, I drive back to the N 340 and proceed on my way.

On the other side of the bay, the road turns left and climbs upwards, around the edge of the Cerro Gordo. At the top, on a bend, stands a squat, grim-looking guardhouse which acts as home to the Guardia Civil. In front of it some stone seats benefit from the shade of a large tree. A sign, nailed to its trunk, reads *Mirador*, or 'vantage point'. I do as the notice suggests and stop to take a peek. From this position, looking over the tops of pine trees, there's a different perspective of the bay. The spectacle from this angle is even more remarkable. Whichever way you look the views are stunning! After remaining there, lost in wonder, for a minute or two, I turn about to discover that the coastline towards Málaga is just as mind-blowing. My head starts to spin. It's all becoming too much.

As I stand there, doing my best to take it all in, I catch sight of a conical, 15-metre high structure, positioned a short way up the hill behind the Guardia Civil barracks. On my travels, I've come across many such towers, each one standing in a commanding position, looking out to sea.

Henry Avellan's *Moorish Cavalcade* (1978) tells us that the Moors erected many of these towers during the reign of Abd-ar-Rahman (822–852) to help keep watch for the Vikings! These feared Nordic seafarers had already pillaged and ravaged towns and villages all along the northern and western coasts of Europe as far as the Straits of Gibraltar and then, in the early 9th century, they started pushing their way into the Mediterranean. With their terrifying appearance, fearsome reputation and bloodthirsty ways, these blond, horn-helmeted, giant marauders were considered demons. When guards in the towers spotted Viking longboats approaching, a message, sent by carrier pigeon, gave warning of their approach. These literally 'airmail' winged dispatches enabled a defensive force of Moors to be gathered together and sent to repel the attack.

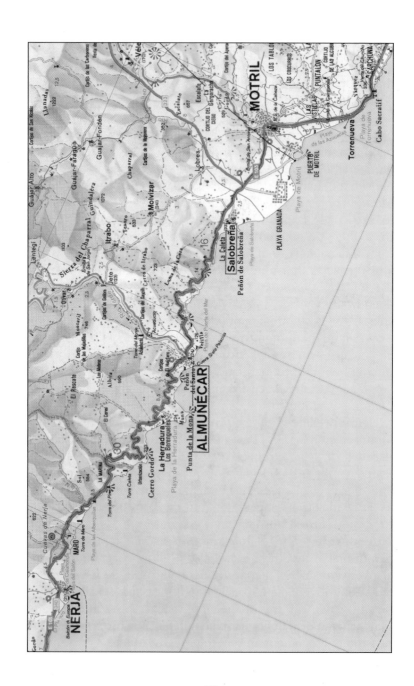

Six centuries later, the same structures were used by the Christians to watch for raiding Moors. Then, instead of carrier pigeons, fires were lit as a signal. Nowadays, it's difficult to know which of these towers are original and which aren't, for quite a few replicas are being built to act as water depositories for new estates.

A kilometre further on, past a bar-restaurant called, appropriately enough, *El Límite* (The Limit), I drive over a small bridge which takes me out of the province of Granada, and into that of Málaga.

The following stretch of the N 340 is still reckoned to be one of the most attractive on the south coast of Spain. In 1966, without present-day tunnelling and bridging, the twisting, turning journey between Almuñécar and Nerja takes at least an hour. The small, rock-lined coves along its route might be tempting to look at but, with dozens of hairpin bends, hardly any barriers and sheer drops to the rocks below, most sensible drivers keep their eyes fixed firmly on the road in front of them.

The best way to appreciate the coast's rugged enchantment is to make the journey by bus. In order to relax, though, travellers are advised not to sit too far forward. As I have already observed on the road down from Granada, the front wheels of a bus are set quite a way back from the bonnet, so, in order to make it round tight corners the bus is forced to poke its nose over the edge of the cliffs. It can be terrifying for passengers sitting in the first few rows of seats to glance down at that precise moment.

As more local people start to own their own transport, the amount of traffic on this section of road increases and it becomes quite commonplace to see the crumpled remains of some vehicle or other being hauled up from the rocks below. The only thing to be said in favour of this hazardous section of highway is that, during the '60s and '70s, it acted as a natural barrier to development further east, in places like La Herradura, Almuñécar and Salobreña. (Roland could have held the Saracens at bay here!)

I don't get as far as Nerja. On its outskirts, I pass through a cluster of newly-built, ugly-looking houses and, a little beyond that, come to another site, swarming with workmen, where foundations for more of the same are being laid. Posters advertise properties for sale by a company called Capistrano. Deciding I've seen enough of Nerja, I turn around and head back, stopping off for lunch at a pretty little village I passed through on the way: Maro.

Maro has recently seen a large increase in the number of visitors due to the discovery of enormous caves, stumbled upon in 1959 by a group of schoolboys out on a bat-hunting expedition. As well as the usual stalactites and stalagmites, evidence in the shape of skeletons reveals that these caves were occupied as long ago as 2000 BC. This news has brought excited archaeologists rushing to Maro from all parts of the world. As the search continues, their scholarly hearts beat faster as pottery, ornaments, tools and, to top it all, rock paintings, are found.

When I pay a visit in 1967, these huge grottoes are still being explored. For a small entrance fee, sightseers (if they can be called that) are given permission to look around inside but the ramshackle conditions leave a lot to be desired. A local guide leads a short line of people (no more than five), trailing behind him clinging on to a rope. As these poor souls slip and stumble their way along in the pitch black, they are brought to a halt here and there in order to squint at something faintly illuminated by the leader's small, hand-held torch. I find the experience quite eerie. The dancing shadows conjure up all sorts of ghostly images, especially as visitors are told that, all those centuries ago, a major earth tremor created a landslide, blocking the cave's entrance and sealing the occupants inside. What a story those bones could tell! Edgar Allan Poe would have been inspired.

Forty years later things are somewhat different. Everything has been tarted up and revamped. A large car park, souvenir shops, a restaurant and small museum have been built outside, and visitors can now stroll safely around the paved, brightly-lit interior to the sound of piped music. It has lately become a venue for concerts. I see in the local newspaper announcements of a flamenco night, the Los Angeles Jubilee Singers, and a performance by Julio Boca and his Argentinian Ballet.

My trips along the coast have just about convinced me that either Almuñécar or La Herradura must indeed be the place to look for a property. Just about, but not quite. Even though other places I've seen haven't been a patch upon that fantastic bay, in the back of my mind there still lingers a slight suspicion that perhaps some little jewel has been overlooked. So, before finally deciding, I come to the conclusion that it might be a good idea to chat things over with someone who knows this area like the back of his big hand: John the Plumber.

I met this character the week before while waiting for Anthea at the Cafetería Al Quirós. On this particular morning, among the usual crowd of hopefuls waiting for the Poste Restante to open its doors, I catch sight of someone I have not seen before, sharing a table with Felix, who calls out, "Roy, my fren', come to meet my goot fren', John. He Englishman, too."

Straight away I see that the Belgian's 'fren'' is a different kettle of fish from the usual types congregating at Al Quirós at that time of day. He stands out like a sore thumb. To start with, he doesn't look in the least 'hippie'. No beads. No jeans. No sandals. Instead, he wears baggy corduroy trousers, check shirt and suede shoes. About my height and weight, the man has short, untidy hair and a beaten-up looking face, and his nose appears to have been broken and badly set.

As I approach, he leans across, holds out a huge hand and smiles, showing a couple of gaps in his front teeth.

"Pleased to meet you, Roy! What'll you have to drink, mun? Felix tells me you've not long arrived. Not a bad little place, is it, mun?"

He speaks with a strong Liverpudlian accent.

I would have liked to spend more time with this character, but, at that moment, Anthea turns up. Putting her arms around my shoulders, she bends down and softly murmurs a few seductive words in my ear. I'm being summoned. So, with a 'see you later' to my friends I go with her back to the workshop and up the stairs.

Later, as we lie together, I ask what she knows of this John. After a short silence, she answers, "The guy's a bit of a mystery. He's hard to fathom. Nobody seems to know much about him – even his full name. Apart from believing that he comes from Liverpool – and from his accent that's not hard to tell, and the fact that he's a plumber, not much more is known about him."

Anthea wriggles her body a little closer, places a hand on my knee and slowly inches it upwards.

"I suppose he's a decent enough bloke. Lives for the moment, it seems. When he's got pesetas in his pocket, he buys. A lot of the sponging bums around here take advantage of his generosity and tag along for the handouts."

She pauses for a moment to nibble my ear, then her head slides lower.

"Don't get on the wrong side of him though, Roy. He's one tough hombre. Keep well away when he's had too much."

Anthea takes a break from giving me further information about John, due to the fact that her mouth is now full. My concentration has shifted, as well. Later, though, she goes on to tell me more.

It transpires that John arrived in town some years earlier, carrying his tools of trade in a leather doctor's bag. As a plumber, he manages quite well to earn his keep. With a reputation for being good at his job and, more importantly, reliable, finding commissions is no problem. His unusual practice of turning up on time makes him popular, and besides, there are plenty of English customers delighted to find a craftsman who speaks their language. News of John the Plumber's arrival in town brings a stampede from those seeking his services. Those that employ him know the score. If the job cannot be finished in one day they must provide bed and board for as long as it takes. As some of the customers are women, Anthea says, his 'services' are not always restricted to plumbing.

When she finally stops talking, I turn and ask her, meaningfully, "As you're very well informed, just how well do you know this guy?"

She laughs, "Not that well. Anyway, he's not short of a girl or two. They say he's got a string of them dotted along the coast. A girl in every port, like a sailor. You should know all about that, Roy."

Since meeting with John at Cafetería Al Quirós that first day, I've had no further opportunity to speak with him. He left Almuñécar to work somewhere or other and has only just returned. Knowing how much he travels up and down the coast leads me to believe that he will be worth consulting. I want to look as much as possible before I leap. As well as that, the little I know about the man, I like.

A tour of the drinking establishments leads me eventually to catch up with him in 'The Bicycle Place', where I find him talking nineteen to the dozen to a couple of Spaniards in what sounds like fluent, Scouse-accented Spanish. Once he has finished chin-wagging with his mates and we've knocked back a few drinks, I explain my dilemma. I give John an account of my exploratory trips and then ask his advice. Where, in his opinion, would be the best place to buy a property in these parts and what does he know about the village of La Herradura?

He ponders for a while before answering.

"The Horseshoe, eh? Well, mun, I suppose it depends on what you want to do down here. Not much goes on in that sleepy little place. Mind you, I don't know it too well. I've been out that way once or twice but there's not much in the way of work for me there, you know, mun. Not too many foreigners yet. It's certainly a beautiful spot, though. That goes without saying. There's nothing finer along the coast, for sure. Have you spoken to Antonio or Donald? They've just started building houses there, mun."

I remember that Anthea has told me something of this. The news needs to be followed up.

"Are you busy at the moment, John?"

He gives me a broad, toothy grin.

"I'm busy having a drink. No, mun. I've got nothing on that can't wait."

"Fancy a trip out there then? I'd really appreciate your company."

"Nothing I'd like better, mun," and off we go.

On the way, I ask if he knows of anything that might be on offer on Punta de la Mona. I rather fancy the idea of getting hold of something there, for it would mean being able to look out across the bay in a westerly direction and witness the wonderful sunsets.

To my surprise, John breaks into a little ditty. He has a terrible voice.

"Punta people are the best,"
"No-one can deny it.
If you want a bit of class,
That's the place to buy it."

I look at the man at my side more closely. He hasn't drunk too much, as far as I know.

"What's all that about? I'm not looking for a bit of class."

"I know, mun. The lyrics weren't meant for you. You don't look like a Punta person. It's just that the posh lot up there, with their grand abodes, gardeners, cooks, house-cleaners and so forth, tend to piss me off. Quite a few living up on the Punta arrived here from places like India, where they were used to having servants and suchlike at their beck and call. We say it's 'from the Punjab to the Punta' in their case. You know how it is with that type of person, Roy. They're usually the sort that knows the price of everything and the value of nothing. If any of their number, with their airs and graces, happens to come within earshot of us bums, we give them a blast of our little number. There's more to it. Do you want another verse, mun?"

Before I can say anything, he starts again.

"You may live on the highest hill,
You may even see Gran-a-ada
But if you don't live on Punta Point
You don't amount to na-a-ada."

As he pauses to take a breath. I jump in.

"Um, perhaps a little more later, John."

"Perhaps I've exaggerated a bit, mun. They're not all like that. Have you heard of a guy called Andrés Segovia?"

I reply that I know him to be the most famous classical guitarist in the world.

"Well, mun, he's got a house up there, along with a lot of other wealthy types. Mostly, Punta people keep themselves very much to themselves, like others I can mention."

He hesitates before carrying on.

" A little word of warning, mun. If you come across any middle-aged Germans out this way, looking as though they aren't short of a peseta or two, it's best not to ask what they did in the War. They can do no wrong in this country. Quite a few came out here at the end of the War with a couple of art treasures under one arm and a sackful of Jewish gold teeth under the other, if you know what I mean, mun. Our General Franco welcomed them with open arms, for he appreciates the help they gave him in the Civil War. If you ask the 'Krauts' out this way too many questions, it might lead to a knock on your door from the guys with the shiny hats."

With a little chuckle, he adds, "They don't have it all their own way up on the Punta, though."

A short while ago, he tells me, a large boulder needed to be removed to make space for a swimming pool. To achieve this, builders decided to blast the obstacle away, using a bountiful supply of dynamite. The huge explosion had the desired effect but, at the same time, brought down much of the hillside, including several newly constructed villas. Luckily, the houses were unoccupied at the time. The huge rock, which had been acting as anchor stone, rolled down the hill and can today be seen resting on the beach just below the road that curves its way up Punta de la Mona hill.

6

1966

In which I learn more about building methods, agree to buy a house at San Nicolás and am visited by a long-legged physiotherapist.

My heart gives a jump for joy that late December day as, once again, I feast my eyes on the glorious, glimmering, horseshoe-shaped bay. I challenge anyone not to be moved by the sight.

When John and I reach the turning that leads into the village of La Herradura itself, I am directed a short way past it, to a freshly surfaced, narrow road curving off to the right of the main road. Up a steep slope, we pass between an impressive, ancient-looking building and a terrace of three small white houses, to where a line of men stand like prisoners in a chain gang, swinging pickaxes at the hard baked earth. Others are following along behind, scooping out the débris with what look like giant hoes. Carrying on past them, to the very top of the hill, I park the Land Rover in the shade of a tall, round, stone structure, built in the shape of one of the old look-out towers. Here, John gets out and goes across to talk with one of the excavators while I stay put. To my left stand two gleaming white houses, seemingly completed, while finishing touches are being given to a third. At the base of a still unpainted, grey, cement-rendered wall, a short, square-built man is struggling with a long bamboo pole which has a brush tied to its end. On tiptoe, with arms at full stretch, he just manages to reach, and paint white, a section seven metres above his head, then he painstakingly turns the long pole upside down and dips the thick wad of bristles into a pot at his side. Having accomplished this, he twists the whole thing round the other way and carefully begins to raise the paint-soaked brush aloft again. As it goes up, hand over hand in little jerky movements, white dollops rain down on the man's head and shoulders and I understand why he is wearing a cap with protruding peak. Not only does the head-gear stop his hair from turning white but, more importantly, the peak offers protection to the cigarette dangling from his lips. Suddenly, a spatter of brown liquid showers down from above to mix with the white. At this, the painter momentarily flinches but, after taking a deep draw and blowing out a cloud of blue smoke, carries on as if nothing has happened. Somehow, his fag escapes the deluge. Glancing upwards, I catch sight of another two figures on top of the sloping, wooden roof. Both are bent double, with one slapping down vertical lines of what looks like a mixture of mud and straw while the other follows behind, covering his mate's messy handiwork with rows of slightly tapering, half-rounded, orange tiles. They are being laid in such a way that the downward curve of one overlaps the upward curve of the other, thus keeping it in place. At intervals, a third man makes an appearance with fresh bucketfuls of muck, which he puts down near the tilers and scurries off with the empties. The whole routine ticks along like clockwork. None of the workers seems to hurry himself but I anticipate that it will not take long for the roof to be covered.

John comes back, saying we are in luck. The people I need to speak with are at La Tartana.

"La what?"

"Oh, that's the place we passed on the way up, mun. It means a sort of coach, I think."

(The name refers to a two-wheeled carriage, as used by Washington Irving when he departed Granada.)

Before leaving, I motion towards the work in progress on the house opposite.

"Why doesn't that guy with the long-handled brush use a ladder? It looks to me as though it would make his life a lot easier."

La Tartana

La Tartana

John laughs.

"They haven't been invented here yet, mun."

I point to the men on the roof.

"How did those two characters manage to get up there then?"

Another chuckle.

"Follow me, mun. I'll show you."

In a small plot of land behind the unfinished house, two workers are busy mixing a combination of straw, water and freshly-dug earth into a lumpy paste. The end result puts me in mind of the 'wattle and daub' used, in mediaeval times, to plaster the walls of English houses. John nods towards a long length of timber with horizontal pieces of wood nailed to it, leaning against a wall.

"Heath Robinson's got nothing on these guys."

As I watch, one of the mixers, slopping bucket in each hand, uses the improvised ladder to climb up to the roof. The long plank wobbles and bends so much, I think it might break in half.

"Phew! Rather him than me!"

"Oh, you'll get used to it, mun. I couldn't believe how they went about things out here myself when I first arrived, but they get things done, you'll see."

Instead of driving back down the hill, I leave the Land Rover where it is and follow behind my friend, slithering and scrambling down through the almond trees to the imposing building I passed earlier. Before going inside, we dust ourselves down as best we can, then cross over a cobbled entrance patio and enter by way of two heavy wooden doors. I find myself in a pretty quadrangle where bougainvillea trails its purple and pink flowers from the gallery above and a variety of potted plants are dotted around on the polished, tiled floor. On the other side of this delightful area we pass through an archway into an oblong room furnished with comfortable cushioned seats. Carrying on through to the outside, we find the people we are looking for, seated on a bright, sunlit terrace in the shade of a pomegranate tree. A blueprint plan lies spread out on the table in front of them.

Two of their number I recognise, having already met them on my first day in Almuñécar, at the bar Al Quirós. Antonio, resplendent in a flowered Hawaiian-style tunic, open at the neck, exposes a tanned, hairy chest, and dapper Donald, longish blond hair neatly brushed back, wears a crisp blue pin-striped shirt. It fits him so perfectly that I reckon it might have been tailored for him in Savile Row. The other man, Juan, is new to me. He wears a white linen jacket over a light-blue singlet. Sitting there, giving us the once-over through dark glasses, looking as cool as cucumbers, these three suave characters make quite a picture. I reckon that if Sergio Leone were to walk in at that moment, he would sign them up at once.

In 1964, Leone made use of the desert-like terrain along the coast near Almería to shoot a film called *A Fistful of Dollars*. The following year he used the same landscape to make another tongue-in-cheek 'spaghetti' western, *For a Few Dollars More* and then, in 1966, the classic *The Good, The Bad and the Ugly*.

A few years later, in 1968, news came to Almuñécar that work would soon be starting on another of his motion pictures: *Once Upon a Time in the West*. Rumour had it that blond 'extras' were in constant demand, so I and a couple more fair-haired hopefuls, made the trip to Almería and waited in a certain recommended hotel reception room in the hope of being 'spotted' and offered work. (My horsemanship might come in useful at last, I thought.) After three days of waiting we gave up. Nobody had 'spotted' us. The film company had missed its chance!

The elegant trio on the terrace do not seem particularly over-joyed at seeing us. They just sit there staring, without saying a word. John may have noticed the cold reception but, if so, does not appear to show it.

Stepping back a pace and throwing up his arms in mock alarm, he cries, "What have we here, mun? I do believe it's the bloody Mafia!"

He then waves his hand in my direction.

"If you want a hit man, my friends, look no further. I'm sure

Roy here has had experience in that line of work." (Had Anthea been talking, I wondered?) "I've brought him over to take a gander at your Mickey Mouse houses. If you play your cards right you might be able to flog him one. You can pay me my cut for the intro later."

His words loosen things up a little. While the other two remain seated (I overhear Juan questioning Donald as to the meaning of 'gander' and 'Mickey Mouse') Antonio stubs out his cigarette, gets to his feet, comes over to me and holds out his hand.

"Is it true, Roy? Are you interested in buying a property here in La Herradura?"

I've already noted that the proper way to pronounce the name of the village involves rolling the first double 'rr' but not the second. Donald has acquired the knack but John, who speaks Spanish as well as anyone I've met, doesn't seem to bother. It takes a long time and a lot of practice for me to enunciate the word correctly.

Before I can reply, John makes mention that all this shinning up and down dusty slopes has given him quite a thirst, whereupon, at this unmistakable hint, we find ourselves being ushered into the cushioned, oblong room where we sit ourselves down. From a little bar in the corner, Juan fishes out five glasses and a bottle of wine. As he pours, Antonio asks again whether I seriously intend buying a property in Spain.

"That's my aim. That's why I came to this part of the world in the first place."

I feel pretty sure that one of the three must have heard something of my visit to Velilla. Philip Ashby would have mentioned the event to someone or other and I know how fast news travels in this neck of the woods. I give an account of my exploration along the coast and say that, as far as I am concerned, the other places I've looked at are not a patch on La Herradura. In answer to the question – yes, I am interested.

"The thing is, how much would a house cost? I haven't got a lot of money. In fact, originally, I had in mind to look around for a run-down ruin and try to do it up myself."

Donald steps in here. He leans forward, taps the ash from a large cigar, which, I can see, has taken the place of his cigarette. The way he turns statements into questions leads me to think he might be Welsh. It turns out he's Australian.

"Well, Roy, there are properties like that to be found. And, it's true, they can be bought for a song. But, in nearly all cases, they're without water or electricity, you see, and, in the long run, by the time you've paid for these amenities to be laid on, assuming it's possible, you'll find the eventual cost runs into more than buying something we're building here on San Nicolás."

He goes on to tell me a sad tale of a couple who arrived in these parts about a year ago. After hunting around, they did find, and buy, a cheap, derelict place three or four kilometres away, back in the hills.

"They thought they had it made, didn't they? Peace and quiet. Fantastic views. Just the job. However, they didn't want to keep driving up and down a rough track to buy supplies all the time, did they? No fear! They decided they must buy a fridge to keep things fresh. Quite right! For a fridge they had to have electricity, didn't they? Well, as it proved impossible to connect to a mains power supply, off they go to Málaga to buy themselves a brand, spanking new generator. After a lot of hassle, with everybody's help, they managed to drive and drag the thing up to their house. Then, you see, in order to get the fuel needed to operate the machine, they were forced to pay for a proper access road to be built. The one that existed was scarcely more than a footpath, meant only for mules, you see. With water, they were quite lucky. A local farmer, for a certain consideration, allowed them to connect to his reservoir. Even so, this meant laying hundreds of metres of piping across pretty rugged territory and, even then, a dispute with the farmer or a prolonged drought might well have resulted in the precious liquid being cut off. In the end, torrential rains caused part of their newly surfaced road to cave in, which meant they could no longer drive to or from the village. No fuel equals no generator and no generator equals no fridge, doesn't it?"

Donald stops for a moment to take a long pull on his cigar, then carries on. From the way he rambles on, non-stop, he reminds me even more of Mr. Bloch-Watson.

"They didn't give up that easily, though, did they? Nil desperandum and all that. No, they hoofed it down to the shops, got in a supply of candles and foodstuffs and set about repairing the damage."

"Are they still there?"

Donald sighs. "No, poor souls. They managed to put up with things for a while longer and worked like billy-o on their house but the final crunch came when the water supply went kaputt, along with their pesetas. The last thing I heard was that they'd bought a new apartment in Torremolinos."

Taking a sip of wine and another puff on his cigar, he looks across at me.

"The house is still up there, gradually falling apart, and I think it's for sale. I'll tell you where it is, if you like. You'll have to walk, though, won't you? There's still a wide gap in the road, you see."

Do I discern a twinkle in his eye? Anyway, I've heard enough. I only want a small place, I tell him – just for myself. How much would a little one-bedroom house cost? He pulls a sheet of paper from a folder and starts work. Very rapidly and skilfully, he sketches the outline of a single-storey bungalow, showing the layout of bedroom, bathroom, living room and kitchen. When he's finished, he tosses the drawing acros to me.

"How about something like that? It'll include an outside terrace and small garden."

"How much?"

"Ah, you'll have to ask Juan about that, won't you?"

Juan has not contributed much to the meeting yet, but now all eyes turn in his direction. With Donald's plan in front of him, he starts measuring the dimensions while, at the same time, writing down and adding up figures. When he's finished, he passes his calculations to Antonio, who studies them for a moment or two.

"For you, Roy, we can build something like this here for three hundred thousand pesetas."

It's my turn to work with the pencil. The present rate of exchange stands at 168 pesetas to the pound so 1000 pesetas, in round figures, equates to six pounds sterling. Therefore, a house built on the lines of the one Donald has just drawn, will cost approximately £1800.

As I sit there thinking things over, Antonio speaks.

"If you want a better idea of what you would be getting for your money, Roy, why don't we go over the road to Donald's place? The room sizes are about the same."

It sounds good. We finish our drinks and head out from La Tartana and cross the road to the three houses opposite. As we climb the steps leading up to them, I notice an impressive-looking insignia sculpted into the wall above one of the front doors. This turns out to be Donald's house and the emblem, according to him, his family crest.

The ground floor has two rooms. A small kitchen, just inside, and to the right of, the entrance and beyond that, a living area, about 4 by 4 metres square with a fireplace built into one of the walls and patio doors leading out onto a terrace on another. Upstairs consists of a quite spacious, tiled bathroom and a wooden-ceilinged bedroom. Two half-glazed doors open from this onto a small terrace. The house has been furnished and decorated by Donald and his wife Evelyn in a simple, traditional style and I can see at once that something like this would suit me down to the ground. Small, maybe, but comfortable and easy to manage.

Antonio then proposes we go up the hill to take a look at one of the finished properties. I go along with that idea for, back in England, having spent some time working on building sites, I've learned a thing or two about house construction and feel it will be interesting to make comparisons.

As soon as we arrive, I note one pleasant difference. The smells are the same – newly turned earth, drying cement, paint, varnish, sawn timber and all that sort of thing – not much out of the ordinary there – but, most noticeable by its absence, is noise. No clattering cement mixers, deafening pneumatic drills, creaking cranes. I can even hear birds singing!

Donald's house

Searching around the site, I see that quite a few of the materials being used are different from those back in England. Bricks, for example, as well as being smaller in size, are of a completely different design. Those being employed here have square holes running through them longitudinally, which makes them not only lighter and easier to handle, but also, I notice, allows for electric cables to be passed through their middle. This method of wiring worries me a little, though, for I see no evidence of conduits. (Better watch out when drilling holes, I think to myself!) Still, burying cables inside walls seems to be an improvement on most other places. Here in La Herradura and in Almuñécar, just about every bit of electrical wiring I've come across has been simply tacked to the outside of the wall.

All house surfaces, inside and out, are either tiled or rendered, so I reckon it does not much matter how evenly the bricks underneath are laid. Very few appear to be used for face-work. In place of the more familiar shovel, all the workmen use an *azada* – the long-handled hoe seen earlier. I guess their action of pulling different constituents together to mix them, instead of our traditional English method of lifting and turning, puts less strain on the back.

Floors, like those in Donald's house, are all covered with large, reddish-brown tiles, with matching half-tiles fitted around the bottom of the wall to act as skirting. Vocabulary used to describe the many different varieties of tile can be a little confusing. Whereas in England we simply add a location, such as 'roof tile', 'floor tile', 'bathroom tile' etc., in Spain wall tile comes across as *azulejo*, roof tile as *teja* and floor tile as *mosaico* or *baldosa*. But then, tiles have much more significance in Mediterranean countries. Not only are they laid on just about all floor surfaces, but, in many buildings, they form a high dado, covering walls up to a height of a metre – inside and out. This prevents the flaking of plaster and, at the same time, hides damp patches which would otherwise appear on solid walls built without damp-proof courses. (In bygone days, English houses were fitted with wood-panelling for the same reason.)

Almuñécar in tiles

Of course, in a hot climate, tiled surfaces are much more acceptable than in cold northern Europe, where we reserve that sort of thing for public toilets. The colour and design of tiles has hardly changed at all over the centuries. Traditional Moorish examples showing complicated geometrical patterns and rough outlines of birds, trees and plants are still being fabricated. (No human form, of course: this is strictly forbidden by the Qur'an.) The pomegranate motif, too, is widely depicted, especially in the south, for the fruit is not only the national emblem of Spain, but the word translates into Spanish as 'granada'. The Arabs, always masters of tile technology, introduced in the 11th century a technique whereby surfaces could be multi-coloured and then lead-glazed, thus making them impermeable to liquid. One of the best examples of their remarkable skill is the ornate decoration on display at the Alhambra Palace in Granada where many different configurations are on display, including six-pointed stars, diamonds and wheels. Tile production became an important industry for Spain, with factories in Málaga, Granada, Seville and Manises in the province of Valencia. They were, and still are, being exported to many parts of the globe.

Outside, on the sloping piece of land at the back of the unfinished house, a deep hole has been dug three metres deep and two metres wide. This crater, after being lined with rocks, serves as a soakaway or *pozo negro* and into its depths runs all waste from toilet, bathroom and kitchen. Many newcomers to Spain learn the hard way that this drainage system has to be used with a certain amount of mindfulness. Only biodegradable material can be flushed down the lavatory. Nothing in the way of plastic bags or cellophane wrapping can be disposed of in this way, otherwise gaps in the rocks around the edge of the *pozo negro* will block up and not allow liquid to filter its way into the earth. In other words, the soakaway will not soak away. If a lot of water is likely to be used (and this can prove expensive, for every house is metered), waste pipes from the washbasin, *pila* or washing machine are often directed straight onto the garden. This not only stops the *pozo* from filling too quickly but also gives the plants a soapy drink. If treated sensibly, these age-old dumping pits cause no problem. The hot sun and dry earth will suck up liquid faster than it accumulates.

Windows, unlike those in England, open inwards. At first, I deem this to be bad design for, without an outer sill, they will let in rain. But then I observe that they cannot open outwards because wrought iron bars or *rejas* are fixed to the wall directly in front of them. Also, by opening inwards, they allow the traditional roll-type blinds or *persianas* to be fitted externally. When down, these slatted blinds not only prevent nosy neighbours from looking in but, at the same time, allow air to circulate in the hot summer months.

At first, I imagine the *rejas*, which appear common to most dwellings, are fitted to prevent burglars from breaking in. How-

Rejas, La Herradura

ever, Gerald Brenan gives a different reason. In *South from Granada* he writes that, traditionally, for a young man to court the girl of his choice, he must follow the young lady home and talk with her through the grille at her window. Strict custom forbids anything like embracing, kissing or even touching. If their ardour proves lasting, the young Lothario would, after a decent period of time, be invited into the girl's home to be introduced to her parents. Eventually, if the relationship continues, both their families meet and, after certain formalities have been approved, consent is given for the couple to become engaged. They will then be known as *novio* and *novia*.

When apartment blocks start to appear in Spain, parents living on the third floor and above find it very difficult to marry off their daughters – unless her suitor has a very powerful voice! The best singer of a serenade is the likeliest to win the fair lady, as Rossini illustrates in *The Barber of Seville*.

After vetting everything as closely as possible, I tell Antonio that I approve what I have seen. Using modern materials, a traditional 'feel' has been maintained and, in particular, I like the generous use of timber. I know this to be an expensive commodity here in the treeless expanses of southern Spain.

"You can thank Donald for that. He watches over everything. Not a brick can be laid without his approval. Anything constructed here must fit in with his plans for the whole future village. He won't allow for any modifications. If you do decide on a property here, Roy, and have your own ideas about design, you will have to argue things out with him."

I shake my head. "From what I have seen so far, there won't be much to argue about."

Juan comes across and joins us. He speaks English nearly as well as Antonio does. It really frustrates me to hear the way everybody communicates in each other's tongue, with me being the exception!

"The first thing you must do, Roy, if you want to buy, is to choose a site. Individual houses are being built on plots of round about 6000 *palmos*."

Donald sees my puzzled expression.

"Let me explain. *Palmos* is an old way of measuring areas. It means, as you would imagine, palm of hand. The plot Antonio is talking about would measure six thousand times the size of someone's hand, you see?"

I see – and add, with a little chuckle, "I think I get the picture – but how about letting John here be the someone? Have you seen the size of his *palmo*?"

They understand what I'm getting at as a smiling John holds up a huge hand. Donald laughs. "Well, I know it's not very accurate. We go on an average of 23 *palmo*s per square metre. The plot Antonio spoke of would be 15 metres by 15, which works out at roughly 6000." I try doing some mental arithmetic, but give up.

"What's the cost of one *palmo*, then?"

"Ah, well, you see, that depends on the location. Up the coast, nearer the airport, they're paying 50 pesetas. Here? Well, I mustn't give away too many secrets now, must I?"

Antonio interrupts.

"I don't want to rush you into anything, Roy, but so far things have been moving pretty fast here at San Nicolás: much faster than in San Juan. And, I must remind you that the plots up here on top sell first, of course. They have the best view, naturally."

I see what he means. With a panoramic scan of the bay to the south and splendid mountains to the north, the higher the better. Our present position could not be improved.

Although I haven't seen Antonio's first building project, Anthea had made mention of this San Juan. She told me that the small estate of houses rested on the side of a hill on the other side of Almuñécar, facing north, plantations of fruit trees. This, I guess, probably accounts for the slower selling rate. Most folk buying property in Spain, including myself, want a sea view. I stand there weighing things up. Decision time. The layout of Donald's house certainly had impressed me. I have a sudden thought.

"Tell me, Antonio, would it be possible for you to build me a place exactly like Donald's – that is, with an upstairs and down-stairs – for the same price?"

I had been thinking how great it would be to live in a house where I can get up in the mornings, throw wide the terrace doors, stand out on the balcony and take in the wonderful view. Being on top of the hill, and on a first floor, would mean that nobody could build in front and spoil my field of vision. The three partners huddle together for a few moments. No problem: they would be able to erect a two-storey house in place of the bungalow type discussed earlier, for the same amount of money.

I tell Donald how impressed I am by his home and the way things are shaping up on the estate in general. He is doing a grand job. Does he encounter many problems?

"It's not easy. Folk living hereabouts are not accustomed to building this style of house, you see, and getting hold of the right people to do the right work is no easy task." Looking around, Donald points to someone bent over, sawing at some metal tubing.

"Take that fellow over there, for example. Last week he work-ed as a car mechanic. Now he's a *fontanero* (plumber) – and that's only because he's the only person in the village with a few spanners and a hacksaw, you see? The same's true of electri-cians. When they've finished wiring a house, we hold our breath when we first turn on the light switch. If a light actually comes on it's celebration time: drinks all round. More often than not, all we get is the sound of a little explosion from somewhere inside one of the walls and we have to start hacking away to find out where the two wires are touching. Luckily for us, these novices are learning from their mistakes and are now starting to get the hang of things. Labourers are easily found, because they can earn more here than they do fishing, but tradesmen are harder to come by. Still, I mustn't complain, must I? Carpenters and roofers are damned good and tilers are bloody fantastic. And then, as a bonus, there are always guys like that, who can run rings around all the other bricklayers."

Donald points towards a fit-looking, middle-aged man, cap on head, cigarette in mouth, building a wall. His body moves in smooth, easy fashion, plonking down a dollop of mortar with the trowel in his left hand, then almost casually tossing a brick

José María de Haro, Master albañil

on top with his right. A quick tap with the trowel handle, then a scrape at the sides and the clockwork action starts all over again. For an instant, his mechanical movements bring back memories of my dreaded Guardsman days. I can almost hear the Corporal-Major shouting, 'Up, two-three! Over, two-three!' I look away.

The man I've been watching lay bricks is a master *albañil* – in his case, a craftsman in stone masonry – and I learn that he, José María de Haro, is the person largely responsible for all the fancy brickwork at La Tartana.

So Donald finds it difficult to find tradesmen, eh? I nod towards John.

"If you want a good plumber, what's wrong with him?"

The plumber speaks for himself. "Me work for these guys, mun! You must be joking! For a start, they couldn't afford me. You know what these crooks pay those *peones* (labourers). I'll tell you. Eighteen pesetas an hour – if they're lucky. *Albañiles* (bricklayers) get maybe twenty-five pesetas. I wouldn't get out of bed for that sort of money, mun."

Donald looks hurt.

"I pay the going rate, don't I! Anyway, have you seen how the majority of these so-called bricklayers lay bricks? Agricultural workers swap their rake for a trowel and turn up ready to start, knowing they can earn twice as much here as they can on the land. The same applies to fishermen. Construction work is pretty steady employment for them compared to fishing because they don't have to rely on the weather so much, you see? Strong winds keep them shore-bound half the time and, when this happens, they earn nothing, do they? If you want to know the exact figures, Roy, it works out at about 2,500 pesetas (£15) a square metre for us to build. That's without the cost of buying the land, architect's fees, electricity supply, access road and so on. And then there's water. Antonio luckily managed to get hold of a stretch of sugar-cane field just back from the beach, which has a well underneath. From there, water is pumped up to the estate's *depósito* (reservoir)."

He waves his hand in the direction of the round tower where the Land Rover is parked.

"Without a supply of water, nobody can do anything, you see, Roy. We have to invest a lot of money, you know. Laying on amenities and getting the site ready for building is not cheap. You work it out."

John has had enough.

"Stop! You're making me weep, mun!" He turns towards me.

"Look here, mun. I've heard enough of this bloody sales talk. Why don't you just go home, put on your thinking cap and mull it over?" But I have no need to think or mull it over. Facing Antonio, it's my turn to hold out my hand.

"Where do I sign?"

Back in the snug little cushioned room at the coaching inn, aided by another couple of bottles of wine, we sit discussing the course of action British subjects are obliged to follow in order to purchase a property in another part of the world. The three developers seem to know all about it, having sold to English people before, at San Juan. Before we start getting down to details, Antonio looks across the table.

"You want to do this legally, I suppose, do you, Roy?"

Legally?

"I'm no rich bank robber, if that's what you mean."

I get the gist of his question, though, having heard tales of people turning up in Spain with bulging briefcases, ready and able to pay spot cash for a property. They take a chance with the Customs, but, as long as the seller gets what he wants, no questions are asked. Whether it helps matters or not, I don't know, but I decide to give a full account of my financial affairs and spell out how I hope to live on the income from my house in Twickenham.

They listen with interest.

In that case, Antonio reckons, once I've finished my story, the best and easiest way to buy a property here is for me to simply inform the authorities back home in England that I wish to set up home in Spain. That way, after a bit of form-filling, I should be eligible for an external bank account and legally be able transfer up to £5,000 to this country. My local bank can sort it all out for me. It sounds too much like plain sailing.

"Doesn't a person have to be retired or something to do that?"

Nearly all the other British owner-occupiers I have come across have been elderly. Antonio shakes his head.

"I don't see why that's so important. Anyway, can you not be retired? From what you tell me, you lucky man, your house in England would provide you with the means. I can see no problem."

Another method, he says, entails buying 'investment dollars'. This would mean paying a premium of about 11 % (an amount varying according to the supply available) but once in possession of these dollars, I could use them to buy real estate anywhere I liked. The thought of paying a supplement turns me off that idea.

Buying from someone who legitimately owns a property, having already gone through the rigmarole with the authorities, is another possibility. There are opportunities to do this sort of thing farther along the coast in the more popular resorts, Antonio says, but here, where foreigners with something to sell are thin on the ground, it would be like looking for a needle in a haystack. Anyway, I've already set my heart on having a house built here on this hill called San Nicolás, so that option is ruled out.

His first suggestion sounds my best bet. From what I have seen, my £30 a month will be more than enough to live on. In fact, half that amount would probably suffice. Spanish wage-earners manage to provide for a wife and large family on 500 pesetas (£3) a week, while I should have more than double that to look after myself alone. Food, whether eaten at a restaurant or bought in the market, costs very little. Why, with three-course meals, including wine, priced at thirty pesetas, I could eat out all the time if I chose. Recently, I had been to a party where the hosts served up a splendid meal of grilled *sardinas*, *boquerones*, bread, salad and, of course, copious amounts of the red stuff, at a cost that must have been trifling. Fish, on average, costs 50 pesetas (30 pence) a kilo, and no more than two kilos were needed to feed the ten hungry guests; a salad of lettuce, tomatoes and onions, works out at 40 pesetas (24 pence); and good mountain wine, ten pesetas a litre. So, all in all, with a large loaf of bread at 4 pesetas (2.5 pence), the total outlay would have amounted to 250 pesetas (£1.50).

I give an average price for *sardinas* and *boquerones* because their value varies according to the weather. If it blows up rough and smaller boats can't put to sea, fish have to be purchased in Motril, and this, naturally, makes them more expensive.

Yes, although I learn later that owning a property in Spain results in a few extra disbursements, the cost of living in this part of the world suits most pockets. Quite a few people simply make the annual travel allowance of £250 per person last as long as possible, and that can be the whole year, if careful. At this rate, of course, it might seem perfectly feasible for an English family of four, with a total of £1,000 between them, to buy a property abroad. Some do, but thereafter live in fear lest the Inland Revenue might find out, for the authorities regard such an act as illegal.

In 1970, a rumour spread along the coast that inspectors had been despatched to Spain to seek out these wrongdoers and, for a while, panic reigned. Holidaymakers, knowing nothing of the investigation, were sometimes surprised to find that an innocent question, such as, "Do you spend much time here?" caused the person asked to down his or her drink quickly and hurriedly clear off without so much as an *adiós*. An honest Joe like me, though, has no need to do anything surreptitiously. I am able to buy my property quite openly.

Once we have finished discussing the alternative ways of buying in Spain, Antonio disappears into another room and comes back with a typed sheet of paper.

"This, Roy," he says, passing it across to me, "is a *por prepuesto*, or fixed-price contract. You see I've put down the right amount. Three hundred thousand pesetas."

What does he mean? Why should it show anything but the right amount? The others must notice my puzzlement and tell me that normally, when it comes to selling, the *escrituras* or deeds show a price much lower than the amount actually agreed by both parties. This, they explain, reduces, or does away with altogether, the *plus vale* or capital gains tax applicable when a property changes hands. Purchasers have to be careful. Although the vendor should be responsible for tax on the profit (for, after all, he is the one making the gain), if he fails to pay what is owed, it falls to the new owner to fork out. Once started, this practice of putting a low price on the sale document continues in future sales, otherwise, if, at any time along the line, the correct price is shown, the calculated profit will involve a tax of 15%. With a new property, however, things are different. As no capital gain is involved, the full amount paid can be declared. If and when I come to sell, and a large profit might accrue, I may find it better to adopt the customary practice.

The contract Antonio hands me is written, of course, in Spanish so, before signing, I slowly go through all the details with him. I gather that I am undertaking to pay one third before work starts, another third when the roof has been put on, and the final third on completion. A third of £1800 amounts to £600.

"Does this mean that I agree to pay you a hundred thousand pesetas here and now?"

Donald answers.

"That's the usual procedure, you see."

I turn in his direction.

"Well, I can't. I haven't got it."

John has been watching all this with a grin on his face.

"There goes my commission, mun."

In the end, after deliberating for a while, I let it be known that all I can come up with, at that moment, is £100, and then send the balance of £500 from England. If there's any problem with the bank formalities, I will let them know at once. Would that be OK? Donald lights another cigar, Juan pours more wine and Antonio takes a deep breath.

"We don't usually start work on a property without the full deposit being paid, Roy, but," and here he looks across the table at his two silent partners who, after a quizzical glance at each other, nod their heads, "but, in your case, we'll start building on the strength of your promise."

So, after altering the deposit figure from 100,000 pesetas to 16,000 pesetas, I sign on the dotted line and Antonio does the same. He then hands me a copy of the document, saying,

"There's your receipt for the £100, Roy."

"Thanks. Um, there's one other problem, though, Antonio. I'm afraid I haven't got it on me at the moment. I'll give it you tomorrow, or later today, if you like."

At this, John bursts out laughing.

"What can you do with this man, mun? He's bought a house without handing over one peseta! He's got you down from 100,000 to 16,000 and now he's reduced it to bugger all! He'll be getting you to pay him next!"

Antonio, with a sigh, reaches over and takes the receipt back.

"Perhaps we can meet up later, Roy."

I realise that by paying the £100 deposit I shall not be able to stay in Spain as long as I intended and shall have to leave soon after Christmas. Never mind, I think to myself, my objective has been achieved. I've found an ideal spot here on the Costa del Sol and actually agreed to buy a house!

On the way out from La Tartana, as we cross the fabulous, galleried courtyard again and pass through the ancient-looking gates on to the cobbled entrance patio, I remark to Donald,

"What a terrific old place!"

"It's to be opened up as a lodging house-cum-bar/restaurant for those on the estate, you see."

"How long has it been standing there?"

He holds his hand up to his forehead, as if deep in thought and I notice the others are amused by my question.

"Well, let me think for a moment. How old, you ask? According to my calculations, we finished building it about three months ago."

As we drive back to Almuñécar, I ask John what he thinks of my headstrong action.

"It doesn't seem such a bad deal to me, mun. Like I said before, I don't think you'll find anywhere that has as much going for it along this coast. You saw the sort of buildings they were putting up back there. If I'd been in your position, and had your lolly, I think I'd have done the same as you, mun. Things are just starting up in La Herradura. You won't go wrong buying there, and those plots on top of the hill won't be around for much longer, I can tell you that for a fact, mun."

He goes on to say that Donald didn't just spin me some sales pitch with his woeful story of the couple up in the hills. His plumbing travels have brought him into contact with others occupying such remote, deserted farmhouses.

"They make me laugh, mun, with the image some of those phonies try to put across. I've seen them slowly sidle their sandal-shod way into town wearing those long Moroccan night-shirts – *jellabahs*, I think they're called. You know the sort of thing, mun. These drop-out types look like something straight out of the Bible, with their long straggly beards and uncombed hair, usually carrying heavy-going reading material under their arm. Books by Carlos Castañeda and all that. They sit themselves down at some place that's popular with the hippies, and stay there doing their damnedest to look mystical and interesting. I've watched these guys, mun, and spoken to one or two. Sooner or later they strike up conversation – usually with some chick – and let on how they want to be on their own. After all, it's not much use being a wise hermit living all alone in the mountains if no one knows, is it?"

"What do they live on?"

"Live on? Why, whatever they can get. A bit like our friend Felix."

"Yes, but he does earn his keep, what with his guitar playing and painting and all that."

"Oh, for sure, mun! Our Felix makes out OK. But he's involved with a few other money-making schemes as well."

John pauses for a moment before continuing.

"Keep this to yourself, mun. Felix used to be one those characters I've been talking about. He and a gang of weirdos formed a sort of commune back in the Alpujarras, somewhere north of Elmira. There are plenty of deserted houses, even villages, up there. Local farming folk, being the sort of people they are, imagine these young people have nothing much to eat and so give them handouts of stuff like potatoes, tomatoes and so on. Some of Felix's crowd, himself included, had been living in North Africa and knew all there is to know about growing 'grass' – and I don't mean the kind cows munch – so they started cultivating the stuff. Before long they got quite a little enterprise going on up there and made good dosh 'pot-peddling' down on the coast here. What they didn't smoke themselves, they sold. Mind you, from the amount they used, it's a wonder there was ever any surplus. Felix told me that a person could get high just by standing downwind of their hideout. After a while, though, the authorities heard about it. Some arrests were made a while ago but most of the gang just moved on somewhere else. You'll notice that Felix disappears for a few days from time to time and when he returns to Almuñécar he's a very popular man. Take my advice, mun. If he asks you to drive him anywhere, find a reason to turn him down."

"I've already been warned by Anthea."

Not all abandoned dwellings are occupied by bearded, sandal-shod phonies. Some years later, in 1973, a shy young English couple called Mark and Jane arrive in La Herradura and move into an isolated, unoccupied house situated a few kilometres inland from San Nicolás. Among the impoverished people around at the time, these two take the biscuit when it comes to eking out an existence on limited funds. Somehow, by diligently watching every peseta, they manage to stay put for the next two years on a budget averaging one hundred pesetas (60 pence) a week. By 1975, their original stake of a hundred and fifty pounds sterling is almost halved and with the capital they have left, they decide to buy a Spanish *burra* (mule) and walk (yes, walk!) home to England through Spain and France. After an adventurous journey of four months, all three manage to arrive safely back in the UK where the mule, Amapola (Poppy) by name, is donated to an animal sanctuary.

While living in their house in the hills, Mark and Jane adopt two ducks. With water in short supply and ducks being aquatic rather than land creatures, they and their owners make a point of coming down to the coast twice a week during the summer months for a cooling swim in the sea. On one of these little excursions, Juan, the owner of a nearby hostal, notices that one of the ducks paddling near the rocks shows signs of distress. Quacking loudly and fluttering its wings furiously, the animal is being dragged under the water. Juan rushes across, rows out in his boat, pulls up the struggling duck and retrieves a large octopus hanging onto its leg. The rescuer, Juan of Peña Parda, can authenticate this story.

Back at the Hostal Victoria I lie on my bed and try to work out exactly how much longer I can stay. Allowing for petrol, overnight stops, cross-channel ferry ticket and so on, I could, if I watch my purse, have enough pesetas to see me through until the New Year. Then I shall have to return to England, sort out the emigration business and, more importantly, find a way to earn enough money to pay for the house I've just agreed to buy. With about £800 in my bank account back in England, I need at least another £1,000. Back to work for a while appears to be the only answer. Oh, no!

Christmas Day arrives. 25 December is not commemorated in Spain as it is in England, although it is one of the eighteen Spanish public holidays. Christmas Eve is celebrated by a larger than normal turnout for midnight mass, but the big day itself is a pretty low-key affair as far as the locals are concerned. Festivities are reserved for 6 January (Epiphany or Three Kings' Day). This date is extra-special for children as it is the day they are handed their long-awaited presents, delivered the night before by the Three Kings who ride into town on horseback. There's not a lot of difference in the setting, I suppose: it's just that horses take the place of reindeer.

We foreigners, of course, keep to our recognised, traditional date. On that special day, Antonio kindly invites me to a party and dinner at his apartment in Almuñécar and there I meet his mother, Manola, sisters María and Silvia and two brothers, Eduardo and Jesús. Among the company are many I already know, including Juan, accompanied by his very pregnant English wife, Patricia, and Donald with his French wife, Evelyn. Felix and I take turns with the guitar and while he plays a variety of music, including some very fine flamenco, I stick to my English folk songs. As the evening wears on, a few carols slip into the repertoire. These are very popular with the English contingent and before long we all let loose with *In the Bleak Midwinter, The Holly Bears a Berry* and Sydney Carter's *Lord of the Dance*. A German, Hans, delivers a lovely rendering of *Stille Nacht*. Aided by plenty to eat and drink, we all make merry.

The next day, to my surprise, a letter arrives from Rosalind, a girlfriend of mine back in England, informing me that she will be flying into Málaga on Monday, 9 January, the day after my thirtieth birthday. Since Anthea's departure I have suffered a somewhat chaste existence, so news that a beautiful, long-legged trainee physiotherapist will be spending a week in my company does not exactly displease me. However, as I'd intended leaving Spain before the date of her arrival, I write back at once asking her to bring some extra cash. By some miracle my letter reaches her in time and so, belatedly, we are able to celebrate my anniversary in style. In order to augment the coffers a little more, we stop off at Nerja on our way back from the airport and sell her return air ticket. She will have no need of it as she is accompanying me back to England in the Land Rover. The purchaser of her ticket, whose address I got hold of from Anthea, seems to have quite a thriving business. In those days, airline tickets can simply be exchanged for boarding-passes at the flight desk and passengers continue on through to the departure lounge to board the plane. After a later spate of hijacking, however, the authorities tighten things up and the checks and double checks make using someone else's ticket impossible.

A few days before our departure, Antonio asks a favour. Will I take his sister María back to England with me and help her find employment as an *au pair*? She wants to learn English. Any expense incurred on her behalf can be subtracted from the balance of £500 owing on the first payment for the house. What can I say? His family have been very kind and hospitable to me, especially over Christmas. He goes on to say that he has every confidence in me and feels sure I will see to his young sister's well being. Perhaps his faith in me would not have been so resolute if Rosalind had not been accompanying us. Escorting a pretty, seventeen-year-old *señorita* on a three-day and night journey through Spain and France on my own would be like asking a confirmed alcoholic to look after a brewery!

The three of us leave Almuñécar on the morning of 16 January, though Rosalind and I are both suffering bad hangovers. At a farewell party in La Ventura the night before, we had sat drinking most of the night away with a gang of well-wishers. As on the eve of Anthea's departure, the drinks kept appearing in front of me and I kept knocking them back. Felix seemed to be in a particularly inspired flamenco mood that evening, sitting hunched over his guitar, completely lost to the world. I have a suspicion that his passionate, full-blooded delivery may have stemmed from something other than alcohol.

"Ees ze sadness I feel, Roy. You lif so soon and wit you tek two luffly *señoritas*."

John the Plumber behaved himself pretty well at first, spending much of his time chatting with Rosalind who, I can see, attracted him. But, as time passed by and drinks went down, his mood gradually changed from being good company to becoming a pain in the ass. I've learned from my sea-going days that too much booze can make a man (or woman) sleepy, amorous or, as in John's case, belligerent. He started off by challenging anyone in the room to a 'wrist wrestle' and, finding no takers, demonstrated his dislike of 'hippies' by referring to them, in a loud, sneering voice, as, "A bloody load of lazy poofs!"

The beaded brigade sitting at one particular table quietly got up, settled their bill and left. Tommy tried to calm things down. He came from behind the bar, went across to John and placed a hand on his arm.

"Now then, my friend, we don't want Roy's last night here spoiled, do we?"

The question seemed to confuse the plumber. He stared, glassy-eyed, in my direction for a moment, then angrily swept Tommy's hand away, reached into his pocket, tossed a few notes and a handful of coins on the counter and, with a shake of his head, staggered out through the door. After that little episode, things were not quite the same and, before long, we, too, bade goodbye to those left in the bar and made our wobbly way back to the hotel.

7

1967

*In which I sort things out in England, return to Spain,
meet Pedro and settle into Casa Roy at San Nicolás.*

So, with two pretty ladies at my side, I motor my way, once
again, through Spain and France – only this time heading
north. The weather is still pretty cold, but without John's con-
tinual chatter and Cynthia's moaning and groaning, I enjoy the
trip much more.

Awaiting me in England are the joys of colour TV, with *Dr
Who, Softly, Softly* and *Till Death Do Us Part,* plus music from
the likes of The Beatles, The Rolling Stones, Jimi Hendrix and
The Monkees. A Mr Billy Graham is at the ready to evangelise
me, a Mr Harold Wilson (whose Labour Party has recently won
its second term in government) promises to make the country
a better place from which to escape, and there is news that the
situation in Vietnam, between the Communist North and the
American-backed South, is deteriorating.

Lindsay Anderson, the film director who, the following year,
in 1968, made the classic film *If,* puts it like this:

'Let's face it: coming back to Britain is always something of
an ordeal. It ought not to be, but it is. And you don't have to be
a snob to feel it. It isn't just the food, the sauce bottles on the
café tables, and chips with everything. It isn't just saying goodbye to wine, goodbye to sunshine...'.

I've only been away for a couple of months, but that's long
enough to know what he means. It is not all bad news, though.
Mini-skirts appear to have become even more 'mini' and a new

crowd on the scene, the 'flower power' people, are urging us to make love instead of war. I do my best to co-operate.

Rosalind kindly takes María under her wing and gives the young girl board and lodging while helping her look for work as *au pair*.

Things seemed to have gone pretty smoothly in Twickenham during my absence. My trusted accountant friend, Lenny, has diligently seen to everything concerning the general running of my guesthouse and the only hiccup, he says, concerns a certain tenant, two weeks behind with the rent, who did a 'moonlight flit.' More importantly, he took with him the key to his room and another to the front door. A few days later, as Lenny and I are walking down the street, this naughty man is pointed out to me. I run across and politely ask for the return of the keys and the money owing. He replies with a couple of well-known rude words, one beginning with 'f' and the other ending with 'off'. I try asking again – this time, less politely. After a little gentle persuasion he hands over the debt and faithfully promises to bring back the keys within the hour. Instead of the key thief showing up, two uniformed policemen call to the house and invite me to accompany them to the local police station, where I am charged with assault and battery. Oh, dear! Only in the country a matter of days, and already I find myself in the doghouse. Luckily, as my former tenant decides not to press charges, the case is dismissed. I consider a move back to Spain as soon as possible to be my best option. Much more of this and I could lose my passport. Firstly, though, I have to earn enough money to pay for the house at San Nicolás and sort out the transfer of capital.

Everything goes without a hitch. The friendly manager of the local Barclays Bank kindly helps me with the paperwork. A fit, good-looking man of about middle age, he seems very interested in my plans.

"How much do you say the house is costing you?"

I tell him the price: eighteen hundred pounds.

"And what do you reckon it will cost you to live in Spain?"

I give him a figure: I reckon no more than five pounds a week. "Mmm. Really? Is that all?"

A dreamy look comes over his face. He makes notes.

I discover that the information Antonio gave me is correct. As long as I intend to become resident in Spain and make it my permanent home, there should be no problem. My Twickenham property will be looked upon as a business and income from it will be taxed, but the balance, or any part of it, can go into an external account and be transferred to Spain. However, consent for me to live abroad still constitutes a concession, not a right, and I keep my fingers crossed that my application will be given approval.

Meanwhile, back to the grindstone. By mixing door-to-door selling with occasional sessions of 'film extra' work, I manage, in the space of seven months, to save enough money to meet my obligations. Then, as soon as I hear that the Bank of England's Exchange Control Department has granted my request, I forward the balance owing on the first payment for the San Nicolás house to Antonio (minus María's expenses). Later, on receiving news that the roof has been put on, I send another £600, on the understanding that the final instalment will be paid on my return.

So, by the end of July 1967, I'm all set. I make tracks across the Channel once more, this time driving a Morris Minor pick-up. The vehicle has been equipped with a sturdy frame onto which is securely lashed a sleek blue and white fibreglass yacht known as a 'mini-sail', just introduced to the market by a company called Richmond Marine. I have no idea how to sail it but have visions of myself out there on the sunny bay in La Herradura, slicing my speedy way through the clear blue sea. The length of hull exceeds that of the pick-up by about 3 feet, so I take to the road looking like some giant battering ram and half expect to be stopped by the police. I am lucky in that department, but the journey has its moments. Up in the Pyrenees, strong headwinds waft under my load and cause the front wheels of the pick-up to leave the ground, making it practically impossible to steer. Once or twice, that blustery day, I almost end up going over a cliff edge. Driving very slowly, with my heart in my mouth, I just about manage to keep to the road. From then on, thank goodness, conditions are calmer. Still, with all its drawbacks, looking on the bright side, the overhead protrusion serves as a giant visor and does, at least, keep the sun out of my eyes!

Accompanying me and my yacht and sharing the dubious excitement, comes a young lady called Stella whom I had met while working as an 'extra' on a Hammer Films production called *Quatermass and the Pit*. An aspiring actress, she gripes pretty much non-stop all the way. Firstly, she kicks up a fuss because I didn't drive through Paris so that she could sightsee a little. Then, she swears that the alarming windy episode on the mountain has made her a nervous wreck. Along with numerous other grievances, she finds Spain is too hot, its roads too bumpy, the food too greasy, my driving too jerky and her seat too uncomfortable. Her constant nagging gets on my nerves so, as soon as I can, I try to give her the slip. On the pretext of going to the toilet, I leave her sitting in a restaurant while I creep out the back way. Either I stay away too long or she smells a rat for, while I'm standing by the car wondering what on earth I can do with her luggage, she suddenly appears and asks what the hell I am doing. Thinking quickly, I reach up to the bindings on the roof rack and tug on a knot or two.

"Just checking."

The angry look in her eye leads me to think she smells a rat and doesn't believe me. From that point on things get even worse.

We somehow make it as far as Granada. There, Stella slams my car door as hard as she can and hobbles off in a lopsided way, lugging a heavy bag in her right hand.

Driving straight on, past Almuñécar, I take the little turning that leads into the Punta de la Mona and stop, once again, to look out across the fabulous bay. I've not been imagining things. At times, during my stay in England, I wondered whether my

San Nicolás

mental picture of the horseshoe-shaped cove had, perhaps, become a little exaggerated. But no: there it lies in all its glory, fully living up to my expectations. After standing transfixed a while longer, overjoyed at the thought that this part of the world will, henceforth, be my new home, I continue to San Nicolás.

Driving up the curving road, I see that the builders have been busy. When I last saw the estate, it consisted of only a few buildings at the top of the hill, along with La Tartana and the three small terraced houses at the bottom. Now, most of the almond trees in the sloping field that I scrambled across with John the Plumber have been replaced by bricks and mortar. I carry on to the summit and pull up alongside a gleaming white two-storey property standing on the plot I had chosen. The front wall faces me and the flank wall runs to the side of some steps. As I stand there, gaping, a black Labrador dog comes bounding up, wagging its tail. The door of the house stands open. Together, we go inside.

An inspection of the ground floor shows the layout to be, as expected, identical to that of Donald's. Apart from rubble littering the floor, everything appears to be perfect. Followed by my new friend, I climb the stairs to find a splendid, tiled bathroom, with bath and shower, and next to it, a quite spacious bedroom. French windows open onto a little balcony. I take a deep breath. Can this be true, I ask myself, as I slowly move my gaze from Punta de la Mona on the left, across the bay to the Cerro Gordo on my right? Do I really own this place? Will I be able to wake up to this every morning? As I stand there, lost in wonder, a voice calls out from below.

"¡Hola, Luis!"

The dog immediately runs out from the bedroom and down the stairs. I follow. Framed in the doorway stands a tanned wiry-looking man, dressed in shorts, singlet and sandals. He has a high cheek-boned face, wide mouth and, from what I can

Casa Roy, San Nicolás

see behind thick horn-rimmed glasses, brown eyes. I guess his age to be in the mid-forties. The voice and dog belong to him. He thrusts out a hand.

Pedro the Norwegian

"Bienvenido, I know you comink. You are Luis, I tink. You mit already my dock, Tel, ya?"

I tell him that I am not Luis. My name is Roy.

"Ah! Ya! *No importa*, Luis."

I learn later that this man, Pedro, a Norwegian, gives everybody a Spanish name, including himself. Besides, he finds it difficult to get his tongue around the word 'Roy'. He goes on to say, in a mixture of languages, that he, too, lives on the estate, in one of the houses I passed on my way up the hill. Antonio has given him news of my imminent arrival. His next question leads me to wonder what else has been said about me.

"Pliss, you vant drink of somtink, ya?"

I can think of nothing better. The drive down from Granada has been a hot and thirsty one. Firstly, though, I ask Pedro if he will kindly help me unload the mini-sail from the pick-up. I'm not sure how much heat the thin fibreglass can take. Together, taking hold of one end apiece, we manage, after a struggle, to manoeuvre the long hull through the front door, along the narrow passage, across the living room, out through the French windows and lay it down on the back terrace, away from direct sunlight. By the end of it all we are both puffing and sweating and I can see that bringing something that length in and out through the front door each time will be quite an effort. (The problem is eventually solved by having a side gate installed in the garden wall.)

Having recovered our breath, we make our way down the steps, past a couple of half-completed buildings, to arrive at a large *hacienda*-style property. A painted sign fixed to the wall announces it to be 'Casa Pedro'.

(Later that evening, the subject of house names crops up. Pedro maintains that, unless a house is called something easily understood, the prospect of anyone finding its location is minimal. Where he lived before, he says, the number of 'Casa Blancas' on the estate led to many deliveries, messages and visitors going astray. Taking note of his advice, my house henceforth goes by the name 'Casa Roy').

Casa Pedro

Casa Pedro is built lengthways, bungalow style, and rests at the very edge of the urbanisation, overlooking a large field of olive trees. The house has larger rooms than mine, more of them, and is provided with an integral garage. After proudly showing me around, he pours two cold beers and leads me outside onto his front terrace, where we sit ourselves down on stone seats that have been cleverly built into his boundary walls. For added comfort, cushions are fitted inside shallow troughs on top. I like this idea and determine to do the same. Leaning back, beer in hand, I begin to unwind, but not for long. After no more than a few minutes the scorching sun, by now almost directly overhead, begins to burn my exposed skin. Noël Coward's song, *Mad Dogs and Englishmen,* comes to mind so I move back to join a very sane black Labrador lying in the shade. Panting heavily, long pink tongue hanging limply from his mouth, the dog looks up at me with his big brown eyes and nods his approval.

For the next hour or so, the three of us stay quite contentedly where we are, Pedro and I knocking back our drinks and Tel, every now and then, giving little snuffles and odd twitches as he chases something or other in his dreams.

By this time, I am starting to feel quite hungry and ask my host if he knows of anywhere nearby that serves food. He apologises for having nothing to offer me in the way of *tapas* but suggests that we make our way to a local bar, which he assures me provides good, cheap meals. He fancies something to eat as well so, letting sleeping dogs lie, off we go.

Instead of taking the road, we nip over his boundary wall and make our way across the adjoining field, along a grassy little track bordered with a pretty selection of wild flowers. The only ones I recognise, at that time, are yellow buttercups, white daisies and red poppies. Later, though, on my rambles in the hills behind the village, I learn the names of many others.

Because of its position, midway between Europe and Africa, Andalusia provides a climate encouraging the growth of a tremendous variety of plant life. Half of the 10,000 types of flower known to exist in the whole of Europe are found in Spain. Of these, 150 grow nowhere else in the world.

Pedro and I do not have too far to go. On the other side of the N 340 we descend a slight slope, cross a dry riverbed, and there, on the corner of a road that leads into the village, stands El Salón. The only indication that it is a pub or restaurant is a large Coca Cola sign in the shape of a bottle-top on the wall outside. Pushing aside a curtain of hanging beads, we go in.

At first, having walked straight in from the brilliant sunshine, I find it difficult to see anything at all. A thick blanket of cigarette smoke hangs over everything and the only light enters by way of two small, dirty windows and the curtained doorway we've just passed through. Gradually, as my eyes become accustomed to the murkiness, I make out, at the far end of the room, a collection of short, weather-worn characters either perched on high stools, or standing in front of a long wooden counter. On either side, sitting on rickety chairs, groups of elderly men are

El Salón

banging dominoes onto equally rickety tables. Yellowed, peeling, uneven walls are plastered with faded calendars showing pictures of handsome, tight-trousered bullfighters or elaborately dressed women, holding fans. As we approach the bar, two of those on stools stand up and offer their seats, which we gratefully accept. Sitting down makes me feel less conspicuous for, standing, I tower at least a foot above the others in the room and must look a veritable giant – almost as if the Vikings have returned. I understand how Gulliver must have felt when finding himself in Lilliput.

From the number of *holas* he receives and the way a glass of beer is placed in front of him without being asked for, it looks like my Norwegian friend is a 'regular' here. Pedro then proceeds to satisfy everybody's very obvious curiosity by introducing me all round and, for a while, I hear the word *inglés* floating around the room. First, I shake hands with Manolo, the squarely-built, curly-headed proprietor, and then with our barstool neighbours, except for one man who stands all by himself. He is not presented to me. In fact, quietly smoking his cigarette and sipping a red wine, he seems to be ignored by all.

Pedro asks Manolo for two *menús del día*. There does not seem to be much in the way of choice – other than taking it or leaving it. Straight away, a most palatable meal, consisting of a starter, *sopa de picadillo* (chickpeas, ham, potatoes, rice and egg), followed by a large plate of grilled sardines, is served up. Fresh figs and oranges come as dessert. With wine and bread, the bill amounts to the grand total of fifty pesetas (30 pence) for the two of us.

The combination of food, booze and heat is starting to make me feel very drowsy. The *Mad Dogs and Englishmen* stanza by Noël Coward may have been appropriate a short while ago but the ending to the same verse – 'Englishmen detest a/ Siesta' – does not apply to me at that moment.

Nothing would please me more than the chance of a little lie-down, so I ask Pedro if he knows of anywhere locally where I might find a room for the night. At this, he shakes his head and waves his index finger from side to side.

"No, no, Luis, wiss me you stay. Iss goot, ya? In *España* zey say, *mi casa es tu casa*. My 'ouse iss your 'ouse."

Later that evening, after a refreshing snooze in Casa Pedro's spare room, I go outside once again to join my hospitable friend on his terrace. The sun has disappeared behind Cerro Gordo, taking the heat of the day with it, and I find the temperature perfect. The two of us sit there chatting and drinking away, with bright stars twinkling overhead, for the rest of the evening and well into the next morning. Pedro has been living at San Nicolás for the last four months and during that time has picked up plenty of facts, historical and otherwise, about the village and its people. I ask him what he knows of the man I saw standing alone back in El Salón. His seemingly self-imposed isolation intrigues me.

"Ah! Dat man. He iss secret poliss. Dat iss why he iss *solo*. I tell you, Luis, dere iss secret poliss all over. Dey watch all."

It turns out that these individuals do indeed watch and listen to all. Very little escapes their notice. There is nothing 'secret' about their identity, though. They are merely looked upon as part of the fixtures and fittings by the locals. An offshoot of the *BIS,* or *Brigada de Investigación Social,* this band of official government agents was originally set up after the Civil War to take note of any political dissent. Their function nowadays is more concerned with keeping an eye open for drug activity – although their ears would still prick up if they overheard too much in the way of political chat. Two others of his type are stationed in La Herradura and are, of course, known to all. The one in El Salón that afternoon is called Antonio. He has a wife and five children (three boys and two girls) living in Burgos, is aged 32, speaks a little French and English, drinks too much cognac, lusts after foreign *rubias* (blondes) and is known to carry a small pistol in a leather holster under his shirt.

I learn that La Herradura has much in common with Almuñécar. Before the arrival of the Moors, the Phoenicians and later the Romans farmed both areas. Two kilometres to the west of present-day La Herradura, a settlement called Jate or Xate came into being on the banks of the River Jate. In the 7th century, with the departure of the Visigoths, the Arabs took over and changed Jate's name to Alquería (farmstead). It remained that way for the next 700 years, as the busy Arab community continued to trade in products like fish, fruit and minerals, even after the Reconquest. They might have carried on a while longer had it not been for the Arab rebellion of the Alpujarras in the 16th century. This act provoked neighbouring Christians from Almuñécar to sack the area, destroying dwellings and burning boats. A little later, in 1609, Philip III gave orders for all Moors to be expelled from Spain. After that, the bay Jate, Xate, or La Alquería, became known as La Herradura, due to its distinctive horseshoe shape, and a new colony sprang up where it is today.

At this point, perhaps believing he has taught me enough local history for one day, Pedro changes the subject and asks me to tell him more about the load he helped carry into my house.

"Iss sailink boat, ya, Luis?"

I tell him he's right but, before I can say anything more, he steps in.

"Wit sailink iss *mucho peligro*, Luis. Listen. I tell you anoser story."

On 19 October 1562, a squadron of 25 Spanish galleons, making their way eastwards from Málaga, found themselves heading into a powerful headwind that, before long, developed into a fierce storm. To give the exhausted rowers a break, they decided to shelter in the lee of Punta de la Mona but, while they stayed at anchor, the wind suddenly changed direction and started to blow strongly from the southwest, driving the flotilla on to the rocks. Of the 25 vessels, only three survived. The number killed, either by drowning or being smashed against the cliffs, is reckoned between 3,000 and 5,000.

Quotation from Don Quijote outside church of San José, La Herradura, referring to the shipwreck of 1562

Cervantes makes mention of the shipwreck in *Don Quixote*, saying that the *hija* (daughter) of Don Alonso de Marañón, a Knight of Santiago, drowned in La Herradura. This extract from the book can be seen inscribed on tiles outside the parish church of La Herradura, named for San José, or St. Joseph.

In 1990, the bronze statue of a naked male figure, half-lying, half-sitting, with one arm held above his head, is erected on the beach, midway between Punta de la Mona and Cerro Gordo. A plaque bolted to a rock underneath reads;

'Este monumento a los hombres de la mar conmemora el naufragio de la Armada Española en 1562. Fue inaugurado el 18 de marzo 1990 por los vecinos de La Herradura siendo Alcalde D. Juan Carlos Benavides Yanguas'.

'This monument to the men of the sea commemorates the shipwreck of the Spanish fleet in 1562. It was inaugurated on 18 March 1990 on behalf of the citizens of La Herradura by the mayor, Don Juan Carlos Benavides Yanguas.'

Anyone viewing the statue will immediately be aware of something glistening in the sunlight. On closer inspection they will see that it is where the green patina from the man's dangling penis and testicles has been rubbed away, exposing the brass-like metal underneath.

Pedro supposes the ill-fated fleet of ships to have been part of the Spanish Armada, assembled to invade England, but I find out later that he's wrong. The attack so ably repulsed by Sir Francis Drake did not, in fact, take place until twenty-six years later, in 1588. With the Spanish word for any fleet being *armada* it's easy to see the misunderstanding.

Pedro tells me that he too has a boat, a dinghy, brought with him from Norway. I ask him if he fishes from it.

"Fishink! *Naturalmente!* Vot else I do wiss a boat, Luis?"

This news interests me. I have great hopes when it comes to fishing and ask Pedro if he knows what types of fish are found

Bronze statue, La Herradura

in these waters. The question seems a difficult one for him to answer. I think perhaps he doesn't know the English names.

"Ach, der is so many, Luis. Iss better you com wiss me for fishink – maybe *mañana*, if wesser goot."

The next day then, with the sea looking like a millpond, we put to sea in his red fibreglass dinghy, but I learn very little about the art of catching fish from Pedro, for I soon discover that he lacks the one essential ingredient that makes a good fisherman: patience. We move from one spot he selects to another, each time dropping our improvised anchor of a heavy stone tied to a rope, followed by squid-baited hooks. After no more than a few minutes, Pedro claims, pointing,

"Iss not goot 'ere. We go zere."

I must have pulled up that stone at least a dozen times and at the end of the morning I find myself back on the beach suffering from a sunburned back, aching arms, sore bum and no sign of a fish.

Pedro and I have much in common. Back in Norway, he worked as a motor mechanic and, by frugal living and diligent saving he too managed to accumulate enough money to buy his own business: a garage-cum-repair-workshop. Then, once he'd got the affair ticking over, he rented the whole lot out, lock, stock and barrel, and moved here to Spain, accompanied by his dog, 'Tel'.

His first port of call was Nerja, where he bought one of the houses on the estate I had seen called 'Capistrano', but the ever-growing number of neighbours induced him to look for somewhere quieter. He travelled a short distance along the coast and, like me, fell in love with La Herradura at first sight. "Iss *magnífico*, ya, Luis?"

Being an active, industrious sort of person, Pedro uses his skills as a welder to make and sell metal-framed, tiled tables for outside patios. Built to last, there are still many around today. Alas! The same cannot be said of poor Pedro.

Some years later, a change took place in his state of health. Normally a vigorous, outdoor type, he suddenly started to complain of feeling tired all the time. His friends, myself included, advised him to lay off the booze and try going to bed earlier, for he tended to be the sort of person who gets up early, spends his days working at table-making or out in his boat and then parties the night away. Burning the candle at both ends must stop, we warned him. Although he did as we suggested and took things easier, his fatigue continued. Then, after a short period of feeling better, when it looked as though he might be on the mend, he fell ill again and started to lose a lot of weight. Leaving his dog in my care, a worried Pedro returned to Norway. There, the result of several blood tests revealed that he had picked up a disease called 'Malta Fever'. The specialist doctor, on learning that he had been living in the south of Spain, asked whether he had eaten goat's cheese or drunk goat's milk. When my friend answered that he had partaken of both, he learned, to his dismay, that this could well account for his condition. Apparently, the infection is found around the shores of the Mediterranean, hence its other names: Mediterranean, Undulant or Gibraltar Fever. It has been known to exist since 1886 but not until 1904 did a man named Bruce discover that eating or drinking unprocessed products of cows, sheep or goats spreads the Brucella bacteria. The ailment became known as brucellosis.

In his book *Journey to the Alcarria* (1948), Camilo José Cela mentions the malady. Arriving tired and hungry at a village called La Puerta, the traveller searches in vain for somewhere to eat. On his return to the inn, the woman of the house can only offer him a meal of cooked goat's meat and a glass of goat's milk. By now, ravenous and very thirsty, the traveller takes his chances with Malta Fever and eats and drinks anyway. Although he is aware of the risks of contracting the disease, he says, 'the horn of hunger bores deepest of all'.

The shop in La Herradura sells the soft, creamy, white goat's cheese and, if desired, a daily supply of goat's milk can be delivered straight to the front door – inside the goat! The goatherd simply squeezes milk straight from the animal's teat into a container of your choice, right there and then, on the doorstep. It

Goat's milk delivered to the door

Goatherdess, 2001

seems that, over a period of time, local folk have become pretty much immune to infection, but newcomers to the area have not.

Brucellosis is not usually fatal but, on his return from Norway, Pedro's condition deteriorates and, a short while later, in 1977, the poor man dies. Many of his friends, myself included, attend the funeral service, after which we accompany the coffin to the nearby cemetery. There, his body is placed into one of the stone honeycombs of oblong spaces and then sealed. These *columbarios* have been used as a place of entombment since Roman times. Gerald Brenan, in *South from Granada*, describes them as 'masonry chests-of-drawers'.

To be interred alongside locals suggests that Pedro must have been of Catholic faith for peoples of other religions have their own designated cemeteries. In the 19th century, the burial of non-Catholics proved no easy matter. Richard Ford, who lived

Ruins of columbarios

in Spain between 1830 and 1833, tells us in his book *Gatherings from Spain* (1846) that local folk wanted nothing to do with the body of a dead Protestant. Considering the corpse to be that of a heretic, they thought it might taint the surrounding soil and stop corn growing in its vicinity. As a concession, in coastal villages, authorities allowed the remains of a non-Catholic to be placed in a hole in the sand at low tide, but this act upset fishermen who feared that the soles of their feet might become poisoned. These superstitious people also felt concerned when the late Mr Hole (having been refused permission to be buried on land) ended up being lowered to the bottom of the sea in a casket. Believing this deed would stop them catching fish, fishermen hauled the box to the surface again and threw the man's remains 'to be devoured by the fowls of the air'. Even for those of Catholic faith, it is said that 'bodies find a place in catacombs for those that can pay – an open ditch for those that cannot'.

A century later, in the 1920s, Gerald Brenan finds that many of his neighbours in the Alpujarra region where he lives think Protestants are possessed of tails! Of course, conditions are different today. With hundreds of thousands of foreigners all over Spain, there are plenty of graveyards for people of every faith.

I spend the next couple of days buying furniture. I have my heart set on getting hold of some old, folksy samples but find that anything considered to be even slightly 'antique' costs a lot of pesetas. Gypsies from Granada are busy scouring the neighbourhood in the hope of snapping up vintage items. One man I know, copying the character from *Aladdin*, drives around the countryside in his van, calling at village houses, swapping shiny, formica-topped, aluminium-legged, easy-to-clean tables for old, hand-made, time-honoured pieces of furniture that have been in the family for generations. His business prospers. People think him mad to offer such a deal. Antique dealers in posher resorts near the airport are eager to give a good profit on anything they consider worthwhile, for the wealthier residents setting up home locally provide a ready market. With more and more homeowners looking for something with a bit of age and character, container-loads of Victorian artefacts are soon being shipped from England to meet demand.

The only traditional Spanish item I do manage to come across, and buy, is a beautiful old, engraved chest of drawers, complete with marble top. On closer inspection, however, I find parts to be covered in tiny holes. It looks to me like the dreaded woodworm! Fortunately, Pedro has a can of killer-cum-preservative liquid which he gives me to paint the piece of furniture all over. With doors, window frames and roof of my house made of pine, precautions are necessary. Woodworm, or any number of other wood-boring insects that abound locally, can reduce a piece of timber, especially soft timber, to a pile of sawdust in a very short time. One species in particular, known as a longhorn beetle, makes such a racket with its munching and crunching that it keeps people awake at night.

A hollow-eyed friend of mine became so incensed by this irritating sound that, one night, he took an axe and chopped a chair into little pieces to get at the noisy perpetrator. Once found, he deposited the two-inch, finger-thick white grub into a jar of wood shavings, where it lived for a number of months, chomping away quite happily, and would have survived even longer if it had not been for his cat. Antonio assures me that all the timber in Casa Roy has been treated with something that makes it insect-proof, but I check regularly for holes, just in case.

From the start, I suspect that getting hold of the right size of bed might prove a problem. I try in Almuñécar, but have no luck. The one likely shop there has only the standard 1.82 metres length, whereas my 6 feet 3 inches equals 1.875 metres. (In later years, when young Spaniards eat a better diet, their growth in stature is acknowledged by manufacturers, who increase bed length by 8 centimetres, to 1.90 metres.) From my experience of sleeping in Spanish lodging houses, I know how frustrating and downright uncomfortable it can be not to be able to stretch out my legs, particularly first thing in the morning. Divan beds, the type that have no baseboard or headboard, are just as bad. With my feet dangling over the end, I usually wake up with sore Achilles tendons.

Having a bed made to measure is one answer, of course, but as this will take quite a long time, I decide to take a trip to Málaga and shop around. Until then, I have been sleeping uncomfortably on an inflatable, rubber lilo on the hard, tiled floor of my house.

En route, I discover that quite a few changes have taken place since my trip seven months ago, when I passed this way to pick up Rosalind from the airport. The twisting, turning section of the N 340 between La Herradura and Nerja has been made a little safer, with barriers installed on some of the more dangerous hairpin bends, and most of the larger potholes filled in, but, apart from that, my discoveries are not good news. Capistrano has expanded its building programme by studding the hills to the north of the road with more 'little boxes' and the village of Torre del Mar is now a concrete jungle of apartment blocks. The last time I drove through the main street, little coloured fishing boats could still be seen pulled up on the beach but now they, and the shoreline, are completely hidden from view by these high-rise monstrosities.

The number of private automobiles on the road seems to have increased as well. Those I come across, apart from tourist models, are nearly all 1400 and 600cc Spanish-manufactured Seats. As their cost works out at 155,000 (£925) and 75,000 pesetas (£450) respectively, I can see that folks in these parts are already benefiting from the effects of tourism.

At the start of the so-called 'development years', in 1961, only one person in a hundred owned a car. By 1973, this number increases to one in ten. Down here in the south, in 1967, they are still considered a luxury. Petrol (85 octane) costs 9.25 pesetas a litre and, as a small car uses 5.7 litres per 100 kilometres, the expenditure for a return journey from Málaga to Madrid, a distance of 1,000 kilometres, will amount to the then average weekly wage of 530 pesetas. By train, the outlay is about the same.

On the subject of cars, I realise that sooner or later I must consider the merits of keeping a foreign car in Spain. The law, as it stands, stipulates that if I remain in the country for more than eighteen months, I will be obliged to 'import' any vehicle I have with me at the time. This means paying an import duty of 68%, a fiscal tax of 8% and a luxury tax of 16%, each one being added to the sum of the previous amounts. In all, a total of an extra 110.47%! What is more, because second-hand cars are few and far between, the assessed value of something like my Morris pick-up will be very high. The price I paid in England, £90, will not count. Its worth is reckoned on how much it will fetch here in Spain. How about a mule, I wonder?

After searching high and low in Málaga, I finally manage to get my hands on a giant of a bed. It lies, in pieces, in one of the many junk shops that line the streets close to the port. By standing upright alongside one of the metal side supports, I estimate its length to be at least two metres and the width of the intricately engraved headboard and end section measures about the same. It looks, almost, to be the twin of the one I shared with Anthea in Almuñécar. After a bit of haggling, I hand over 200 pesetas and load everything on to the pick-up. Pillows, sheets and blankets I buy from a nearby department store and return to La Herradura.

My huge bed serves me well. It turns out to be very comfortable and provides a good night's sleep – with night being the operative word! Again, it's almost a repeat of my experience back above the carpenter's workshop in Almuñécar for every day, at the crack of dawn, my slumbers are rudely interrupted. This time, however, the sounds of hammering, sawing and singing have been replaced by those of scratching, pecking and tweeting. The first morning, still half asleep, I try dragging my hands from under the bedclothes and clapping them together as loudly as I can. This results in a piercing shriek coming from the boarded ceiling overhead, accompanied by a frantic scuffling noise. Then all goes quiet. Just as I manage to drop back to sleep again, the irritating hullabaloo starts up once more. In vain, I strive to find a way to get rid of the pesky birds who, I discover, are nesting in the mud and straw under the roof-tiles. To start with, I try keeping a large, heavy stick by the side of the bed and, when disturbed, use it to clout the timbers above my head. This sends the little devils on their way for a while but, at the same time, brings an eyeful of dirt falling from between the gaps in the tongued and grooved planks. Next, I try chucking a fluffy child's toy bear onto the roof. This keeps the birds guessing for a while and allows me a few blissful mornings' peace, but it doesn't take long for them to work out that the strange object holds no danger. They end up pecking the bear to pieces and using the bits for nestbuilding. In the end, I have to admit defeat and have the mud and straw under the tiles replaced by cement. Donald laughs when I tell him the story and we both agree that, although traditional building methods are fine in theory, they sometimes cause problems.

The rest of my furniture I buy locally. My old mates, Paco and Pepe, come up with a splendid table and three chairs made from local almond wood and I manage to get hold of a heavy, mirror-fronted Victorian wardrobe, a chest of drawers and various other useful items from an elderly English couple. They, and their belongings, had been shipped from Somerset to their house in Almuñécar, but after only a matter of months, health problems made them decide to sell up and go back home to the West Country again. Being too big and cumbersome to carry up the narrow stairway, the wardrobe has to be dismantled and hauled up to the bedroom via the balcony.

The few cooking utensils I need are obtained from the one and only shop in La Herradura, which stands on a corner opposite El Salón on Camino Real. This small general store stocks just about everything from fishhooks to bread. A little farther down the road towards the beach, fresh fruit, vegetables, meat and fish are sold from a row of covered stalls. They open for business very early in the morning and close down before the sun has had a chance to warm things up. As well as an assortment of other utensils, I make sure to purchase a small, round, terracotta charcoal grill known as a *parrilla*. This simple little cooker, which I've seen blazing away outside people's homes in both Almuñécar and La Herradura, has never failed to fascinate me. I've watched as bundles of olive or almond twigs are burned down to glowing embers then, sandwiched in a wire frame, fish or meat is placed on top and grilled to perfection. This ultra-efficient barbecue has been in service for many hundreds, if not thousands, of years. Archaeological evidence has proved that the Phoenicians used a contrivance of exactly the same design as long ago as 400 BC.

Since it looks to me as though these *parrillas* have stood the test of time, I make up my mind to continue with the age-old custom. Most evenings, therefore, find me out on my back terrace, happy as a sandboy, grilling whatever took my fancy that morning on my visit to the market. Half a dozen *sardinas*, a piece of *pollo*, and a slice of *cerdo* (pork) sizzle away while I wet my whistle with a glass or two of *vino del terreno*. Everything is kept as simple as possible. A couple of tomatoes, a slice of onion, a hunk of *pan de campo* (bread baked with little or no yeast, which keeps fresh longer that way) complete the menu. Not bothering with plates or cutlery, I use my fingers. Who likes washing up?

The charcoal retains enough heat for me to boil a saucepan of water for coffee. Then, cup in hand, I sit back, puffing on a cigar, to gaze up at the mind-blowing display overhead. As yet, with hardly any light pollution from neighbouring houses to interfere with the wonderful starlit spectacle, the sight reminds me of my days at sea, when on night watch in mid-Atlantic.

In Spanish houses, during the colder, winter months, *parrillas* are also used as a form of heating. A round, communal dining-table, common to most homes and known as a *mesa de camilla*, has a round hole cut into its base into which the hot, glowing canister is placed. A small amount of lavender, rosemary or thyme sprinkled on top gives off a delightful aroma. On particularly chilly evenings, a thick tablecloth can be drawn up over the knees, trapping the heat underneath, thus keeping everybody warm – below the waist, at any rate! Nowadays, this method is still used, though in quite a few cases electric heaters have replaced the charcoal.

Until the 1950s, most of the country's inhabitants were obliged to burn some sort of solid fuel as a means of cooking. Only in a few of the larger towns, which had their own gas works, did people use anything else. A wood-fired *horno* (oven) in the kitchen saw to roasting and baking and a metal *hornillo* (hob), built into a tiled surface above, accommodated pots and pans for frying and boiling.

This *horno* sounds a bit like the coal-heated kitchen range my mother used in our 'two up, two down' terraced house in West Ham. Its fitted side-oven cooked our Sunday roast, pies and casseroles while vegetables were boiled and bacon, sausages and eggs fried on the fiery hob above. The 'hot-plate' seemed permanently to support a steaming kettle, ever ready for a cup of tea. Apart from a fireplace in the 'front' room, lit only on very special occasions, our house had no other provision for keeping warm. The whole family drew close to this friendly, glowing cooker during the winter months, keeping company with the socks and underwear dangling down from a line strung out across the mantelpiece above.

After the war, however, in order not to seem 'old-fashioned' and to 'keep up with the Joneses', most people living in the street, including my parents, had their old, black-leaded, range taken out and a gas fire fitted in its place. For cooking purposes, gas cookers were installed in the scullery. This change-over, although lamented by many, did at least cause less smoke to spout from the thousands of chimneys in the area and consequently reduced the choking fog and smog which covered many London boroughs at certain times of the year. A joke going about at the time reckoned that it felt great to wake up in the morning to the sound of birds – coughing their little hearts out! Nowadays, an expensive cooker called an Aga seems to be the favourite choice for the discerning homeowner. Whether gas, oil or coal fuelled, it seems to me that they don't differ too much from the old kitchen range.

In much the same way, in Spain, the traditional *hornos* and *hornillos* continued to prepare family food until 1960 when, with the introduction of bottled butane gas, new properties were built leaving space in the kitchen for a modern gas cooker. At the same time, a socket wired into the wall provided electricity for a fridge. During the '60s, the number of homes with a refrigerator leapt from 4% to 66%. Before that, food had to be bought fresh every day or kept in an ice-box.

To qualify for a supply of bottled gas, customers are obliged to sign a contract and pay a deposit of 1,000 pesetas. They are then given their allowance of two bright orange containers, costing 135 pesetas apiece. In our locality, empty bottles can be exchanged for full ones either at the depôt in Nerja or from the delivery lorry, which tours the environs of Almuñécar and La Herradura, stopping at particular locations on certain days of the week. Most sensible folk always keep a spare, topped-up gas bottle ready to replace the one being used. In my case, I find that one full container gives me enough gas to heat the water for my kitchen, bathroom and cooker for at least two months. Mind you, I do not use a lot of hot water and light the cooker only to occasionally make a cup of tea or coffee, thanks to my charcoal grill.

Initially, water-heaters, or *calentadores de agua* (which heat the water as it passes through a copper tube inside) were sold and installed with no regard to safety. In Casa Roy, for example, each time the pilot light ignites the gas jets, the water heater explodes with a loud bang. Only after some terrible accidents do the authorities insist on a metal tube being fitted above the heater, running through the wall to the outside of the house. This *ventosa* or vent allows any build-up of gas to escape. My kitchen, built before such safety regulations were introduced, has no such feature.

Some years later, I sell Casa Roy to a Mr. Tom Weeton. When it comes time to change his empty gas bottle for a full one, Tom asks, in his limited Spanish, if the butano man will kindly show him how to go about connecting the replacement. Once inside the kitchen, however, and seeing no obligatory *ventosa* above the *calentador* (gas-heater), the carrier starts to carry the full bottle of gas out again. Tom grabs hold. Now, these delivery men, due to the nature of their work, are robust, hefty individuals and it does not take much of a tug-of-war before weedy Mr Weeton finds himself without a butano-bottle. Unable to cook or heat water, a down-in-the-mouth Tom runs to me for help. I promise to do what I can.

Taking the N 340 towards Motril, we find what we are looking for on the other side of Almuñécar: a lorry, laden with orange bottles, standing parked outside a roadside bar. With Tom left in his car, I go inside, order a coffee and stroll across to where two burly men dressed in blue overalls are seated at a table. I keep my voice low – but not low enough, it seems.

"¡Hola, señores! Muy buenas."

They look up, surprised.

"Excuse me, *señores*, I wonder if you can assist me. You see, I am looking to buy a bottle of gas. Mine have been stolen. Can you do me a favour by selling me one?"

The men look at each other, then glance around the room. Unfortunately, some of those standing nearby must have overheard for they are staring in our direction. The sight of a foreigner always arouses interest anyway. The butano man speaks out. His voice is loud and clear, so everybody can hear.

"Sell you a bottle, *señor*? Certainly not! Without the right papers, such a thing is impossible." His mate joins in. "Impossible!"

Thanking them anyway, I return to my coffee. Before long, the two men drink up and leave. I follow soon afterwards to find them leaning against their lorry, waiting. A few hundred pesetas lighter, Tom, accompanied by a bottle of gas, returns home a happier man.

❀　❀　❀

8

1967

In which I raise a few eyebrows, muck about in boats,
catch fish and find myself 'denounced'.

The sweltering heat of August puts paid to any plans I might have for the patch of earth and rubble at the back of the house, for I decide this is definitely not the month for doing too much in the way of physical work. Even furniture hunting is put on hold. Instead, I decide that a refreshing swim is more the order of the day.

Not knowing the coastline too well, I start off by heading for the nearest and most convenient spot: the junction where the beach road meets with the one leading into the village, the Acera del Mar. However, it doesn't take long for me to find out that I'm not the only one who favours this location. It also seems to be popular with a group of gossiping old women who sit together in a black huddle, keeping a close eye on a noisy, laughing, gang of children frolicking at the water's edge. Clucking away at each other, they look for all the world like a cluster of mother hens guarding their chicks. Some have open umbrellas in their hands, angled to keep their head shaded. Others wear broad-rimmed hats. I can well understand why. From what I've seen locally, unless precautions are taken, the fierce heat from the sun shrivels a person's skin, especially on the face, from plum smoothness to that of a wrinkled prune in a very short space of time.

On my first day, as I crunch my way across the pebbles towards them and the sea, heads swivel, eyes glint from the shadows and the chattering stops dead. For a brief moment, children are forgotten. The staring continues as I walk on past, strip off and, with towel around waist, slip into my swimming trunks. This unheard of and most outrageous act precipitates the hubbub again, only this time the cackle is interspersed by loud tut-tutting sounds and an occasional screech. From then on, I find it more comfortable for me and less embarrassing for the ladies to take my daily dip further along the beach.

These watchful-eyed *señoras* are, for the most part, grandmothers or even great-grandmothers of the playing children. Their role in the family is not only to care for youngsters, but also to lend a hand with cooking and cleaning, thus giving their daughters or granddaughters the freedom to bear and care for babies while husbands go out to work. In this way, they are not looked upon as a liability – quite the reverse.

This traditional extended-family system has persisted here in the south of Andalusia for a lot longer than in other parts of Spain for lineage has always been, and still is, all-important. Even today, I don't know of any Spanish friends in the village who would contemplate, for one moment, the idea of putting their parents into an old people's retirement home, even if one existed. But a recent survey shows that this is not true of the country as a whole. Things are very much on the change, especially in the north. Whereas, in 1970, 71% of people over sixty-five lived with some member of the family, by 1992 the figure had fallen to 23%.

From mid-July to the beginning of September, others join me on the beach and in the sea. A few are young men and women from the village but, for the most part, their number is made up of *granadinos* who come south to escape the discomfort of Granada. There, tall buildings trap and radiate the savage summer heat which can push temperatures up to, and above, 40 degrees Centigrade, making it impossible to work, play or even breathe comfortably. The sensible course of action is to move away from the city in August to holiday on the coast, where the sea cools the air. La Herradura and Almuñécar are the chosen resorts for *granadinos*. The luckier ones lodge with relatives, while others, not so fortunate, take rooms in the three lodging houses on offer. Two, La Caleta and Peña Parda, are situated on the beachfront and the other, Pensión La Herradura, is in the Camino Real, just up the road from El Salón.

For beachwear, women dress themselves in the old-fashioned one-piece costume, while their husbands wear baggy swimming trunks that look like stitched-up underpants. Only in the last few years have men been able to bare their chests. Before that, male torsos had to be covered. Due to the fact that both outfits are made from thin, wool-like material, a soaking in the sea makes them cling to the contours in such a way as to leave nothing to the imagination. Coming forth from a swim shows off so many curves, bulges, bumps and knobs that many of the locals just stand and ogle. (When bikinis are donned, a few years later, eyes almost drop from sockets!)

It does not take long for these black-haired, brown-eyed village folk or their *granadino* counterparts to develop a flattering suntan. I am most jealous. While their bodies seem to go brown almost overnight, I have to be very careful about how much time I spend in the sun and can sunbathe only for short periods at a time.

By the middle of September, however, I reckon my skin to be conditioned enough for me to try my hand at mini-sailing. The summer may be officially over, but the weather is still fine and hot. After checking things out, I deem the Cerro Gordo end of the bay to be best for launching my boat, for there the beach shelves more gradually and the projecting point offers shelter from the prevailing south-westerly wind.

For the first couple of days I persevere at trying to work out how to handle the rigging. Ropes, rudders and centreboards can be confusing to a beginner. Eventually, mostly by trial and error, I manage to get the hang of things and, after spending more time in the sea than on it, eventually end up skimming merrily across the bay to my heart's content. It takes a while longer to fathom the weather, though. The sea might appear perfectly calm in the morning but, by midday, huge waves can be crashing down on the beach. Wind strength changes from a slight breeze to storm force in the twinkling of an eye and I see in my mind's eye the sudden shipwreck of 1562.

However, I soon find that holding back, waiting for weather conditions to be perfect before putting to sea, leads me to spend most of my time hanging about, doing nothing. It is either too calm or too rough. Flat seas and gentle breezes are a rare combination.

After a while, impatience leads me to take chances. To hell with the weather, I think to myself, and remember two sayings: one by the SAS, '*Who dares, wins*', and the other, by Bernard Shaw, '*In this world there is always danger for those who are afraid*'.

Bearing this in mind, neither blustery winds nor turbulent seas stop me from setting out. I find that, by pushing the mini-sail in front of me and swimming out past the breakers, I am able to scramble aboard, hoist the sail with one hand, grab hold of the rudder with the other and, my toes hooked under a foot-strap and my body stretched out at full length, I can whirl over and through the waves at a terrific rate of knots. What an exhilarating experience! Gradually, becoming bolder and stupider as time goes by, I try for greater stimulation by taking more, and bigger, risks. Over-confidence leads me to try my luck when I should know better. Sometimes, when I am attempting to launch in blustery weather, the tremendous force of the rollers tears the mini-sail from my grasp and sends it, and me, crashing back through the surf, head over heels onto the beach. Twice a local carpenter manages to put together facsimiles of broken rudders and centreboards, but, in the end, the aluminium mast ends up bent to such an angle that I have to accept the fact that my poor mini-sail has finally had its day – as a sailing boat, at least. Its long, sturdy base still enjoys a life on the ocean wave – as a canoe – and is being used as such to this day.

Skating over the sea by wind-power proves great fun but, from

Pulling in the nets

the outset, my heart is set on getting hold of another type of boat: one from which I can fish. The fishing bug bit me as a kid at school and still bites.

In an effort to learn more about the fish found locally, I start off by going down to the beach early some mornings to lend a hand at bringing in the nets. Closely-knit and small-holed, these have been rowed out the night before and dropped overboard in the shape of a semi-circle, with a line of floats holding their tops on the surface of the sea while the rest dangles down underneath. When enough people have gathered, the hard work begins. Men, women and children from the village take hold of a rope at each end and strain and struggle to pull the heavy net ashore, with whatever it contains then being shared out. As I watch the puffing, sweating recipients walk away, each with a few tiddlers flopping about in the bottom of their buckets, I wonder whether their effort has really been worthwhile. This method of fishing does not seem to have improved much over the years. Laurie Lee, who spent some time in Almuñécar just before the Civil War, in 1936, notes in his book *As I Walked Out One Midsummer Morning* (1969) that it was 'a labour without mercy, dignity or reward'. Fifteen years later, he returned to the same village to find matters just the same. In *A Rose for Winter* (1955), he watches an auction of fish that have been dragged up the beach in nets. 'It was all over; the pathetic price was shared, and the stunted men, still blown from their labours, took their few pence in silence'.

One man from the village, called Joaquín, does not need a boat to fish this way. Very strong and a good swimmer, he swims out with his net and hauls it in on his own.

At other times, in the evenings this time, I make a point of meeting up with a different sort of fisherman: the few that still fish out at sea. Once their boats are beached, I help them slide them over greased lengths of wood to a higher, safer position away from the water's edge and, in the process, try, as best I can in my limited Spanish, to pick up a few tips. What are the names of the fish? Where have they been fishing? What do they use as bait? What size hooks? Although the poor guys must be pretty

Six, eight, or even ten fishermen rowed out together

worn out after their long period out at sea, they inevitably do their best to satisfy my curiosity. One day, perhaps appreciating my physical assistance, or maybe just fed up with my constant questioning, these kind gentlemen ask if I would like to go with them on one of their trips. Would I, indeed? I jump at the offer.

Early one morning then, before the sun has risen over the Punta de la Mona and with the bay of La Herradura bathed in silvery, rippling shadows, four of us set off, an oar apiece. We row in a south-easterly direction towards a lightening horizon, with the line of hills to the north sharply silhouetted against a star-spangled, vermilion sky. After about an hour and a half, covering a distance I calculate to be about five kilometres, we come to an area known as Las Rocas, so called because a line of rocks lies on the seabed one hundred metres below. Five or six other brightly painted boats from Almuñécar, Salobreña and Maro have anchored there before us and, as we get closer, I see, with my heart beating a little faster, that their crews are pulling up fish after fish. I can't wait to get at it myself. Before attempting anything, though, I watch attentively as one of my shipmates carefully threads a piece of sardine onto each of the six hooks, spaced roughly ten inches apart, which are attached to a strong, weighted nylon line. Next, he lowers the whole lot over the side, letting the sinker fall until it reaches the bottom. He then pulls back up a few inches. Almost immediately, the hand holding the line is pulled seawards in a series of little jerks. One! Two! Three! A fish has taken the bait. "Quick!" I feel like shouting. "You've got a bite! Strike! Bring the line in!" – but the man doesn't seem at all concerned. He calmly waits as, once again, his fingers are yanked down. Still nothing. Only after the fifth or sixth bite does he haul up three nice-sized, struggling, gleaming fish. The scheme of things seems to be to wait until at least three or four fish have been hooked before troubling to bring in the catch. No easy matter. When I try, I find it difficult to determine whether the tugging on the line comes from one large fish or three small ones, and waste a lot of time and energy landing one fish after the other. Not that it matters; I enjoy every minute.

The most adept fisherman of our bunch is a diminutive, crinkled, toothless man called Francisco. He outfishes everybody and never bothers bringing up fewer than five fish at a time. Whenever he feels a bite he gives a flick of the wrist to the cry of *¡Olé!* Five *Olés* result in five fish being hooked. Although slight of build, there seems to be plenty of strength in Francisco's thin, wiry arms for it's no easy matter to raise a kilo or two of fish from a depth of a hundred metres. It amazes me to see that, even with all his energetic movements and loud shouting, a smoking cigarette never leaves his lips.

By holding up my catch, raising my eyebrows and asking, *"¿Cómo se llama?"* I slowly get to know the names of the different fish flapping about in the bottom of the boat. Among their number are a variety of bream, including the red sea bream (*besugo*) and couch's sea bream *(pargo)*, a fish similar to the English whiting called *brótola* (also known as 'forkbeard'), *merluza* (hake) and the highly prized, delicious, *salmonete de roca* (red mullet). Eels, both moray (*morena*) and conger (*congrio*), sometimes take the sardine bait and are hoisted, twisting and turning, out of the water, to be grasped firmly by the tail and have their spine cut through, just behind the neck, with a sharp knife. These needle-toothed fish are considered very much a nuisance, for not only are their snapping jaws very dangerous but also they manage to make a terrible tangle of the line. Sometimes its whole length, with hooks attached, has to be replaced. Once unhooked and sliced, these evil-looking contortionists are severely bashed over the head until their wriggling stops. Finally, the slimy creatures are stuffed, with care, into a lidded plastic container, well away from bare feet, for they have a reputation for suddenly springing back to life. Another little devil treated with much respect, the *cabracho* or red scorpion fish, has a row of poisonous spines along its back. When caught, it too receives a merciless beating and is then tossed in to join the eels.

I return home a happier and wiser man. My introduction to Las Rocas could not have been better. While out there, I have

Easy to see the Viking influence

seen dolphins, basking sharks, a turtle or two, the weather has stayed perfect, and we've caught fish a'plenty. We had luck that day, though. Quite frequently, unforeseen winds can spring up, forcing fishermen to quickly up-anchor and head back to shore. At other times, powerful currents can mysteriously sweep over the underwater rocks and carry weighted lines away, making fishing impossible.

For as long as the local people can remember, going back before the time of the grandfathers of their grandfathers, Las Rocas has been a favourite venue for practising this method of 'hand-line' fishing. Although on subsequent trips I never come across more than four men together in one boat, I am told that, in bygone days, six, eight or even ten fishermen rowed out together in much larger vessels. A sorry, windswept example lies rotting on La Herradura beach. With its high prow and distinctive 'longboat' design, it doesn't take much to see Viking influence.

I am keen to get hold of a boat of my own as soon as possible. There are plenty to choose from. With their owners now working on building sites, a whole line of them lie neglected and looking pathetic, pulled up on the shingle. Individually hand-made, each is different in size and shape. One example stands out from the rest. Three metres in length, with a metal strip running along her base, the vessel's lovely, sleek, rounded – almost feminine – lines make it a question of love at first sight. As the song goes – '*she stole my heart away*'. (At that moment, I can well understand why boats are referred to as 'she').

I seek out the owner and we strike a deal. Due to the fact that the boat has been lying out of the water for quite a while, the sun's heat has shrunk and opened up her timbers, so I end up paying only a few hundred pesetas. Although the vendor, Salvador, has no further use for it, I can see that he still treasures his former breadwinner and offers to help me scrape, caulk and paint it back to its former condition. When we've finished the restoration, he lights up a cigarette, stands quietly for a while, then slowly walks around the boat's edge, running his eyes almost caressingly over her glistening sides.

Restored to former glory

Later that evening, I answer a knock at the door to find a smiling Salvador standing there holding a magnificent pair of oars. Foolishly, without thinking, I raise my hand and rub my forefinger and thumb together in an attempt to ask how much he wants. The grin leaves his face. He looks me full in the face, shakes his head, wishes me *buena suerte* (good luck) and walks away without another word, leaving the oars leaning against the wall.

Owning a boat is one thing: catching fish from it is quite another. At first, I row to a point halfway between the beach and the tip of the Cerro Gordo – a place where I've occasionally seen other men trying their luck – and there I anchor and have a go at 'bottom fishing', baiting the hooks with squid and pieces of sardine. This results only in tiresome, constant nibbling by little, striped *cabrillas* (known as *vacas*, or 'cows', locally). Further attempts at different places bring the same outcome. What am I doing wrong, I ask myself? Am I using the wrong bait? Fishing at the wrong depth? Realising I need advice, I turn to a person who always seems to come ashore with a sizeable catch: a fisherman 'extraordinaire', my old friend, El Mudo.

Born deaf and dumb, this man can be found, depending on the weather, either out at sea or busy working at something or other on the beach. His talents, besides fishing, include shoe and boat repair, herb-gathering, toy-making, cutting and supplying bamboo, laying stone mosaics and others too numerous to mention. In constant demand are his splendid walking sticks, made from the wood of the *acebuche* (wild olive) tree. To obtain the curve for the handle, he loops and ties selected branches into the right shape as they grow and then cuts them when ready. As a gift, for me, he fashioned an extra-long example. I still have it. For someone who can neither speak nor hear, El Mudo spends a lot of time 'talking'. By using his hands he manages to deliver an easy-to-understand sign language, enabling him to chat away quite fluently. No language is 'foreign' to him.

Physically very strong, the deaf and dumb man puts up with no nonsense from anyone foolish enough to make fun of his affliction. Once, in El Salón, he notices someone imitating his little grunts and hand movements. To the amusement of every-one in the room, El Mudo walks straight up to his impersonator, points down to the man's groin and wiggles a little finger in the air. The implication is obvious and so embarrasses the mimic that he very soon slinks shamefacedly out of the bar to hoots of laughter.

One day, El Mudo invites me and one or two others to accom-pany him on a trip in his large, heavy, flat-bottomed boat. On the way around Cerro Gordo, he rows to the base of the cliffs, leans over the side, hacks a quantity of mussels from the rocks, then continues round the point to the next beach, known as Cantarriján. Once we have collected enough driftwood, he makes a circle of large stones, lights a fire in the middle and places a large, battered, iron frying-pan on top. Into this he pours half a bottle of white wine, adds some garlic and then tosses in the mussels. Before long, the blue shells open to reveal

Author (second from left) with Daniel, with hand aloft, and El Mudo (far right)

their tasty orange meat inside. After being given a hunk of bread apiece, we dunk and eat. Delicious!

I can thank this man for teaching me an easy and reliable way to catch certain types of fish. His technique entails the use of something known as a *panera*. This device consists of a rounded piece of cork, about 10 cm in diameter and 3 cm deep, with four hooks tied around its edge. Atop this, another, smaller, circle of cork is placed with five metres of strong line wound around its middle, the end being tied to the larger cork underneath. Small squares of bread are then baited onto the hooks and the contraption is floated near to where surface-feeding fish are known to congregate. As an enticement, a few scraps of bread are tossed in around the floats. Before long, the fish start nibbling at this 'groundbait'. Then, all of a sudden, one of their number finds itself with a mouthful of hook sandwich and, in panic, dives down under the sea, pulling the larger piece of round cork with it. As it plunges deeper, the section with the line attached is left spinning on top. It is then a simple matter to row, as fast as possible, grab the smaller cork and pull in the catch.

Fish such as mullet and several sorts of bream can be taken using this system, close to the rocks, at either side of the bay. Of the seven species of Mediterranean mullet, the most common found locally are the thick-lipped, grey variety, known as *lisa* – good to eat, either baked or charcoal grilled. A sprig of rosemary adds to the taste. Although I've never seen it happen, it is said that a captive female mullet is sometimes used to lure a shoal of male mullet – an age-old method, practised since Greek times. The 2nd century Greek poet Oppian, author of a didactic poem on fishing called *Halieutica*, writes: (Mair's translation) 'A like doom does love bring upon the mullet, for they are beguiled by a female trailed in the waves. ...For so, when they behold her, they gather round in countless numbers and, wonderously overcome by her beauty, they will not leave her'. Oppian is said to blame or praise fish according to behaviour rather than taste.

Fishing with panera

The bream family is even larger. Unesco records twenty-two different species. Some, like the *besugo* and *pargo* found at Las Rocas, are 'bottom' feeders while other varieties, those that look for food nearer, or on top of, the sea, can be caught with the *panera*. The most common of these are saddled sea bream (*oblada*), the two-banded sea bream (*mojarra*), the white sea bream (*sargo*) and the little annular sea bream (*raspallón*). Good to eat, they can be cooked in the same way as mullet.

If a really large specimen, or two at a time, become hooked, the frightened fish can pull both the top and bottom corks out of sight. This is when the episode becomes really exciting. Eyes must be kept peeled for the top cork to bob up from below for, when the buoyancy of two corks proves too much for the struggling, weakening fish to hold down any longer, the smaller of the two floats re-surfaces. Then a thrilling chase takes place. Sometimes, just as the hand reaches over the side of the boat to grab the floating cork, the quarry below finds enough energy to plunge deeper again, dragging it out of reach. This sometimes takes place two or three times before, finally, the wriggling fish is heaved out of the water and into the boat.

I find it best to fish early in the morning or late evening. The trouble is, the visual delights of the bay at these times of the day are so distracting that concentration on the corks is difficult. As the sun rises, the sea reflects all the colours of the rainbow as it changes from dark crimson through to coral pink and, when going down, from flaxen gold to a fiery, burning red.

Other, larger, types of fish are to be found in and around the craggy edges of the bay. One species, the dusky grouper, or *mero*, grows to a huge size – sometimes a metre or more in length and weighing as much as 30 kilos. These monsters can be caught either by lowering a large, sardine-baited hook, attached to a strong line, into underwater caves or crevices or, if lungs are powerful enough, by diving deep with a spear-gun. In the days when only simple masks, snorkels and not over-powerful, elasticated spear-guns were used, few *meros* were taken, but later, with the introduction of sophisticated scuba diving

Mero

equipment, complete with air-bottles, wetsuits and high-powered pneumatic guns, the poor fish stand no chance. Too late, conservationists decide to outlaw this latter method, so today, in the early 21st century, *meros* have become scarce. Their delectability could be responsible for their demise, for they are most delicious to eat and, if and when available, expensive to buy. Firm of flesh, delicately flavoured and without too many bones, they can be cut into steaks and grilled or poached.

Late one evening, on my return from a fishing trip, I am surprised to find two Guardia Civil officers, rifles slung over shoulders, standing at a point on the beach where I usually come ashore. My companion, a Belgian called Daniel, is likewise bemused. As soon as we have landed, the men in the shiny hats step forward and give a polite salute.

"Good evening, *señores*, may we make an inspection of your boat?"

Daniel, who speaks good Spanish, translates. An unnecessary question, I think to myself, for how can we stop them?

It doesn't take the men long to sort through our two buckets. One contains our *paneras* and bread and the other is full of fish.

While they poke around, trying to avoid getting too many fish scales on their black leather gloves, I try to figure out a reason for their actions. Can it be anything to do with drugs? I remember hearing tales of fishermen meeting with boats out at sea and bringing narcotics ashore at night. It is true, we have rowed out of sight around the point of Cerro Gordo – and it is getting dark. The two officers finish their search, brush themselves down, pick up their rifles and turn to face us.

"Do you possess a permit to fish, *señor*?"

This time, I understand the question. *Permiso* and *pescar* are easy enough words to follow. As the question seems to be directed at me, I have to give my answer via Daniel.

"But we are only fishing for pleasure. Surely we don't need permission to do that, do we?"

I am informed that I most certainly do. There must be some mistake. Once again my companion speaks on my behalf.

"Do you mean to say that a person coming here for a holiday needs a permit to do a bit of fishing. Even with with rod and line from the rocks or the beach?"

We are advised that, whosoever it might be, he, she or they need precisely that. They will let us off with a warning this time, but, if caught fishing again without a permit, we will both receive a fine and my boat will be confiscated. I can't believe my ears.

"Are you sure that's what they said, Daniel?"

He assures me that the Guardia have made things very clear. I start to get angry.

"In that case, tell them…"

But my friend has had enough. I can see that he is a little nervous.

"I think I've done enough telling for now, Roy. It might be wiser to just do as we're told."

It turns out that the guards are right. Under normal circumstances, the authorities take no notice, but, in my case, I learn that someone has made a *denuncia* – a complaint – about my gifts of fish to a local restaurant. So that's it. Quite often, on calm evenings, when they are 'on feed', I have ended up with more fish than I need for myself and have donated the surplus to a nearby restaurant. This, I guess, must have upset someone or other – possibly a local fisherman. Here is he, trying to earn a few pesetas by selling his fish in the market, and here am I, giving them away for nothing.

In truth, the restaurant sometimes gives me a free meal, so in a way, I suppose, this can be looked upon as payment.

Having now been warned of the dire consequences if found to be fishing without the required papers, Daniel and I drive next day to Motril to try and sort things out. Getting hold of correct documentation is never an easy matter in Spain. That's why *gestores* (fixers) are so popular. First of all, after a lot of running around, we find a place that deals with permits, only to discover that it issues them for just about everything under the sun, except fish or fishing. Then, on the far side of town of course, we visit another place that handles nearly all matters concerning fish and fishing – other than permits. Eventually we locate the right building. A scruffy wooden hut, down in the old port. Inside, we join a file of characters, all looking like clones of our expert fisherman friend, Francisco. Sitting behind a large desk at the head of the queue, a chubby, bespectacled man questions each person in turn, recording the answers on a printed form. When, after shuffling our way forward for an hour, to the head of the line, we listen carefully to the man in front of us being interrogated.

"Length of vessel?"

" Eighteen metres." (Sixty feet)

"Weight of vessel?"

"Fifty thousand kilos." (Fifty tons)

"Engine size?"

"Forty horse power."

Then it's our turn. The tubby man looks up when we appear before him, a little surprised at the sight of two unmistakable foreigners. He begins with preliminary enquiries, asking, and writing down, our names, addresses and so forth, but when he comes to, "length of vessel" and Daniel replies "three metres", the man nearly drops his pen. Next, "two hundred kilos" to his question about my boat's weight almost sends his glasses shooting off the end of his nose as he jerks his head up to stare. Those waiting behind, who overhear all this, burst out laughing.

Eventually, after giving the bemused official details of our little run-in with the *Guardia Civil*, we hand over fifty pesetas and, in return, receive an official permit to fish in Spanish waters, covered in stamps and signatures. I see that the heading *propulsión*, relating to engine size, has been crossed through and the word *remos* (oars) put in its place. The permit has a special, allocated number attached to it and we are told that this, accompanied by a name, is to be painted on the side of my boat. When asked what the name is to be, I answer 'Roy' and the man writes down *Hoy* (today).

9

1967

In which an invasion by American 'draft-dodgers'
upsets the plumber.

With no hotels large enough to interest the new breed of 'package-deal' operators, both Almuñécar and La Herradura remain predominantly Spanish and people from other countries, few and far between, know each other by sight. Usually then, by the end of summer, when the *granadinos* have returned to a cooler Granada and transient campers, mostly French and German, have up-pegged and moved away, things return to normal. The trickle of new foreign homeowners like myself does not upset the Spanish/non-Spanish ratio to any great extent and, as I discovered when I first arrived, new arrivals in the area are noticed at once. All of a sudden, however, in the autumn of 1967, both villages, and the surrounding neighbourhood, see a batch of new faces. They belong to Americans known as 'draft-dodgers'.

As long ago as 1945, a month after the Japanese surrender in World War II, troubles started in Indochina when the North Vietnamese leader, Ho Chi Minh, declared his country's independence from France. The French did not approve of this and from 1946 to 1954 the two countries fought each other for possession. After a disastrous French defeat at the Battle of Dien Bien Phu, an international committee negotiated a cease-fire. Both sides agreed to a boundary line, known as the 17th Parallel, being drawn across Vietnam, to separate the communist north from the non-communist south. A few years later, in 1956, the Geneva Accord stipulated that free elections should take place for the whole of Vietnam. However, as the communists looked as though they might very well win, Diem, the American-backed Prime Minister of the south, refused to allow voting to take place. At this, Ho Chi Minh, the northern leader, threatened to unify the country by force. Americans, or, at least, the American Government, were not amused. Fearing the spread of communism, they made up their minds not to allow this part of Southeast Asia to fall to the 'Reds'. President John F. Kennedy sent economic aid to the South Vietnamese, accompanied by a gang of his 'advisers'. These US personnel numbered 900 in 1960, increasing within two years to 11,000.

The situation deteriorated with Diem's assassination, Kennedy's murder, and an American destroyer's attack on a Viet Cong patrol boat in 1964. In November 1964, the USA (now under President Lyndon Johnson) started conscripting or 'drafting' young men into its armed forces and, by the end of 1965, had dispatched 180,000 troops to fight in Vietnam. By 1967 this number had risen to 400,000. The fierce fighting brought heavy casualties to both sides of the conflict, and in 1973, the unpopularity of the war within America, with growing protests all over the country, ultimately led to the start of troop withdrawal. By the end of it all, more than 47,000 US soldiers had been killed and 300,000 wounded.

Those young Americans lucky enough to have well-heeled parents, or some other benefactor willing to provide financial support, considered the mid-'60s might be a good time to leave home for a while and set off to see more of the world. They may have suspected that fleeing the country to escape conscription could ultimately lead to some sort of punishment, but coming back home in one piece made the risk seem worthwhile. As it happened, a day after his inauguration as President in 1977, Jimmy Carter granted a pardon to draft-dodgers. These escapees made their way to all parts of the globe and southern Spain, with its good climate and low cost of living, saw its share.

My introduction to these draft-dodgers comes one morning, while waiting at Al Quirós with Felix and John the Plumber for the midday post to arrive. Three of their number amble on to the terrace and plonk themselves down at the table next to ours. As is the usual case, they immediately become the centre of attention, but, although all eyes are fixed upon them and the tumult of sound around the terrace increases, the tall, blond, healthy-looking young men don't appear to notice. They just sit, denim-jeaned long legs stretched out in front of them, seemingly oblivious to everyone else. Something about the swagger and extreme confidence of these lanky lads reminds me a bit of the officer types from my guardsman days. I jerk my thumb in their direction and ask my two companions quietly,

"Who's that lot?"

John, who has also been silently watching the new arrivals, gives a little snort and answers, not lowering his voice at all,

"I bet they're bloody Yankees, Roy, mun. I was wondering when they'd show their faces in these parts. They're starting to bloody take over."

The chat at the next table stops dead in its tracks. I sense the icy silence behind and swivel in my chair to find three pairs of blue eyes glaring in our direction. The tall trio are taking notice now. For a moment or two all six of us sit silently eyeing one another up and down. Al Quirós has become the OK Corral of Andalusia. Felix breaks the ice. Holding up his glass, he wishes one and all *salud* (health) and takes a long swig of beer. His simple little act eases the tension a little. One of the Americans leans across towards us and gives us a somewhat forced smile.

"We're from California, my friends. That's in the south, y'see and 'Yankees', as you call 'em, are up in the north."

John seems intent on stirring things up. He doesn't return the smile.

"I don't care where you're from, mun. You're all bloody Yankees as far as I'm concerned. And what're you doing out here then? Draft-dodging, is it?"

I anticipate trouble, but to my surprise, John's question appears to unsettle the three Americans. They seem lost for an answer. Instead of taking offence, they look first at each other, then all at once find something interesting to look at down by their feet. After a few moments, one of them raises his head.

"Um, no man, no. Yuh got it all wrong. Yuh see, we – that is, I'm out this way studying the, er – the Islamic influence on the Spanish – "

John doesn't let him finish. He sounds angry.

"Why not admit it, mun? You're bloody draft-dodging. Nothing to be ashamed of. In your shoes, I'd be doing the same."

I can see that the three young Californians don't want to continue with this line of talk. They look decidedly embarrassed. After sitting a little while longer, they finish their drinks, get up and go. Once they're out of earshot, I ask John why he is being so difficult.

"Why didn't you give the poor buggers a break, John? They weren't doing us any harm. It can't be easy for them out here on their own, a long way from their family and all. What's the point in rubbing them up the wrong way?"

The plumber bangs his glass down on the table with such force that I wonder it does not break.

"Difficult? Me? You don't know what you're talking about, Roy. I've seen their kind moving in all along the coast. There's hundreds of 'em in Torremolinos. They've just started showing their faces around here but before long you'll have plenty of chance to see how much they mind their own business."

Felix joins in here.

"Sí, sí, and in Nerja zere are many, too."

I can't make out why these Americans have made John fly off the handle so.

"So what, John? What's wrong with that? It's a free country – well, sort of."

The plumber calls for another round of drinks. His last beer is all over the floor.

"I'll tell you what I don't like about it, mun. First of all, they won't admit to being draft-dodgers – you've seen that already. They always give some stupid reason for coming to Spain, like they're studying or something. I ask you, mun, how can they possibly imagine anyone believes their story? How is it that hundreds of young Americans turn up by chance, all at the same time, for the same purpose?"

I agree that it would seem too much of a coincidence.

"Well, perhaps they feel a bit guilty, John. It can't be much fun being called a draft-dodger, can it? I'd probably think up some excuse for being here, too, if I was in their shoes."

John hesitates a moment before carrying on.

"It's not only that, mun. Look, let me give you an example. I got to meet some of these characters some time ago while working on a job along the coast in Marbella. They were new to me then. In fact, I guess they must have been some of the first to turn up in these parts. The three I came across were sitting at the bus station looking pretty pissed off and, at the time, I felt the same as you. One of them asked if I could spare a cigarette so, after handing over the packet, I invited him and his mates for a drink. They told me they'd just flown into Málaga from the States and asked if I knew of a cheap place to eat and somewhere they could doss down for the night – that sort of thing, you know, mun. Well, they convinced me they were pretty much on the breadline and, being a soft touch, I treated them to a meal and gave them a handout. Well, bugger me if, a few days later, I didn't see the same three sods roaring through town on shiny new motorbikes, looking like something out of *Easy Rider!* I learned from someone, later, that they weren't hard up at all. They had plenty of lolly but liked to pretend they hadn't, thinking it cool to look busted. Since then, I've met others who've been conned this way, too. It appears that these Yanks like to put on an image of being peseta-less hippie bums struggling to make ends meet but, all the while, they've got a fat wad of American travellers' cheques tucked away, plus a rich Daddy back home ready to send them more. Mark what I say, mun. There'll be more of their kind here soon. Don't be fooled by them."

By the time he's finished his little speech, John seems to have worked himself into quite a state. I come to the conclusion it might be a wise plan to give the dangerous mixture of Yankee draft-dodgers and Scouse plumbers a wide berth in future.

Judy is one of the customers sitting on the terrace of Al Quirós that particular day and she can't help but notice John's set-to with the three Americans. When I bring up the subject later, she gives me another reason for his little outburst. It seems that one of their fellow countrymen, by switching on the charm and bringing forth the fat wallet, managed to win the heart, or at least body, of the plumber's ladyfriend in Marbella. When he found out, John blew his top. It all sounds a repeat of events that took place in the UK during World War II. With a bountiful supply of dollars, scarce foodstuffs and coveted silk stockings to dole out, US GIs managed to persuade many an English girl to dump her absent Tommy sweetheart in their favour. The saying floating around at the time reckoned the Yanks in Britain to be 'overpaid, over-sexed and over here'.

10

1967/8

In which I give the 'evil eye', have a haircut, collect firewood and eat lots of baked beans.

Setting up home in La Herradura, with no radio, TV, telephone or newspapers, pretty much cuts me off from what is happening in the rest of the world. News of the Arab/Israeli War and the closure of the Suez Canal is brought to my attention six months after the events take place. I'm living in a sort of Shangri-La. Not that I much care: local happenings are of more concern.

As the months drift by and my knowledge of the language slowly improves, I spend more time trying to get to know local inhabitants. Men, at any rate, for it does not take me long to learn that, with the opposite sex, I have no chance. Spanish women are never seen in bars, alone or accompanied, and the ones I come across on the street or at the market place hardly ever answer when I speak to them. My greetings of *¡Hola!* or *¡Buenos días!* are deliberately ignored and pretty young *señoritas*, heavy, shiny, jet-black hair hanging down their backs, either lower their big brown eyes or give me a cold stare back if they catch me eyeing them up. With a haughty toss of the head, away they stride, buttocks swaying seductively. Their untouchability excites my imagination, conjuring up images of dark, curly hair growing on other parts of their body.

What does it take, I wonder, to get to know one of these young ladies on a more intimate basis? I broach the subject when next speaking with my learned plumbing friend, John.

"It would be a great way to learn the lingo, John, wouldn't it?"

"Oh yeah! – and a great way to get your balls cut off as well, mun!"

He looks serious for once.

"Let me give you a word of advice, Roy, mun. Leave the village girls well alone. Don't ask any of them to meet you anywhere for a drink or anything like that, and don't, whatever you do, invite one into your house."

"You know what it's like around here, mun. Everybody would know of it immediately. When word got out, the poor kid would be looked upon as 'tainted' and never treated the same way again. The local lads expect to marry a virgin and the thought of their future wife associating with the likes of you, me or any other foreigner, would make them think the worst. As well as that, your name would be 'mud' in the village and you'd probably find it advisable to clear out. It's like the Mafia down here, mun, I tell you. They're all one big family. You upset one and you upset the lot. The only thing you could do if you wanted to stay put after upsetting the Godfather would be to marry the

Young ladies of La Herradura

girl and – take it from me, mun – that's going too far. I've known some try it but it never seems to work out. No, mun, stick to the foreign girls. What we do amongst ourselves is accepted: perhaps envied by some. We are thought of as different."

He finishes his little speech with a laugh.

"Take it from me, mun – we're living in the land of the untouchables!"

Women here may be considered untouchable, but they certainly know how to 'touch'. They do not consent to sexual intercourse before marriage, even when betrothed, for to become pregnant before marriage would bring terrible shame on themselves and their family. However, in order to keep carnal desires at bay until after the wedding ceremony, girls see no harm in masturbating their boyfriends.

In his book *The Pueblo* (1973), Ronald Fraser meets a young man, Juan, who admits that, in his village, 'wanking' between sexes is as 'normal and ordinary as giving a kiss'. Girls talk quite freely about it. His wife, Encarnación, says that this might be true in the south of the country, but in the north, masturbation is not really enough to satisfy men and couples therefore marry at an earlier age.

Fraser's story is corroborated by a middle-aged Scotsman named Bill who, living alone and having no car, employs a local woman, María, to cook and clean the house for him. After a period of about six months, during which time she prepares splendid meals and keeps the house spotless, María walks into the bedroom one morning and catches Bill, literally, with his pants down. Instead of turning about and leaving the room the middle-aged, rather portly *señora* walks boldly up to him and, looking him full in the face, asks,

"Do you not have needs, *señor*?"

It takes a few moments for him to realise what she means. The idea excites him and, as María's eyes drop lower, she sees that, by now, he does indeed have a 'need'. Bill says that he had not thought it possible for a man to be brought to a climax so quickly and expertly. Word of the Scotsman's experience spreads around town and he henceforth becomes known as 'Willie the Wanked'.

Another friend of mine, Mike, learning of Bill's delightful experience, tries a repeat of events with his cleaning woman. With a towel wrapped about his middle, he stands in front of her, declaring that 'as a man, he has needs'. She guesses what he is getting at and barks back at him, "Well, you'd better find yourself a wife, then!"

Like Almuñécar, but on a smaller scale, the hundred or so properties that constitute the village of La Herradura have gradually, over a period of time, spread to cover one side of a hill. Nearly all face west, towards Cerro Gordo. Climbing upwards, in a series of steps, between the flat-roofed houses, are three main passageways. Several more, much narrower, run off horizontally to the sides. All surfaces are cobbled, to enable mules, the most common means of transport at that time, to gain secure footing. I feel these drowsy-looking animals, often seen tethered outside beaded or curtained doorways, probably

La Herradura: tethered mules

La Herradura: cobbled streets

La Herradura: splendid display of potted plants

contribute unknowingly to the splendid display of potted plants that hang from the whitewashed walls.

During the baking hot summer months of July and August, with menfolk away working, children at school and women and older members of the family inside their shuttered homes, these attractive little streets are depopulated during the day. Then, with the setting of the sun, when temperatures become more bearable, short-legged, rush-seated chairs are brought outside for neighbours to sit gossiping as they make ready their *parrillas* to cook the evening meal.

One fine evening then, thinking perhaps it might provide a better opportunity to make contact with the local community, I decide to take a look around this old part of the village. Mounting the steps and turning into one of the alleys, I put on my best smile and make a beeline for the first group of people I see. At my approach, chatter ceases, people stop what they're doing, stare at me for a moment and then look hurriedly away. Some of the old ladies make a sign of the cross to the mumble of prayer and small children, still as statues, gaze up in wonder until they are scooped up by their mothers to have their heads turned away. There is an ancient and widespread superstition in this part of Spain that certain individuals have the power to harm or even kill a person by catching their eye and holding it for any length of time. Nobody wants to take chances. I might be one of these 'bogeymen' possessed of this 'evil eye'. I can understand why people may think this way – but animals? When dogs see me heading their way, they either run away yelping or start manic barking, while frightened, skinny cats scurry under doorways. Even birds, hanging in cages at the windows, stop chirping. I definitely do not find 'a welcome in the hillside' and empathise with those unfortunates from mediaeval times who carried a notice around their necks informing others they were 'unclean'.

Conditions change of course – but not much. Today, in La Herradura, most tourists still prefer to stay near the beach and seldom venture into the old part of the village. Those that do are treated in much the same way.

In the autumn of 1967, the village's main thoroughfare, the Camino Real, is given a coat of asphalt to render it less bumpy for the growing number of vehicles. This road starts a short distance from the seafront and winds its way up through the western side of the village, past El Salón and Pensión La Herradura, eventually to connect with the N 340. On the last stretch, before reaching the 'T' junction, it cuts through a thick cluster of olive trees and, at this spot, several men are supposed to have hanged themselves from a thick branch which projects over the side of a steep gorge. The locals, who are very superstitious, give the locality a wide berth, for they consider the area to be haunted. I must admit that, with that story in mind, it does not take much to conjure up a picture of a body swinging there in the shadows if I happen to pass by late in the day. While on this gruesome subject, I must tell of an incident that happened that winter.

Driving back from Almuñécar one afternoon, I stop to give a hitch-hiker a lift. The young man, a South African, asks if I know of a cheap place to stay and, on my recommendation, books into the Pensión La Herradura. He thanks me for my assistance and offers to repay my kindness by inviting me to join him for a drink or two the following Saturday evening. Bring along some others, he says: we can throw a little party. He tells me that he has some business matter to sort out which will provide him with funds. The idea sounds OK to me, and so, on Saturday, at the appointed hour, I and a few friends meet up at the *Pensión*. After waiting a while I ask the owner, Gerónimo, if a foreigner still has a room there. The answer comes as a shock.

"The blond one? Oh, don't speak to me of him. He hanged himself this morning – and he hasn't paid!"

On the same road, farther down the hill, nearer to the village, stands the one and only barber's shop. A visit paid to this establishment benefits me in more ways than one. Firstly, it results in a few new words being added to my vocabulary, some of which do not appear in the dictionary; secondly, I learn much more about the ways of the village and its people; thirdly, whether I like it or not, my knowledge of football is greatly enhanced. Besides all that, I end up with a good haircut. Although not very trendy at that time, I like to keep my hair short.

When I first push open the door and peer inside this long, dimly lit, smoke-filled salon, I see at least ten others sitting around its edge, waiting, presumably, for their turn in the barber's chair. Thinking there might be a long delay, I nearly turn round and walk straight back out again. I can always try again later. To my surprise, one of those seated stands up, holds out his hand, gives a broad smile and wishes me, "Goot mornink".

Square-set and slightly corpulent, the man has an authoritative air about him. With thick lips and a bulbous nose, he reminds me of the old-time film star W.C. Fields. The comb and pair of scissors sticking out from the top pocket of his almost-white jacket announce him to be the man himself. The hairdresser. Without further ado, he ushers me into an ancient chrome and leather-padded chair which stands facing a cracked mirror. On the wall to one side I notice a faded sign which promises to deliver 'Haircutting While You Wait'. After carefully adjusting the headrest and, with a flourish, draping a large bib about my neck, the man starts clipping. At the same time he begins rattling away in a mixture of Spanish and broken English, with a few words of French thrown in for good measure. He starts the introductions by tapping himself on the chest with his comb: "Ramón."

I raise my hand from under the drape and point to myself. However, before I can say a word, I hear him pronounce, with a long roll to the 'r',

"Rrroy."

I soon learn that this is the man from whom no secrets are hidden. Not only does he know my name, my nationality, that I have a house at San Nicolás, a boat on the beach and am a keen fisherman, he also seems aware of my previous relationship with Anthea and that I now live alone. Before much longer, he starts on his favourite topic – football. As I am English and

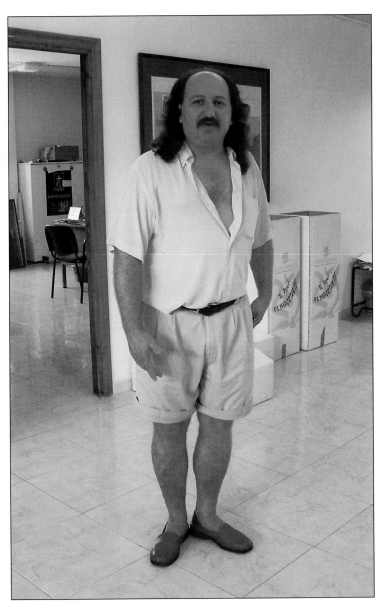

Ramón, the barber

England won the World Cup the year before, in 1966, Ramón incorrectly believes that I, too, must be a lover of the game. He himself supports Real Madrid and proudly gives me to understand (with difficulty) that they brought the European Cup home to Spain five times in a row between the years 1956 and 1960. A feat never again to be equalled!

Football is a very popular game in Spain. La Herradura has a strong line-up of players that year, who compete favourably with squads from neighbouring Almuñécar and Nerja. General Franco, who is known never to miss 'Match of the Week' on television, also loves the game and encourages each little township to field its own team. He reckons that a mind occupied with the merits of football, and in particular Real Madrid and its players, is less likely to be concerned with politics.

His philosophy also applies to picture houses. In Franco's time, there are more cinema seats per head than in any country in Europe and the price of admission is kept, by law, at a level to suit all pockets. Of course, the films shown are heavily censored. Familiarity, such as touching or kissing, is strictly forbidden – on or off screen. One particular feature, I remember, turns out to be most confusing. In order for an unmarried couple to be seen alone together on holiday (shame on them!) the plot is changed to make them brother and sister. Incest, apparently, is acceptable, for by the end of the film they have five children!

Terrible films are shown in La Herradura two or three times a week in a cavernous room on the ground floor of a building in the Calle Real. The projector is very old and spools of film have to be changed five or six times during each programme. Because of this, a trestle table stands in the corner, from which beer or wine is served during the intervals. Quite often, the reels are shown in the wrong order – but it doesn't seem to matter. After five or six drinks, who cares? The beginning has been forgotten anyway.

At first, Ramón speaks slowly and carefully, so I understand most of what he says, but later, as his chatter becomes more animated and the quick-fire mixture of languages gets more jumbled, my head starts to spin. The confusion is probably my fault for, when he breaks off from talking and looks enquiringly at my reflection in the mirror, I find it simpler to nod back at him every time. This affirmative silent response to his question sometimes brings a puzzled expression to his face, followed by a shrug of the shoulders. It soon becomes clear that the barber's unlimited knowledge of the football game encompasses not only names of players in Spanish teams but also those in the English league. His critical analysis of matches, with suggestions of what should have taken place on the field, constantly interrupts his snipping. Suddenly he breaks off from what he is doing and illustrates his ideas by making energetic dribbling movements with his feet or heading-the-ball demonstrations with his head. I find it difficult to follow much of what he says but, not being much of a football enthusiast, I wouldn't have known the difference had he spoken in straightforward English.

I soon come to realise that Ramón's theatrical antics are performed for his audience's benefit as much as mine. Although I try hard to make sense of the football players' names, his strong Andalusian accent makes the task nigh impossible. He makes a sliding, passing movement of his foot on the tiled floor.

"¡Boy Moray! ¡Muy bueno!"

He then breaks off from giving me a haircut, and with his scissors held aloft, clicking away above his head, proceeds to weave his way down the room, finishing off by giving a mighty kick in the air.

"¡Gol!"

The others seated around the room join in enthusiastically.

"¡Gol!"

I smile, again nod my head and poke both my thumbs out from under the drapes. Boy Moray, I learn later, turns out to be Bobby Moore.

Occasionally, one of the others butts in on Ramón's football discourse to offer a suggestion, or perhaps even a contradiction, of his own. When this happens, the expression on the hairdresser's face changes. A deep, serious-looking frown appears on his brow and, abruptly, the light-hearted banter stops. He puts down his implements in a very deliberate manner, walks over to whoever has dared interrupt him and starts a heated argument that can last five or ten minutes, with all the others noisily joining in. Sometimes, a haircut can take all morning.

I soon find another reason why the barber's shop is so popular. No matter how lowly or scruffy a person may be, Ramón treats each of his clients with the same respect. One snip of his magic scissors transforms his chrome and leather chair into a throne and those seated therein are accorded equal royal status. When they open their mouth to say something, Ramón holds up his hand to silence all others in the salon. They must shut up and listen to what his charge has to say. While being lathered, shaved, scented and dusted, his customer's opinions, comments and points of view go unchallenged. His boasts, no matter how far-fetched, are applauded and every joke, funny or not, is laughed at. Ramón makes sure of all this: he rules the roost.

At the same time, it soon becomes increasingly clear that the assembly in the room is not there merely to pass the time of day. In *Gatherings from Spain,* Richard Ford reckons that *'the house of the barber has, since the days of Solomon and Horace, been the mart of news and gossip. It is a club of the lower order'.* This appears to be the case in Ramón's salon. His premises serve as a sort of centre where members of a clique chew over everything under the sun. Every man in La Herradura comes for a haircut or shave at some time or another and, once installed in the leather chair, with only his head showing above the drape, he undergoes subtle, but close interrogation. The assembled crowd gives the man a veritable third degree. All confidences are wheedled out of him. The only taboo subject appears to be politics. The words 'Franco', 'fascist' or 'communist' are never mentioned.

For a brief period, towards the end of 1967, my presence in the barber's shop leads to another subject being raised. What do I think about

'Hibraltar'?

This famous landmark, Gibraltar, once thought to be one of the legendary Pillars of Hercules, had been lost in battle to the English during the War of the Spanish Succession as long ago as 1704. Reports in Spanish newspapers have recently stirred things up by accusing the British of hanging on to the Rock when, according to their investigative journalism, it should be handed back to its rightful owner: Spain. Franco's government, while encouraging such propaganda, has to tread carefully. It does not want to scare the much-needed tourists into cancelling their holidays or stop them buying property on the nearby Costas, but still quietly argues that the British are definitely at fault by twice violating the 1713 Treaty of Utrecht. Firstly, by using the established demilitarised zone between the Rock and the mainland as an airfield, and secondly, although it was agreed that neither Jews nor Muslims would be allowed to take up residence in Gibraltar, people of both religions are now living and working there.

At one stage in 1967, the situation does become quite serious. In some of the larger cities, anti-British riots break out, with consulates being attacked and official vehicles pelted with stones. Spanish irritation at the state of affairs is not lessened when a referendum shows that, of the 12,672 citizens living in Gibraltar, 12,138 vote to stay British.

(A similar situation has just occurred at the time of writing. When, in October 2002, British and Spanish governments discussed the possibility of joint sovereignty over Gibraltar, a survey showed that 99% of Gibraltarians preferred to remain British.)

Ramón brings the matter to my attention on a subsequent visit to his shop when, speaking as though I personally have stolen Gibraltar from him the day before, he pleads, pretending to be angry,

"Roy, *por favor*, give me back Hibraltar!"

I reply, generously,

"It's all yours, Ramón. You can take it back whenever you please as long as you promise not to throw stones at my car."

Although I can understand much more of what the hairdresser says by the time of my second haircut, I cannot always catch the asides made by others in the room. Their mutterings do not escape the hairdresser's ears, though, and if he overhears something he does not think proper he turns on the speaker and lets fly with a tirade of rude-sounding words. While in his shop I have placed myself under his protection. He, and he alone, has the right to make personal remarks.

1967 drifts into 1968. My second Spanish Christmas comes and goes and, although I receive an invitation, I turn down an offer to join the Almuñécar crowd at Antonio's place for the festivities this year, preferring to stay at my house in La Herradura.

Winter temperatures on the Costa del Sol suit me perfectly. It reminds me of a line from a song: '*I'm goin' where the weather suits my clothes*'. The daylight hours are still sunny and warm enough for me to wear shorts, 'T' shirt and sandals but, once the sun has gone down, it gets just chilly enough to warrant lighting a fire. The first time I put match to paper in my untested fireplace I stand back in trepidation, holding my breath, for I know from experience that some fires draw well and others don't. No matter how much trouble a builder may take with a chimney, calculating the wind angle and so on, it still seems to be some mysterious, unknown quantity that decides a hearth's success or failure. In the past, in the belief that it might produce a favourable outcome, a priest was sometimes called upon to offer up a prayer. Luckily, my fireplace provides a good blaze from the start without benefit of clergy, smoke going up the chimney rather than billowing back into the room. Many an evening is spent at my house in San Nicolás, sitting in the warm, comfortable glow of a blazing fire, playing my guitar to the crackle of firewood. Crackles do not come so easy though, for fuel is hard to come by. Initially I guessed that, as all the hills in the immediate vicinity are covered with olive or almond trees, it would be a simple matter to just wander about and collect a few dead branches. Not so. No residual timber is to be found, and I soon find out why.

This part of the country is not short of olives, to be sure, for 80% of Spain's total harvest comes from Andalusia. Of the 800 million olive trees in the world, Spain accounts for 250 million. Harvesting takes place in the autumn, when teams of men, women and children, known as *cuadrillos*, roam the fields, beating trees with long sticks, knocking the ripe fruit into a net, or canvas sheet, spread out on the ground underneath. The gathered crop ends up being either crushed to make olive oil, or eaten. With all this tree-bashing taking place, quite a few branches and twigs fall to the ground but, as the dry, hard wood burns well, the bashers themselves bundle it all up and take it away to fuel their *parrillas*.

Fortunately, I find another way to acquire fire material. Bouts of windy weather result in all manner of driftwood being cast ashore: bits of palm trees, perhaps blown across from Africa; broken sections from rotting boats, gradually falling apart; or occasionally whole lengths of building timber, probably washed overboard from some passing cargo ship. Whatever it may be, as long as it looks as though it might burn, I chuck it into the back of my pick-up, take it home and lay it out on the terrace. In the hot sunshine, it soon dries. I have to search early in the day, though, for there are plenty of others living in the area who also scavenge for firewood.

The black Labrador dog, Tel, loves to accompany me on these scrounging expeditions. I only have to give a low whistle as I pass Casa Pedro for him to come bounding out, barking like mad. He proves a wonderful companion and does his best to help me collect odds and ends as we make our way along the shore. If he spots a piece of flotsam being tossed about in the crashing surf, he waits his chance, then darts into the sea and drags it out. The clever dog has the intelligence to wait until exactly the right moment before attempting this retrieval. I watch anxiously, though. He has to be careful. I know that if he doesn't time things to perfection, he could end up being pulled into the breakers by the strong outgoing current.

Heavy weather is not restricted to winter months. Strong winds can arise at any time of the year and very quickly bring about huge rollers. When this happens, it's best to stay out of the sea. Some holidaymakers, seeing local children diving under the curling surf and coming up unscathed the other side, think it looks a piece of cake and attempt the same themselves. The lucky ones escape with a few bruises. Others, not so lucky, get no second chance. Swept up by a giant wave and smashed back onto the hard, pebbly beach, they end up as an addition to the number of recorded deaths each year from foolhardy people trying this sort of thing. On one occasion, uniformed officers from the *Guardia Civil* barracks traipsed up and down the beach asking sunbathers if they could identify a corpse, dressed only in swimming trunks, found at the water's edge the previous evening. They carried with them the gruesome photo of a man's bashed-in head. The authorities eventually found the body to be that of a young holidaymaker who had come from Almuñécar to La Herradura on a day's excursion.

While on these early morning fuel-hunting expeditions, I meet up with quite a few other windswept characters patrolling the water's edge for the same purpose. After a heavy downpour, the same crowd can be found where the Río Seco joins the beach for, at this junction, a raging torrent of water pours down from the hills carrying with it all manner of combustible material – sometimes whole trees. My trusty pick-up proves invaluable for the collection of such and, as many of the others have no means of transportation, I find myself running a sort of delivery service. The help I give doesn't go unappreciated. Rewards include invitations to stay for a meal, a drink or two in the Salón later or – well, let me put it this way – a single lady, recently moved into a house at San Nicolás, shows her gratitude by finding another way to keep us both warm on cold evenings.

As more of us living round La Herradura become better

acquainted, and with fuel so hard to come by, some decide it makes more sense for the person lighting a fire to invite others to share its heat. Instead of 'bring a bottle' affairs, these gatherings develop into 'bring a log or two' parties. If timber stocks become really low and there doesn't seem much likelihood of a storm or a cloudburst in the offing, a trip up the Granada road to the more forested area beyond Otívar solves the problem. There, we cram as much as we can into our vehicles and share out the spoils on our return to La Herradura.

One enterprising local man sets up a profitable enterprise. As the property business expands, he strikes a deal with builders to remove all the unwanted trees on the land to be developed. Once cut down, he saws up the trunks and branches into logs and sells them by the mule-load. He finds plenty of customers. Most of my friends stick to the old way of collecting firewood, though. We think that getting hold of fuel this way is cheating. Besides, apart from being expensive, buying lacks the romance of beachcombing and doesn't provide an opportunity to strike up relationships.

It's sad to see these age-old trees gradually disappear from the landscape. Originally brought to Spain by the Phoenicians, their descendants have been growing where they stand (or have been standing) for up to 600 years, serving mankind by bearing fruit century after century.

Apart from the lady who occasionally needs warming up, I have few chances to make contact with the opposite sex. Non-Spanish women are in short supply and locals, as I have already pointed out, are no-go areas. The influx of draft-dodgers doesn't help matters. Their presence puts the foreign man/woman ratio at about ten to one and young women living in the area can pick and choose.

It comes as a pleasant surprise, then, when I receive news that an Australian girlfriend of mine will be flying into Gibraltar airport at 4 a.m. on 3 March 1968. The information reaches me just in time. The postmark on the envelope shows the letter to have been posted two months earlier, but it is handed to me in

El Salón on 2 March. It's been in the back pocket of a Spanish builder's trousers for the previous week. Paco, the local postman, not wishing to make the tiresome journey up the steep hill to San Nicolás himself, asked the young bricklayer, who works on the estate, if he would slip the letter under my door. Until he sees me in the bar that evening, the man has forgotten all about it.

By setting off at once, putting my foot down and taking chances on some of the bends in the road, I manage to arrive at the airport just in time to meet the flight. After waiting in vain for my friend to appear through the arrival gate, I walk in through the exit door to find out why she has not come out with the other passengers. In the customs hall I find Patricia standing with three grey-uniformed men. Their attention appears to be divided between her and the contents of a large suitcase. As soon as she sees me, the girl rushes over, throws her arms around my neck, and gives me a long, smacking kiss on the lips. It takes a few moments to recover my breath.

"What's the problem? What are you trying to smuggle in?"

She waves her hand towards the officials.

"I'm trying to explain to these men, but they don't seem to understand anything I say. Oh, you see what you can do, darling."

We go across to where her case lies open. To my amazement, it's packed tight with tins of baked beans! I turn to Pat.

"What on earth – ?"

"Well, darling, you did say that you couldn't get hold of any baked beans here in Spain so I thought I'd surprise you."

The customs men take some convincing. They send to the restaurant for a can-opener and, once the container is unsealed, poke around its contents. Still not satisfied, one of the men pulls off a white glove, scoops out a bean, gingerly tests it with the tip of his tongue and pulls a wry face. The other two look on with concern. The taster pulls a face.

"*Cazuela.*"

Cold baked beans have never been a favourite of mine, either.

Only when I hand them a gift of one tin apiece do the custom officials wave us on our way.

I learn that the kind, thoughtful girl has flown from Australia to London, carting the heavy suitcase of baked beans firstly to

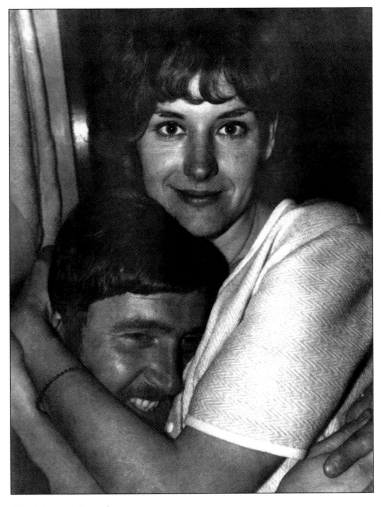

Patricia and I

a hotel in Earls Court and then back again to Heathrow Airport before continuing to Málaga. She tells me later that the excess weight charge she has been made to pay each time she checked in her luggage amounts to nearly one hundred dollars.

On the drive back to La Herradura I ask why on earth she has flown to Gibraltar, pointing out that Málaga airport would have been a lot nearer to where I live.

"Oh, no! You're wrong, I think, Roy. I looked on the map before I left Australia. Gibraltar is only that far from where you live."

Her thumb and forefinger are held about an inch apart. Of course, she had referred to a world atlas.

I had met Pat while ashore in Sydney from the merchant vessel *S.S. Cannanore*, one of the Pan and Orient fleet. Unloading our cargo of car parts and dogs (yes, prize-winners from Cruft's show) meant spending a few days in dock so, one evening, a few shipmates and I took the opportunity to check out the town's delights. Nights ashore, whatever the port, followed a routine. After knocking back a few beers at the nearest drinking establishment, we would call for a taxi and ask the driver to transport us to a house of ill repute. However, on the wall of this particular pub on this particular night, I noticed a sign announcing that a folksong club would be meeting that very evening in the lounge upstairs. Just the job, I thought to myself. Maybe my prowess as a folk singer will sweep some young lady off her feet and lead to a drink or two back in my cabin. With this in mind, I decided to forego the brothel and stay a while. From past experience, folksy types have proved to be pretty liberal when it comes to sexual matters and, anyway, if nothing came of it, I could always join my friends later.

The crowded room above held an assortment of bearded men and baggy-sweatered, bra-less girls, all looking very much like those who frequented folk clubs back in England. While doing my bit with a borrowed guitar on stage, I became aware of a blonde, curly-haired girl staring up at me. Some singers find it difficult to know where to look when facing an audience but, for me that night, this proved no problem. My eyes were held by hers and I sang my songs for her alone. I suppose you might call it 'mutual attraction' at first sight. Later, as we sat together, I found that just touching her hand across the table sent an electric shock up my arm. No lightweight, her breasts were doing their utmost to burst out from her blouse and, when she turned round, I almost choked at the sight of her rounded buttocks stretching her tight trousers. Disappointingly, she turned down my invitation to come back on board for a night-cap, but suggested instead that we meet up the next evening when she would take me home and introduce me to her family. As we were only in port for a couple of days, and meeting parents of young ladies had not been part of my planned schedule, I would normally have made some excuse, but Pat's charms so excited me that I decided to go along with the idea.

All went surprisingly well. Her father, a big, bluff Irishman – a mariner himself in his younger days – liked me from the start. Almost as soon as I arrived, he led me outside to a paved court-yard at the back of the house where we sat swapping 'life on the ocean wave' tales while knocking back 'tubes' of beer and brushing flies away. Her mother took more cajoling. She knew all about sailors: after all, she'd married one. Out of the corner of my eye, I saw her giving me sideways glances as she stood in the kitchen chatting with Pat. Eventually, though, finding it impossible to resist my charisma any longer, she loosened up enough to invite me to stay for dinner. The rest of the family, four boys and two other girls, did not seem to care one way or the other about their 'Pommy' guest. During the meal, Pat told me that she had plans to visit Europe in the near future. Her mother looked concerned.

"I'm sure Roy here will look after you when you get there."

At this, the good lady's husband glanced across the table at me, raised his eyebrows, gave a loud, throat-clearing cough and remained silent.

With Pat's belongings, including the well-travelled suitcase of baked beans, stowed in the back of the pick-up, we return to La

Herradura. I feel pretty tired from a combination of lack of sleep and the long drive – but not too tired. We spend the remainder of the night and all next day in bed, making up for lost time.

The plump Australian beauty lives up to her earlier promise. Although inexperienced in matters of sex, she is a keen student and insists on being taught a new lesson at every opportunity. Her shrieks and groans, wafting out of the open bedroom French windows, give rise to whistles from builders working on the house next door and a bountiful supply of winks and nods when next our paths cross. For a while, our diet seems to consist of nothing that doesn't include baked beans. On toast, with scrambled egg, with *chorizo*, with all three, and so on. The beans also go well with a typical breakfast eaten in Andalusia, made up of toast sprinkled with olive oil, garlic and tomato. Even flying insects give the house a wide berth.

Patricia lives with me at San Nicolás for the next three months. From the start, she falls in love with everything this part of Spain has to offer. The weather, the people, the slow, easy pace of life: all suit her down to the ground. Her open, unpretentious, straightforward manner, along with a willingness to 'muck in', makes her everybody's sweetheart. Unlike some of the fussier ladies, she's not at all bothered by things like dirty hands, unmanicured fingernails or messed-up hair. Scrambling up dusty tracks in the hills behind the village, baiting hooks with sardines, gutting and scaling fish – she loves it all. At the same time, Pat keeps everything at home spotlessly clean, prepares tasty meals and improves the house décor by laying a brightly-coloured Moroccan rug in the living room and another in the bedroom. To complete the happy family scene, while I play the guitar and sing songs of an evening, the industrious girl sews away, making cushions to fit atop the hard stone seats on the terrace, Casa Pedro style.

One day, Patricia lets it be known that she very much wants to look around the old part of La Herradura. Sea and sunny weather are nothing new, but the little cluster of white houses that makes up the village, or any reference to the past, fascinates her. As we make our way up the cobbled steps, remembering my previous visit, I alert her to the sort of reception she must expect.

"You mustn't think them rude. It's just that they're not used to strangers."

But, lo and behold! As we make our way along the narrow passages, Patricia's reception turns out to be completely different from mine. The sight of her brings smiles from the villagers instead of scowls, and caged birds seem to chirp even more merrily. Dogs wag their tails and cats, I notice, that previously scurried away at my approach, stay to rub themselves against her legs. I can't make it out: what has she got that I haven't? Perhaps women don't have 'evil eyes'. After a while, even my four-legged pal Tel jilts me in her favour. On our fuel-hunting trips along the beach, he drops his scavenged bits and pieces at her feet instead of mine.

Speaking no word of Spanish doesn't prevent Pat from bonding with these village folk. One morning, bright and early, she sets off down the hill to buy bread for breakfast. An hour later, hungrier and angrier, I decide to go and look for her. What could have kept her? After hunting high and low, I eventually find my girlfriend sitting in somebody's doorway, bouncing a fat baby on her knee. She looks perfectly at home amid the cluster of chinwagging, laughing, local women who stand about communicating as best they can. Oohs, aahs and other such baby sounds are the same in any language, I suppose. Before long, her growing popularity opens many doors – literally. Welcomed into the homes of many of these friendly ladies, she learns how to cook a range of Spanish dishes, including my favourite, a thick juicy *tortilla de patatas*.

Before long, Patricia melts hearts in Almuñécar as well, especially that of John the Plumber. He can't stop talking about her.

"Mun, you've got a bloody good woman there, mun. What a peach! What a refreshing change from all these bloody skinny hippies, mun. No wonder we haven't seen much of you for a while. Maybe it's time you settled down, mun. She looks the settling down type to me."

Therein may lie the problem. Pat is indeed the 'settling down type'. Her hankering to have a baby of her own leads to our final bust-up. Late one evening, while in a particularly broody mood, she starts, once again, to describe some boring bonny baby she has come across that day. I've heard it all before.

"Look, Pat, don't keep on about bloody babies! I'm not interested."

Another thought has crossed my mind lately.

"And I warn you – don't expect to trap me by getting yourself in the family way. There won't be any 'honourable thing' coming from my direction, you know. And don't forget, it's impossible to get rid of it out here. Abortions are illegal."

The poor girl looks shocked. Her eyes brim with tears. "Get rid of it?"

I realise I've gone too far and do my best to comfort her but, like Anthea, as soon as I place my arm around her shoulders, she lowers her head onto my chest and bursts out crying. Between sobs, with an emphasis on the 'myself', she queries, "If I get myself in the family way? How can I manage that?"

She's right, of course. "Well, you know what I mean."

We do our best to forget the episode but things are never quite the same again. I drive her to Málaga airport on a particularly hot day in the summer of 1968. We've managed to get hold of a return ticket from the man in Nerja. From London she will either fly directly to Australia or perhaps travel a little more in Europe. As we embrace for the last time, I whisper in her ear, "Look after yourself, Pat. Thanks for everything – especially the beans."

Her pretty face, wet with tears, puts on a forced smile.

"My luggage is a lot lighter than when I arrived – but not my heart."

As she walks through the departure gate, she turns to me for the last time and calls out, "Look after Tel."

11

1968

In which Sven's Bar, after battles with officialdom,
eventually takes off – metaphorically, while The Flipper
Bar simply takes off – literally.

At first, the house feels very empty. I think the dog misses Pat
more than I. He scratches at the front door and, once let in,
races round all the rooms searching for his friend. When he
realises she's nowhere to be found, he comes back to where I'm
sitting, flops down on the Moroccan rug and, with his handsome black head resting on his paws, stares up at me with big,
sad, brown eyes. I get the impression that he somehow holds
me responsible for her absence. Perhaps he's right. In an effort
to comfort him, I fondle his silky ears.

"I know, I know. She's gone, old fellah."

Then, to cheer him up a little, I might add, "Never mind. Let's
go down and see Sven."

A few changes have taken place during the three-month period Pat has been staying with me. As well as one or two newcomers setting up home in San Nicolás and several Americans
renting rooms at the hostals, a Swede named Sven has arrived
in La Herradura to build himself a bar on the beach.

Driving along the seafront road one morning, in Spring 1968,
I come upon a very muscular man, dressed only in swimming
trunks, wrestling with a long, thick, wooden pole. His objective
appears to be to plant one end of it into a hole, dug in the shingle. Wobbling unsteadily this way and that, he reminds me of a
competitor at the Highland Games about to toss a caber. Being

quite short in stature and struggling to keep his balance, he clearly has problems so, without further ado, I park, jump out from the pick-up and go across to lend a hand. My height helps and, with two of us on the job, we soon have that post, and then three others, planted in an upright position to make four corners of a square. Once we've finished, I step back, out of breath.

"What's all this about?"

Hands on hips, also breathing deeply, he answers with just a trace of an accent, pronouncing his words in a slightly singsong fashion.

"Thank you for your help, my friend. I am building a *chambao*, you see."

I know this to be a type of beach bar. At the time, the only place of its kind stands a few hundred yards away, in the direction of Punta de la Mona. Its owner, Joaquín (the good swimmer with the net), has been doing quite good business, especially at week-ends and during the summer months.

"Don't you need some sort of permission to do that sort of thing?"

The short man shrugs.

"I don't know. I shall find out, no doubt. John-John there thinks there will be no problem."

John-John? I look about and suddenly become aware of a tall, thin, rather effete-looking character lounging back on a thick pile of sugar-cane leaves, calmly smoking a cigarette. He must have been watching our exertions all the time. When he sees he's been spotted, he gets to his feet, and comes towards me, holding out a limp hand. His voice sounds a bit like one of the RAF pilot types left over from the last war.

"Well done, old chap. Sorry I couldn't help out. Bad back and all that, y'know."

The lah-di-dah accent and world-weary, nose-in the-air manner brings back dreaded memories. I do not answer. Perhaps something in my stiffening of stance or narrowing of eyes induces John-John to think again. He drops his hand to his side and looks away. The other man, seeing something is not quite right, steps in.

"Thirsty work! We go for a drink, yes?"

The three of us make our way to the nearby La Caleta bar where, once seated with beers on the table, Sven introduces himself. Swedish, born in Russia, former sailor, horse-rider, speedboat racer, professional skier (both on snow and water), and lots more. From the sound of it, he has not only done just about everything under the sun, but has been world champion at whatever it is as well. Strangely enough, from the way he speaks, he does not appear to be boasting, merely stating facts. His assured manner and compact, tough-looking physique, gives credence to all he says. Sven goes on to say that he and his companion have together decided to try to set up a beach-bar business here in La Herradura. Apparently, they tried the same thing in Torremolinos but, with tough competition from older established *chambaos*, their enterprise did not prove too successful. I learn later that they had, in fact, been run out of town.

Here, however, with a growing number of foreign visitors and only Joaquín as a rival, Sven feels confident of doing well. He has learned what customers want and intends giving, or, at least, selling, it to them. All the while Sven gives me the low-down on this virgin village's tremendous potential, his partner John-John sits silently chain-smoking cigarettes. His arrogant, slightly sneering expression puts me in mind of someone who has chanced upon a nasty smell. I do not like the look of this man at all.

Pat and I help build the beach bar. Firstly, angled cross-beams are fixed to the uppermost part of the posts, forming a framework for the roof, and atop this, bamboo and sugar cane stems, complete with leaves, are laid and tied securely with wire. Hey presto! – a *chambao*. With Sven's know-how, we have the rustic-looking structure finished in a couple of days – along with self-made sturdy tables and chairs. Next, from the municipal rubbish dump in Almuñécar, we manage to get hold of a large, dented, red and white Coca-Cola container, which we bring back to La Herradura in the back of my pick-up. Once the metal box is filled with broken-up pieces of ice, bottles of beer and soft drinks, Sven's *chambao* manages to open for business just in time for Easter.

At first, all goes well. With plenty of *granadinos* down for *Semana Santa* and the foreign contingent giving support, the beach bar bustles with activity. Even after the busy holiday period, enough *clientèle* from both Almuñécar and La Herradura make it worthwhile for the bar to stay open. The fine, warm months of May and June coax the growing number of residents and American draft-dodgers to spend more time on the beach and, consequently, many stop off at Sven's Bar for a drink. Initially, the *chambao* has to make do with candles and oil lamps to provide lighting in the evenings but, as the money rolls in, Sven pays to have electricity, and then water, connected.

Somehow or other, he manages to get hold of the latest pop music LPs, including those of the Beatles and Rolling Stones. I remember sitting with my arm around Pat, listening to *Sergeant Pepper's Lonely Hearts Club Band* for the first time in Sven's beach bar. Armed with this sort of music, he can do no wrong. The bar really starts to buzz. Scott McKenzie's *San Francisco* proves a great favourite with the young Americans, as do the anti-war songs of Bob Dylan, Joan Baez, Pete Seeger and Julie Felix. Spanish customers are not neglected. To keep them happy, he plays something called '*La, La, La*', sung by a man called Massiel. This lively, popular piece wins the Eurovision Song Contest for Spain that year. Sometimes I take my guitar down to the beach and let loose with *Blowing in the Wind, Don't Think Twice* or *Where Have All the Flowers Gone?*

As with La Ventura in Almuñécar, drinks in Sven's Bar cost at least twice that of Spanish bars, but this does not seem to affect its popularity. In fact, even some of the local lads, wishing to appear 'with it' by mixing with the foreign 'in' crowd, seem happy enough to pay the high prices. On the face of it, the *chambao* goes great guns. A toilet and kitchen are installed, meals start to be served and the Coca-Cola box is replaced by a proper fridge. But, alas! Things are not to last. Dark clouds are gathering. Sven's Bar's celebrity does not meet with everybody's approval. Perhaps jealous of his neighbour's prosperity, the proprietor of the other beach bar, Joaquín, could well be the one to have started the ball rolling.

The day of reckoning arrives when two official-looking men turn up and ask to inspect Sven's 'papers'. He produces his passport, driving licence and insurance certificate. These are not enough. It is 'permissions' they want. Although I feel he must have learned something from his previous experience in Torremelinos, Sven plays the innocent by asking what they mean by 'permissions'. He is told that, before he can continue with his business, he must have:

a work permit;

permission to rent space on the beach;

permission to erect a *chambao*, cut sugar cane, sell alcohol and employ staff.

As well as all this, he needs a statement from the Swedish Consulate declaring that he has no criminal record back in his own country. What is more, add the unsmiling, serious bureaucrats, if he does not obtain these documents forthwith, his bar will be closed down and he will receive a heavy fine. Sven does his best to comply with the order and spends many a long day journeying backwards and forwards to Granada. Eventually, when has what he believes are enough regulatory papers, he tries again with his beach bar, but it is not that easy. Time and time again fault is found with some paperwork or other and each time Sven is threatened with closure and fines. But he will not give in, maintaining that he will, in the end, "beat the buggers at their own game."

Remembering how things were with regards to my fishing permit fiasco and knowing how difficult it is to do things officially, I admire his tenacity. While Franco rules the roost, all ministerial decisions pass through central offices in Madrid and permissions for this, that or the other, in the form of sheaves of paper covered in stamps and signatures, are required for just about anything and everything. Theoretically, it is even necessary to obtain official sanction to wallpaper a room! All this bureaucracy keeps teams of office workers very busy, giving employment to one in four of the working population and accounting for 40% of the national income. By the mid-'60s, nothing much seems to have changed. I'll give you an example.

An elderly gentleman, living at San Antonio, wants to lay a small area of pebble mosaic in between some of the square tiles in his garden patio. He drives to the beach (which is covered with two kilometres of pebbles), fills two buckets with painstakingly collected, oval-shaped, black and white stones and returns home to bang them into the earth to form a star pattern. Finding he needs a few more to complete the job, he makes his way once again to the beach. The Guardia Civil are watching and waiting. They wait until he has gathered the quantity he needs, then intercept him on his way back to his car. Does he have proper authorisation to remove pebbles, they ask? He admits that he does not. In that case, he is told, not only must he tip out the ones in his container, he must return home, dig up those he has laid and put them back where he found them. Then, if he wants, he can apply to Madrid for official sanction to remove pebbles from the beach. They will graciously let him off a fine – this time.

Foreigners soon learn, sometimes the hard way, of the regulatory paperwork neccessary to live and work in Spain. I have already heard horror stories from people who have tried to go about things legitimately. One case involves a man who wants to make and sell little pieces of jewellery. On being told that he needs special authorisation to practise this line of work, he makes his way to Granada and, after being sent here, there and everywhere, finds the building which issues the correct application form. Having written down his passport number, age, height, colour of hair and eyes, distinguishing marks (such as scars), religion, next of kin, marital status, number of children and mother's maiden name, he takes the completed paper to another address. There, he must show his birth certificate, marriage certificate (if any), divorce papers (if any), driving licence (if any), bank reference, a letter from a doctor giving him a clean bill of health and, finally, as with Sven, provide proof that

Guardia Civil

he has no criminal convictions. After a struggle, which entails further lengthy bouts of waiting in queues, he gets hold of all these items, even though the last requires the services of an expensive *abogado* (lawyer). At long last then, his completed dossier is sent to Madrid. After waiting six months for a reply and running short of funds, he takes a chance by surreptitiously continuing with his jewellery business. However, the chance does not pay off. By applying officially, he has made himself a marked man. When I next see him, at the bus stop in Almuñécar, he tells me that he has been forced to sell his tools and equipment to pay a heavy fine and leave enough money for an air ticket. The police have given him seven days to leave the country.

I fear the same sort of thing may happen to Sven, for his bulldog manner and reluctance to toe the line has upset the wrong people. One evening, as I sit with him and one or two friends in the *chambao*, drinking and playing my guitar, a dark green Land Rover pulls to a halt on the nearby beach road and out step two officers of the Guardia Civil.

Instead of coming across to us, they stay where they are and shout, "Sven, come here a moment."

The Swede looks in their direction, spits on the ground and, taking his time, saunters over to where they are standing. It is impossible for me to make out the heated exchange of words but, a few moments later, I hear Sven's voice.

"Roy! What time do you make it?"

I look at my wristwatch.

"One-thirty."

A few moments later, Sven returns carrying a sheet of typed paper.

"Bastards!"

He sounds angry.

"What's the matter, Sven?"

"Oh, the bastards fined me for staying open too late."

"How long can you stay open, then?"

"Till two in the morning."

"But, Sven, I told you the time, it was –"

"Yes, yes, Roy. The time is one-thirty. You know that and I know that, but the guys in the shiny hats over there say it's five minutes past two, and so have fined me."

"They can't do that! You've got witnesses!"

Sven sighs. He sounds resigned.

"The bastards can do whatever they like."

A few days later, I tell John the Plumber what happened that evening. He doesn't seem at all surprised by the news.

"Sven's right, mun. You can complain as much as you like, but if you fall foul of the 'big boys' you might as well call it a day, pack your bags and head for the sunset. The *Guardia* have absolute power, and I mean absolute. What they say, goes. It looks to me as though the little Swede's done something to upset someone in the know or messed with a person with the right connections."

He sits without speaking for a moment, looking thoughtful.

"Look at it this way, Roy mun. The people in your little village don't have a lot going for them, do they? Fishing's finished. Fishermen might still be able to flog a few fish from their stalls in the mornings but their main customers, the restaurants, now buy the frozen stuff delivered from the big fish market in Motril. A few of those with land to sell are doing all right and some of the smarter, better-educated ones, like Antonio and Juan, are cashing in on the building boom, but most of the locals – apart from a few tradesmen – don't see much of this new money sloshing about. Many of them feel they've already been conned out of their inheritance by land developers who have got them to sign on the dotted line. Remember the lines from the old folk-song *Jesse James* – the ones that go,

'If they don't rob you with a shotgun,
It's with a fountain pen.'

Well, that's the way of it in this part of the world. Families down here, especially those in catering, have to make hay while the sun shines and grab as many handfuls of cash as they can while the holidaymakers are about. A lot of them still remember the hard times experienced during and after the Civil War. Now the so-called 'hunger years' are over, they don't want some foreigner cutting in on the act and creaming off what they think rightly belongs to them. They've seen it happen farther along the coast. There, it's the Germans, French and English that are opening all the smart discos, restaurants and hotels. And once they've made their dosh, it's not spent locally, is it, mun? No, it's salted away in some Swiss bank account. I know it's supposed to be difficult for these guys to get hold of work permits and all that. The law states that a foreigner will not be permitted to work at something that a Spanish person can do, but you know and I know how a few backhanders can soon sort that out. We've seen plenty of examples. If you've got enough money to pay for a good *gestor,* the man will get you all the permissions you need from the *Delegación Provincial del Trabajo.* I could have told Sven that, but you know what a stubborn know-all he is. Advice falls on deaf ears. No, mun, I can understand the locals wanting to get their hands on any money being spread about. The little Swede's doing good business. He's got the right idea with his music and all, and there's no denying he works bloody hard – but his prosperity can lead to his downfall. The locals get jealous. It may well be that the guy in the next bar along the beach to him – Joaquín, isn't it? – has brothers in the *Ayuntamiento* (Town Hall) in Almuñécar or maybe a cousin up in Granada or perhaps some relative in the police. If that's the case and old Joaquín gives the word, they'll do their damnedest to get rid of any competition for him. Blood's thicker than water in these parts. If the right people have a down on him, our Sven doesn't stand a dog's chance. No matter how many permits he gets hold of. You mark my words, mun."

I mark John's words, but wonder how it is, then, that he himself has managed to escape the notice of the authorities. After all, he has been living and working in Spain for the last ten years. I ask him to explain.

"I probably haven't escaped their notice. The government guys know what I'm doing, all right, you can be sure of that. It's like this, Roy, mun. Firstly, I don't make the mistake of trying to compete with Spanish plumbers. I only work for foreigners – the ones that prefer to give a job to someone who can speak their language. The locals are aware of this and don't bother me – so far, at any rate. Secondly, mun, I keep a low profile. Although it's true I've been around for quite a while, I've never filled out any of those silly forms you're supposed to fill out – you know what I mean. Once you start with those, they've got you on their register and will keep tabs on you."

I know exactly what he means. The law stipulates that, if a person remains 90 days without leaving Spanish territory, he or she must apply for something known as *permiso de permanencia*. The Guardia Civil barracks deals with these matters in La Herradura and the Town Hall does likewise in Almuñécar. Once this permission has been granted, it lasts a further 90 days and then the whole business has to be repeated. After that, a petition has to be made for an *autorización de residencia* or residence card and, to get hold of this, the requisite forms have to be accompanied by a small fee, a certificate issued by the consulate and three head-and-shoulder photographs. The validity of the card lasts two years, after which a fresh round of form-filling has to take place. Once the first step has been taken, the whole process must be followed through.

The requisite paperwork for someone living in Spain on a semi-permanent basis is nothing compared to the permits and licences needed for anyone wanting to work. I have already seen the problems experienced by Sven and the Almuñécar jeweller. John tells me that for him to plumb legitimately, he would have to apply for a work permit to the offices of the *Delegación Provincial del Trabajo* in the capital of each of the provinces where he wants to work – in his case, Granada and Málaga. I realise what a headache that might be and can well understand his desire to keep a low profile and do nothing. John is not alone in keeping his head down. Plenty of others are surreptitiously trying to earn a few pesetas. Their number also includes many Americans.

Although, by 1970, the number of military personnel in Vietnam has been reduced to 335,000, the fear of the war spreading to Cambodia continues to drive young men of draft age out of the USA and across the Atlantic to this part of the world.

In and around Almuñécar, La Herradura and Nerja, dozens of these young people are busy, toiling away at what they call 'crafting'. Sheets of hide, along with hole-punchers, staplers, needles, strong thread and a variety of leatherworker's tools are purchased in Granada and brought back to the coast where they are used to make everything imaginable. Sandals, bags, wallets, purses, belts, containers for cigarette packets or cigarette lighters, pouches for marijuana, all are 'crafted' and offered for sale to holidaymakers in the summer. Some of the more talented do well but, partly because of competition from Moroccan touts offering much the same wares more cheaply, the majority make no profit at all. It does not really matter. To justify their labour, they buy and sell amongst themselves.

Not all work with leather. One young New Zealand girl (who turns up in La Herradura with a young baby under her arm) earns her keep by making drinking glasses. She fills a bottle up to the required level with old car-engine oil, then plunges a very hot piece of metal inside. Crack! The heated liquid fractures the glass in a neat line. After smoothing the rim of the glass with wire wool and sand she sells the end result to bars or private customers. Their distinctive original design makes the containers very trendy and the industrious girl is kept busy. Coca-Cola bottle glasses have pimpled sides, while others, square in shape, are made from whisky bottles. I have some myself.

As well as leatherworkers and bottle-crackers, there are those in the vicinity that turn their hand to painting or sculpting. Once again, aptitude soon sorts out the people that make any worthwhile financial gain, but there are opportunities in this field. Owing to the number of new houses being built, each with large expanses of white wall needing decoration, good canvases sell well, particularly if painted in bright colours. Many of the finer pieces are bought by wealthier residents who feel it worthwhile to support the 'arty' colony in their midst. They rather like the idea of living in a slightly 'bohemian' community: it impresses visitors. One philanthropic bank in Almuñécar, La Caja de Ahorros (Savings Bank), makes a large room available for an art gallery, organising monthly exhibitions. Unfortunately, the name of the generous bank proves rather difficult for foreigners to pronounce. The 'j' in *caja* should come across as a 'clearing-the-throat-before-spitting' sound, and the double 'r' in *ahorros* is rolled. Because not many non-Spanish can get their tongues around those two inflections, the unfortunate bank becomes known as 'The Chamber of Horrors'.

Artists find another way to sell their works. One of their number is chosen to take a selection of paintings to Nerja (which has more tourists) to put on display on the Balcón de Europa. For this, they pick the most arty-looking person they can find, dressing him or her to look every inch a bohemian, Montmartre-style artist, complete with beret and coloured neck-scarf.

Some coming to Spain, perhaps inspired by the beauty of their surroundings and finding themselves with plenty of time on their hands, suddenly discover a creative talent. Retired bank managers, accountants, stockbrokers and civil servants swap pin-striped suits for smocks, bowlers for berets, biros for brushes and set up as artists themselves. Seeing and seizing a golden opportunity, one enterprising English couple jumps on the bandwagon by opening up their house as an 'art academy'. Later, as the business flourishes, they add more rooms and advertise residential holidays.

Setting up as a teacher of English can be a way of lining empty pockets. An act of 1970 makes it obligatory for all Spanish children to attend school from the ages of six to fourteen but, French being the only language on the curriculum, many parents pay for their sons and daughters to have private English lessons. With so many people flocking to this part of Spain, and English being the common tongue, they realise that an understanding of the language will improve their children's chances of securing well-paid employment. As with the 'art academy', it is not long before private schools make an appearance. Teaching becomes big business.

My knowledge of the Spanish language has improved somewhat over the years and, by the early '70s, I find I can communicate quite easily with local people. Only when travelling to other parts of the country do I discover that the jargon I have picked up leaves a lot to be desired. Folk in this part of Andalusia have a reputation for speaking the worst Spanish in Spain. For example, words like *pescado* (fish) come across as *pecao*, and *cogido* (caught) as *coio*.

An English friend, who speaks very good Spanish, having studied the language at Oxford University, comes to stay. While walking along the beach, she hears a fisherman call to me, "*¿Ha' co'i'o pe'ca'o*, Roy?" ("*¿Has cogido pescado?*" – meaning "Have you caught any fish?")

"*No, he co'i'o na'a,*" I reply. ("*No, he cogido nada,*" – "No, I've caught nothing.") The young lady stares. "What on earth was that all about?" She indicates the person I have been speaking with and asks, "Where's he from?"

When I tell her that the man lives in the village, her brow wrinkles. "Then why doesn't he speak Spanish?"

I reckon my lady friend's lack of understanding might equate to an English-speaking Spaniard finding himself in Glasgow, trying to make head or tail of a Gorbals accent.

Somehow, Sven manages to find a way around the difficulties put in his path and continues with his *chambao* throughout the summer. With a couple of busty girls working behind the bar and another to serve at the tables, there is no shortage of customers – men, at least. Their presence pulls in the women – and so on. His own animal magnetism attracts members of the opposite sex to him like moths to a flame. If his sexual prowess matches his skill at just about everything else, this attractiveness is easily understood.

One way or another, Sven further increases the popularity of his beach *chambao*. He comes up with the idea of having a shower installed for customers' use and when the first water-skiers make an appearance on the bay, it is Sven who floats a few weighted buoys on the sea in front of his *chambao* so that powerboats can tie up. His self-professed expertise as a world-class water-skier is put to the test one day. Egged on by those that doubt his ability, he stuns onlookers by speeding around the bay firstly on two skis, then one, and finally, unbelievably, in bare feet! He also proves to be an extremely competent mechanic. Problems with engines, car or boat, are left in his very capable hands and, if spare parts are unobtainable, as they usually are, he nearly always manages to improvise and come up with a clever repair. Doing his utmost to satisfy patrons, he gives them what they want. Hamburgers? English beers? German beers? No problem. He comes up with these and much more. I become a little suspicious of some of the things he provides when I notice that he occasionally keeps private company with Felix. Ah, well!

With summer coming to an end and the weather turning colder, Sven expands his business ventures by leasing an old, disused stable block and courtyard and cleverly transforming the premises into a stylish, late-night club/bar. He calls the venue 'El Keyhole'. Almost immediately, he finds himself up to his elbows in visits from uniformed and non-uniformed officials, all carrying serious-looking portfolios. To everyone's absolute astonishment, he solves his problems once and for all by marrying a pretty young *granadina* called Conchita, and transferring the ownership of both bars to her name. This completely takes the wind out of all the bureaucratic sails, for they know that, as a Spanish citizen, his wife does not need the permits and papers required from a foreigner. Sven's battles with the authorities come to an abrupt end.

Both the *chambao*, which opens at Easter and stays that way until the end of September, and El Keyhole, which carries on right through the winter months, do excellent business. Possibly because of Sven's success, a few more hastily erected *chambaos* appear the following year, nearly all put up and worked by people from the village. Nearly, but not all. The one exception is the Flipper Bar, an enormous affair, dwarfing all others on the beach, run by a German/Swiss couple named Ralf and Thérèse. As these two seem to have no problems with officialdom, it is widely thought that they must have friends in high places. Instead of the traditional construction method of bamboo and leaves, the giant marquee is put together using a framework of steel tubing with canvas sides and top. Standing there, with a large, jolly, blue, dolphin painted on the outside, it looks as though a circus has come to town. Within, the space has been divided into two sections. One consists of the usual bar sector, dotted about with tables and chairs, but the other half intrigues us all. When we look inside we see it is completely empty! We ask Ralf, a fussy little man with a neatly trimmed beard, the purpose of this large area.

"Aha! Iss for weddink receptions. I haff asked many questions in zee village and, do you know, zere is novhere for people to hold weddink receptions. Zat iss vhat iss needed 'ere."

The room is never used. Villagers hold wedding receptions in their own homes or those of relatives. They have no money to spare for the hire of anywhere special. In fact, people who live up in the mountains behind, who are even poorer, find it cheaper to wait until two or three couples want to wed and then ride down to the church in a group with friends and family in attendance. Not only can expenses for any celebrations be shared, but they know it will cost less for the priest to marry them all at once.

The Flipper Bar does not last long. On a particularly windy day, the huge marquee starts flapping about, making loud, whip-cracking sounds and, as the fierce sou'westerly gains in strength, one or two of its guy-ropes either break or pull loose. Before long, the whole structure is bouncing up and down,

Wedding party

looking as though it might break free of its moorings at any moment. Seeing this, people from neighbouring beach bars, including our gang from Sven's *chambao*, rush across to help. By holding onto the side-rigging, two or three persons at a time, we do our best to anchor the Flipper Bar, but our efforts prove in vain. Every time a particularly strong current of air blows in from the sea, it balloons the canvas to such an exent that we are all lifted off our feet. In the end, as each powerful gust hoists the giant kite, and us, higher and higher in the air, we are forced to let go and the Flipper flies skywards in a shower of bottles, glasses, dishes, knives and forks.

Ralf should have learned his lesson, but no: a few weeks after the airborne Flipper episode, he comes up with the crazy notion of mooring a floating platform in the bay, from which refreshments can be sold to thirsty bathers. He has visions of people swimming out to it, climbing aboard and buying a bottle of something or other – overlooking the fact that swimmers are not likely to carry money in their costumes. He does not give up, though, and tries to work out a plan whereby drinks can be consumed on the raft and paid for either before setting out from the beach or at a later date. He goes ahead with his plan but, a couple of days after a boozy launch, a slight squall flips Ralf's floating bar upside down. Bottles of alcohol are fished from the sea for quite some while afterwards. After that, Ralf and Thérèse give up on beach enterprises and move to Almuñécar, where they open a successful estate agency.

The Flipper may have blown away, but beach *chambaos* flourish year by year, keeping pace with the increasing number of tourists and residents moving into the area. Today, in 2003, at least ten of these little shanty-bars stand dotted along the stretch of beach, all managed by village folk, and all doing well.

Sven's relationship with Conchita is not long-term. For the first few years things seem to run smoothly enough. They work at running the bars, are blessed with two fine sons, Sacha and Eric, and generally appear happy together. But gradually, one way and another, things start to go wrong and they drift apart. Sven tells me that he never feels quite 'at home' with his Spanish wife's family. Whenever he goes to stay at their home in Granada he inevitably gets the impression that they look upon him as an 'outsider'. Perhaps, he says, they fear he might whisk Conchita and the children off to Sweden at any time. Some years later, my friend Sven leaves Spain and returns to Sweden. He has, as far as I know, never again been seen in La Herradura. The two bars he instigated continue to operate but are never the same without his involvement. After a while, Conchita sells both.

12

The '70s

In which increased prosperity brings problems, I change address, marry, return to England and hear news of Franco's death.

As more and more newcomers come pouring into the Costas looking for somewhere to buy or build, Southern Spain changes dramatically – visually and culturally. The trickle of foreigners in the '60s becomes a steady stream in the '70s. Eager purchasers from all over the world seep their way into every nook and cranny, invading previously unviolated, sleepy little hamlets all along the coast, changing the way of life there forever. Some come to stay, but many take advantage of the bargain prices on offer and snap up cheap properties to use for holidays. Others, with money to spare, buy more than one, considering it, quite rightly, to be a wise investment. With capital appreciation and potential income from renting, they cannot lose.

In many of these villages, peoples of the same nationality group themselves together to form little colonies. San Nicolás has its fair share of Scandinavians; an estate called Cotobro, between La Herradura and Almuñécar, consists mostly of Germans; the French and Belgians plump for Cerro Gordo; while the English seem to favour properties in and around Nerja.

As well as new residents setting up home in Spain, there's a dramatic increase in holidaymakers, too. Their numbers rise from 3 million in 1959 to 35 million by 1973. Nearly all head south for the sea and sun, of course, but money spent along the

Costas brings material rewards in varying degrees to all parts of the country. In order to satisfy demand from those further south, factories in the north are kept busy stepping up their output of consumer goods such as cars, fridges, washing machines and cookers.

Inevitably, as the people of Spain become wealthier, their behaviour changes. Instead of keeping to the slow, easy-going pace of the last two hundred years, the tempo suddenly increases. Those employed in the hectic construction industry find they not only have to work longer hours but, in some places, even have to forego their customary siesta. Speed is of the essence, for property developers want to jump on the bandwagon. Pickaxes, shovels, hoes, long-handled paint brushes, handsaws, brace and bit – all once so common on building sites – are put aside to be replaced by cement mixers, pneumatic drills and power tools.

Busy restaurants and crowded bars, once so leisurely and laid back, now employ flustered waiters who rush about, trying to satisfy impatient, clock-watching customers, while the slow clip-clop of hoof on cobble has given way to the irritating splutter from 50cc motorbikes, now a common means of transport for young men and women. The older generation are learning to drive shiny new automobiles.

For some reason, this unfamiliar, nerve-wracking hustle and bustle affects Spanish men more than women. The *señoras* and *señoritas* seem more able to cope with the changing life-style and take the novelties of washing machines, dishwashers and refrigerators in their stride.

In the mid-'60s, a hospital in Málaga has to enlarge its psychiatric wing, known as 'the waiters' ward', to cater for an increasing number of male patients. A 1971 survey shows that nine out of ten men suffering from non-chronic mental illness are those from the countryside who have come to work in hotels on the Costas. One reason, it is reckoned, may be the trauma they experience on suddenly finding themselves in such a liberated, emancipated environment. These unsophisticated, ingenuous young people cannot believe their eyes when they see foreigners slipping in and out of each other's bedrooms at night, for they have been brought up in an environment where moral behaviour is very strictly observed and sexual repression very much enforced. Further shocks are in store. By the early '70s, the police have given up trying to stop women wearing bikinis

Development in La Herradura

or shorts, for the government has made it clear that former regulations must be relaxed in order to encourage even more holidaymakers. Although imports exceed exports at this time, the country's balance of payments stays in the black thanks to invisible earnings generated from tourism. Nothing must interfere with the goose that is laying golden eggs. Imagine, then, what a shock it must be for these young country lads to be suddenly confronted by half-naked women running up and down beaches!

Even with these stresses and strains, the attractions of working in the resorts still tempt waves of young people to leave home and head for the bright lights, where they can earn more money and, at the same time, live a more exciting life. With big new hotels being opened up just about everywhere, personnel is becoming increasingly difficult to find, so waiters and chambermaids can always find jobs. This guaranteed work entices so many people away from inland mountain villages that, by the '70s, many end up completely deserted.

Peasant girls working on the Costas may not suffer the mental breakdowns of their male counterparts, but they risk other dangers. Wishing to escape the humdrum existence of their parents, some refuse to contemplate offers of marriage from local lads and, instead, seek out the glitter and glamour of places like Torremolinos and Marbella. Unfortunately, many of them end up with more than they bargain for and return home pregnant but unmarried.

I sit discussing the state of affairs with John one evening. He still regularly moves up and down the coast, practising his trade at some of the bigger resorts and, during his travels, keeps his eyes and ears open. Not much escapes his notice.

"And do you know what happens to these poor kids when they get back home in the family way, mun?"

I shake my head.

"Why, they get kicked out by their parents, that's what!"

He goes on to say that it is 'honour' that forces the family to do such a thing. They cannot permit the condition of their daughter to bring such disgrace upon their family and the village. It may sound harsh, he says, but it happens all the time.

"And what do you think happens to the poor young chick then?"

I have no idea.

"Well, as you can imagine, mun, it's not too easy for a young mother with a baby sucking at her nipple to find anyone willing to give her a job so, unless they can find someone to look after them, they end up on the streets – as prostitutes. After that, either some dirty, drugged-up pimp gets them under his control and makes their life a misery by getting them shagged to death, or they end up in a brothel – you know, mun, one of those places with fluorescent lighting that you see by the side of the road."

I know. These ugly buildings, often displaying the word 'Club' are usually positioned near to petrol stations or *hostales* used by lorry drivers. Although officially banned in 1956, they continue to flourish quite openly. The authorities turn a blind eye, thinking their presence might be responsible for reducing crimes such as rape. The women there are subject to regular medical examination. A great percentage of Spanish youths have their first sexual experience in one of these brothels. In the mid-'60s, an investigation showed that one in twenty-seven of the female adult population worked as a prostitute: 500,000 in total.

"It makes me sick, mun, the way these poor young country kids end up like that! They come down from their little homes in the hills, drawn like moths to the bright lights, mun, with no idea about birth control. They're nearly all virgins when they arrive but it doesn't take long for those bastard draft-dodgers to take advantage of their innocence. I've seen them in action. I know how they go about it, mun. They chat up the girls and accuse them of being old-fashioned, country bumpkins if they refuse to drop their knickers. This sort of talk makes the poor young things want to prove they aren't old-fashioned country bumpkins."

I know how difficult it is for women to get hold of contraceptives. The birth pill can be obtained only on prescription, for remedial purposes. If the doctor makes them available for any other reason, he breaks the law.

The uptight manner in which the plumber speaks of draft-dodgers makes it obvious that his dislike of them and Americans in general has not diminished over the years. Having apparently rid his system of anti-Yank venom for the time being, John sits quietly for a while.

"Since we're on the subject of knocking shops, how about you, Roy? Have you ever indulged?"

Yes, I confess, I have 'indulged', not in Spain itself, but on the island of Gran Canaria. Our ship, *The British Holly*, en route from the Persian Gulf to Liverpool, had docked in the port of Las Palmas and I had accompanied some of my shipmates to a house which had a glowing red light outside its front door. My innocence must have been pretty obvious to the young lady who grabbed my hand as soon as I entered the building and dragged me upstairs to the bedroom. She had a good time with me that night – but I learned a lot! John listens attentively but wants to know more.

"When would that be, mun?"

I count back the years.

"Oh, let me see. That was back in 1953."

"That long ago, eh? Brothels were legal, then. State run, I believe. How old were you, Roy mun?"

I had not long left school. My reply of "sixteen" surprises even John.

Over the course of the next few years, circumstances change my way of life. While strolling along the beach one day, on one of my fuel-hunting expeditions, the antics of Tel inadvertently introduce me to a tall, attractive young lady. Standing by the water's edge, watching the dog doing his best to retrieve a piece of wood from the crashing breakers, she calls to me,

"Is he yours?"

Explaining that he belongs to a friend, I tell her not to worry and invite her for a drink. One thing leads to another and, to cut the story short, we end up husband and wife. In August the following year, 1972, Catharine gives birth to a bouncing baby boy in a Granada hospital, situated very close to a bull-ring. With a *corrida de toros* (bullfight) in full swing on that particular day, our son, Roland, is delivered to loud cries of '*¡Olé!*' After a short spell in England, my wife returns to La Herradura, where we try to settle down to a life of marital bliss in my little house at San Nicolás.

This is not to be. With only one bedroom and one noisy baby, things soon start to become a little fraught at Casa Roy, so when, in 1973, the chance comes along to buy two joined-together houses on the Calle de Don Gonzalo – a street fronting the beach – I snap up the offer at once. The prospect of getting hold of something like this comes as a pleasant surprise for I know how rarely property of this nature comes onto the market. Usually, village houses pass on down the line and stay in the family. These two properties, however, are not owner-occupied. They have been rented out and it is for this reason, I guess, that the owner, José Martín, wants to be rid of them, for many Spaniards are starting to consider letting a waste of time and money.

In his book *Voices of the Old Sea* (1984), Norman Lewis writes that when he first came to Spain in 1948, he found lodgings which offered full board (of a sort) for 5 pesetas (3 pence) a day! Mind you, then, the daily wage for a tradesman amounted to 21 pesetas (12 pence) and a glass of wine cost half a peseta. Rents were still pretty low in 1966. Furnished houses were available for 150 pesetas (£1) per week. In fact, at these rates, many of my friends questioned the logic of buying a property. They may have been right, but I had my heart set on having a place of my own. I wanted somewhere I could decorate and furnish as I chose.

The low tariffs only apply to simple village houses, of course. Grander abodes, with swimming pools and suchlike, overlook-

House on beach

ing the sea, cost considerably more to lease, if one can be found. Such places seldom become available, for most are occupied by their owners all the year round. Finding somewhere to live in the village is no problem. If they have a choice, Spanish owners prefer to let to foreigners, and usually do so on an annual basis. Firstly, £50 for the whole year shows more profit than the £3 per week they get from *granadinos* in the twelve-week holiday periods of summer and Easter, and secondly, non-Spanish tenants cause less hassle with the authorities. By 1973, with foreigners like me willing to buy, more people like José Martín are putting their properties on the market. Consequently, the number available to rent has fallen, and continues to fall, year by year.

In 1936, Franco stipulated that all rents were to be frozen, not only for the immediate occupants, but also for any relative who happens to be living in the house at the time of the lessee's death. This encouraged younger members of a family to move into the house of an aged parent, aunt or uncle with the prospect of continuing the tenancy. Although a new law, introduced in 1964, allowed the charge to be raised in line with the rate of inflation, owners of rented accommodation still ended up with very little return on capital. It all sounds a bit like the Richard Crossman fiasco (see Chapter 3). Figures show that the number of people living in rented properties fell from 50% in 1960 to 30% in 1970 and then to a mere 12% in 1990. Because of this transition from tenancy to proprietorship, Spain starts to become a nation of real estate owners rather than real estate renters and, as such, capitalists rather than communists. Just what the crafty old dictator, General Franco, had in mind!

Obtaining the *escrituras* or title-deeds to Casa Roy had proved sraightforward enough – or so I thought at the time. I simply handed the pesetas over to Antonio and left all the paperwork to him. When a thick booklet of signed and stamped documents came into my possession a short while later, I assumed the house at San Nicolás had been officially registered in my name. Only later, when I come to sell, do I find that this is not quite the case.

However, the purchase of these two beach houses from José proves a different matter. They are, in fact, owned by six members of one family and I am given to understand that a signature from each of them is required to transfer title. So, with José Martín at my side, I make several precarious trips up into the hills behind La Herradura, slipping and sliding along narrow dirt tracks, to collect his relatives and transport them down to the *notario's* office in Almuñécar. There, each one is required to make his or her mark (often nothing more than a thumbprint) on the *escritura*.

All goes fairly smoothly until the last. At the final little homestead, a fat, grumpy woman, who does not seem at all happy at seeing her brother-in law and a foreigner at her door, informs us curtly that her husband is not in residence. I get the impression that José Martín is not at all surprised by this cold reception. Back in the pick-up, he directs me to a broken-down shack where, outside, sits a miserable-looking, scrawny, scarecrow character, surrounded by a herd of bleating, farting goats. José Martín gets out, goes over to speak to him and, after a moment or two of animated, arm-waving conversation, the three of us drive back to the corpulent lady. Almost immediately, a furious, three-way argument breaks out. It turns out that the fleshy one does not want her husband to sell. The squabble becomes so heated at one stage that I fear for the little goatherd's safety. Every time his wife waggles one of her fat fingers under his nose, the poor little fellow cowers back, holding an arm in front his face as if to protect himself from a blow. I think that only the near presence of José Martín and myself saves the terrified man from something rather worse than being shouted at. In the end, his wife, by now very red in the face from all her screaming, stomps out through the back door, leaving him in our company. As we drive off, the sound of loud squawking along with the sight of feathers flying up from behind the house makes it look as though the chickens are having a hard time of it. We take the still trembling husband down to the village, treat him to three large brandies in El Salón and then deliver him to the Almuñécar office, where he adds his mark to the others.

With the purchasing details finalised, I set to and knock the two houses into one, ending up with a palace of a place consisting of three large rooms on the ground floor with four bedrooms and bathroom above. In all, the total cost of buying and refurbishing amounts to £1500.

It does not take me long to find a buyer for my San Nicolás house. As soon as word leaks out that I intend to sell, two or three people show up and ask if they might make an inspection. After a bit of haggling, I agree a price of £2500 with one of them – a Cornishman named Tom Weeton. Then, once again, with him in tow this time, I return to the now familiar *notario*'s office in Almuñécar to sort out the paperwork.

The functionary there, whom I have got to know quite well by now, flicks through the wad of *escrituras* and, with an apologetic smile, looks at me from behind his desk.

"I am sorry, Señor Roy, but it is not possible for you to sell this house to Señor Weeton."

I cannot believe my ears.

"What do you mean? What's the problem? I've paid for it! I've got the receipts here somewhere!"

I start to fish around inside a cardboard folder, but the *notario* holds up his hand.

"I am quite sure you have, Señor Roy, but the house does not belong to you, I'm afraid."

Does not belong to me? What on earth is he talking about?

"Who does it belong to, then?"

The *notario* looks down at the papers on his desk.

"Well, according to these *escrituras*, the property belongs to Antonio Cefa."

Antonio?

"He's the man who built it. He's the one I gave the money to."

The *notario* pushes across one of the typewritten sheets and points towards an official-looking stamp.

"But he did not sign across here."

Then, dabbing his finger at the bottom of another page, he points again.

"Or here."

Luckily, tracking down Antonio is no problem. He apologises for the error, puts matters right and Tom becomes the new, proud and rightful owner of Casa Roy. Quite a few other residents find themselves in the same boat as I when they come to sell their property. Only then do they find out whether it really belongs to them.

Moving out of Casa Roy saddens me. For the past seven years, the little house has been home to plenty of good times. Rolling up the Moroccan rugs brings Patricia to mind and, as the big wooden bed and mattress is lowered down from the balcony, I think back on the pleasure it has given me. When everything has been moved out, I walk around the empty rooms for the last time. No longer shall I be able to sit on the terrace with my charcoal grill or admire the wonderful view over the bay from my bedroom. Ah well! At least there is a large flat roof at my new home. Anyway, I tell myself, Casa Roy is just too small. A family man needs something larger.

Before finally moving out, I throw a farewell-to-the-house party, inviting just about everyone. As more and more people arrive and continue to cram their way inside I wonder at how many can be squeezed into so few rooms. The future owners, Tom and his wife, look on concernedly as the walls start to bulge. All my friends from La Herradura, including many villagers, turn up, as well as the Almuñécar gang – about fifty in all. José Martín arrives with two of his brothers, but there's no sign of the goatherd's roly-poly *señora*.

Pedro, accompanied by Tel, of course, brings with him a very welcome addition to the merrymaking. Known as *los Cortijeros*, this family, four in number are quite often seen at parties. They

Los Cortijeros

come down from a small community that live in a cluster of houses some kilometres back from the coast. Rather like the Appalachian mountain hillbillies in America, these rural folk have developed a distinctive style of music, played on a variety of instruments. One man strums guitar, another plucks at a homemade-looking mandolin, a woman taps and rattles a tambourine and the fourth, a younger man, scrapes the rough side of an *anís* bottle with a coin. This last sound reminds me very much of the sound created by the rubbing-up-and-down of a washboard in the old 'Skiffle' days of Lonnie Donegan. After a few tunes, the young man stops his rhythmic rasping, the woman puts down her tambourine and, while the lilting melody is continued by the other two, mother and son start to hop and skip around in circles, hands above heads. First, they move to the right, then to the left. Their movements are very easy to follow and before long many more of us are joining in. There is something slightly flamenco in the action and later I ask one of the group how long this sort of dance has been practised. The man on the guitar stares at me for a moment and answers, "Forever."

By 1973, all the plots on San Nicolás have been sold and developed, resulting in a pretty cluster of about forty houses sitting on the hill with their red-tiled roofs and white walls linking together like pieces in a jigsaw puzzle.

Antonio and Juan have started a new project farther along the N 340 towards Málaga. They call the new estate San Antonio. Here, though, the houses are spread out in a random fashion for, by this time, Donald has split from his wife Evelyn and moved somewhere else along the coast. Without his influence or discipline, each newcomer ends up buying as many square metres as he or she chooses and erecting a property of their own design. The result lacks the cohesive, intimate feel of San Nicolás.

The years between my arrival in 1966 and the early '70s do not see too many changes take place in La Herradura. Apart from the odd villa built on Punta de la Mona, the completion of

San Nicolás and, later, San Antonio, the village itself has not changed overmuch. A few new shops and beach *chambaos* have opened, it is true, but the explosion in tourism experienced by towns farther along the coast towards Málaga has not yet spread this far east. The dangers of driving the road beyond Nerja may be one reason, but, added to that, no large hotels have yet been built to accommodate the growing horde of sun-seekers. Package deals offered by tour operators in the late '60s provide an all-in week's holiday for as little as £28 but, for those flying into Málaga airport, only larger resorts like Torremolinos, Marbella, Benalmádena and, more recently, Nerja can accommodate the growing number of holiday-makers.

Yet for some of those living in and around La Herradura and Almuñécar, even these slight changes taking place are too much for them to bear. Disgruntled by the increasing number of what they consider the 'bourgeois middle-class' setting up home in the locality, they decide to set off and seek pastures new. Judging, quite rightly, that it will not be long before everywhere else on the coast will become a target for these despised 'materialistic types', they pack their bags and head inland towards the distant hills. Quite a few end up in the Alpujarras region, where they find plenty of uninhabited houses in mountain villages like Órgiva, Pampaneira or Capilleira. Some properties have simply been abandoned by those who moved to the coast to find employment, while others were deserted much earlier, when the 'hunger years' drove their occupants to look for work in the cities. If owners can be traced, these vacant houses can usually be purchased for a few thousand pesetas apiece. One astute man buys a row for next to nothing, lays on a supply of electricity and water, adds a bathroom and toilet and sells them, one at a time, to people on the coast. The purchasers use them to escape the heat of the summer for, at a height of over 1,000 metres, the Alpujarras region offers a much lower temperature. At the same time, their seaside homes can be let to holidaymakers during July and August, bringing in useful extra income.

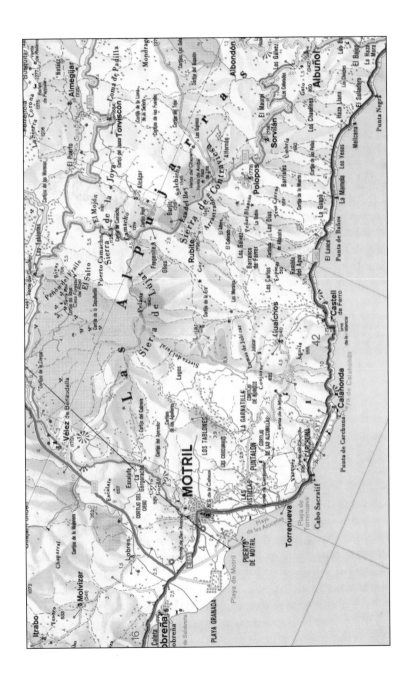

229

I must admit that when I first visit the Alpujarras in the '70s, the wonderful views, crisp mountain air, marvellous colours and complete lack of noise almost tempt me to move up there myself. But I know that, away from the coast, without the sea and my precious boat, I could never be completely happy.

These mountain villages have today, early in the 21st century, become very much a tourist attraction, still partly populated by the self-same groups of hippies that moved there in the early 1970s. Some are now pensioners but, apart from looking older and greyer, their outward appearance has not much changed. Dressed in faded denims, sandals and beads they continue to sit around smoking 'joints', with their hair (if they have any) left long. The 'crafting' and selling of leather goods, learned and practised during their time spent on the coast, has been expanded to include pieces of jewellery, pottery, paintings and rugs, which are snapped up by the coachloads of visitors that arrive daily. (There's nothing new about the rugs, though. They have been made locally since Moorish times.) Unfortunately for those seeking a bit of peace and quiet, Chris Stewart's book *Driving over Lemons*, (1999), which extols the delights of living in the Alpujarras, has brought an abundance of wealthier, more conventional types into the area – although there are still plenty of modern-day 'hippies', known as 'new age travellers', in and around Órgiva. This influx of foreigners, all looking for somewhere to buy and renovate, has led to property prices rocketing and, as happened on the coast, building and development have become big business. Chances of finding a spot where the inhabitants live a simple, rural way of life, as described in Gerald Brenan's *South from Granada*, are becoming rarer. When I paid a visit to the region with Tom Weeton in 2002, he remarked on how much the little whitewashed *pueblos* remind him of fishing villages in Cornwall. With souvenir shops on every corner, tea-rooms and English-style bars serving real ale and Guinness, they resemble places like St. Ives, St. Agnes or Polperro.

Other friends of mine move farther from the Spanish Costas. One writes from a village in Greece to say that the fishing there is just as good, if not better, than in La Herradura – and the cost of living cheaper. And, more importantly, he adds, the country has not yet been invaded by masses of tourists. I ponder the idea of going to visit him and see for myself but, somehow, the thought of my not being able to speak Greek turns me off the idea.

The '70s see some changes take place in Almuñécar. The number of people hanging around Al Quirós at midday remains much the same, but their reason for being there is no longer connected with waiting for the mail to arrive. The shabby building with the Spanish flag hanging from the window has been pulled down and replaced by a brand new Post Office. Now, post is delivered very early in the mornings and can be collected at any time of the day. Those that are left of the old gang, with a sprinkling of newcomers, now gather more out of habit than anything else. Besides, being very central, it makes a good meeting place.

Around the corner from Al Quirós, a late-night disco, Robert's Top, has opened. In the summer months and at Easter, when young people from Granada and Madrid arrive, the place buzzes with activity but, out of season, there are not so many *aficionados* for that sort of music. I paid a visit myself once, but the flashing lights and deafening sound soon drove me out.

La Ventura continues to do well but another late night venue, El Cantador, sets up in competition. With tastefully decorated interior, comfortable seating and reasonable prices, it has all the right ingredients to do well. Unfortunately, its position lets it down for, tucked away down one of the maze of little side streets in the older part of town, it proves difficult for summer visitors to find, and residents, who know its location, are a fickle lot. The proprietors, an English couple called Tan and Cindy, do everything they can to entice customers through the door.

"Oh, what I'd give for a breakfast of bacon, eggs, sausage and beans!" This entreaty can often be heard coming from many of the English and Americans in town, for there is nowhere in Almuñécar that serves that sort of food. With this in mind, El

Maze of little side streets, Almuñécar

Cantador opens early in the morning and Tan and Cindy lay on full English breakfasts. They wait in vain for people to show up. Promises of patronage, made the night before over a few drinks, come to nothing.

Tan and Cindy try again to meet demand by dishing up roast Sunday lunches, steak and kidney pie, and finally curry. A few of us tuck into their dishes with gusto but, after many attempts, the amount of surplus food thrown away each time pledges are broken makes their efforts unprofitable and, after a while, they have to give up.

While the Cafetería Al Quirós remains the favourite midday venue, a new bar, the St. Tropez, now takes over as the 'in' place for early evening get-togethers. It is situated at the far end of the newly-built, beach-front *paseo*, close to the Hotel Mediterráneo. Jean, the Belgian proprietor, has the right idea. He installs comfortable, soft seating around low tables on the front terrace, and keeps the volume of sound and the voltage of lighting to a minimum. An assorted bunch of characters turn up from about 8 p.m. onwards to sit and gossip, play cards, backgammon, chess – or simply relax with a drink and watch the world go by. Some, known as the 'night people', will have just left their beds. From the St. Tropez they will drift on to La Ventura later and stay there until the early hours.

One of the more colourful chess enthusiasts, a white-bearded, aged-looking American, goes by the name of 'Cosmo'. Most evenings, he can be found hunched over a table at the St. Tropez, peering down at the chess board through thick, horn-rimmed dark glasses, dressed in his everyday uniform of blue jeans, khaki T-shirt and denim jacket. He absolutely reeks of 'hippiness'. The leather 'crafters' must rub their hands in glee when they spot Cosmo coming their way, for he is a model customer. Attached to a length of cord dangling from his scrawny neck is a leather pull-string pouch in which he keeps his treasured army-issue lighter and a button-down leather wallet containing his passport, paper money etc. The wide, brass-buckled belt, pulled tight around his narrow waist is adorned with a

Cosmo and Jean outside the St. Tropez

variety of other leather items, including a zip-up purse for loose change, another for his car and house keys, a tube for his multi-gadgeted knife and an oblong container for his packet of cigarettes.

Cosmo showed up in La Herradura in 1968 and moved into one of the three little houses opposite La Tartana. He brought his treasured library of around a thousand books – most relating to philosophy or mysticism. Their content does not much matter to those of us living locally, for we are starved of reading material enough to try anything new. Consequently, almost immediately, this stranger in our midst finds himself badgered by people wishing to borrow. It does not take long for us to discover that Cosmo refuses, point blank, to lend any part of his collection. Those wishing to read his books, he says, are welcome to do so – but only on his premises. On no account will he allow a copy be taken away. As far as I know, the offer is never taken up and it takes only one look inside his front door to understand why. An obsessive hoarder, Cosmo throws nothing away – not even cigarette butts. A large jar of them stands, full to the brim, halfway up the stairs. Never cleaned, his rooms soon become cluttered with odd pieces of junk, dusty old newspapers, empty and half-empty bottles, rotting vegetables and fruit and unwashed clothes tossed about haphazardly one on top of the other. On one occasion, a worried Cosmo asks a friend who works for a pest control company if something can be done about the mice which have invaded his home and are starting to nibble his cherished books. The brave man (who must have worn a gas mask) obliges by placing little oblong cardboard boxes containing poison at strategic places here and there on the floor. A hole at one end allows the mouse to enter, eat the lethal pellets and die – thus allowing both trap and quarry to be collected without problem. Many years later, when Cosmo has departed the property, the same little cartons are found, still in the same places, each containing a mouse skeleton. The weird American survives quite well on a pension awarded him by the US Government for injuries sustained during World War II. We are a little perplexed when we learn that his wounds are to his feet – while he served his time in the Air Force! As far as I know, the riddle has not been solved!

Cosmo is vegetarian. The fact that he is able to stay alive on only a diet of vegetables very much alarms the villagers, who look upon him as some sort of freak. They have never heard of such a thing. In Spanish bars, meat *tapas* will sometimes be deliberately served with his drink so that others present can see for themselves that such a person really exists, for many cannot believe what they have heard and look on incredulously as the dish remains untouched – by him, at any rate. His skinny appearance causes concern. Sometimes, as to a naughty child, he is admonished for his habit.

"Eat! Eat! It will make you strong. Man cannot live without meat."

When eating out, Cosmo normally plays it safe and orders *tortilla de patatas*. In her book *Two Middle-Aged Ladies in*

Andalusia (1963), Penelope Chetwode describes the dish as 'a Spanish omelette which consists of fried potatoes and onions with beaten eggs poured onto them, fried on one side then tossed like a pancake and fried on the other'. She goes on to say that it can be 'leathery or light, according to the hand of the cook'. Cosmo has, over the years, experienced the hands of many a cook and says that he is presently engaged in writing a 'Best Tortilla Guide' for visitors to the Costa del Sol.

One day, as I sit with him at a restaurant in Málaga, Cosmo feels adventurous and decides to try something different for a change. Instead of his usual fare, he asks if vegetable soup is on the menu.

"Sí, señor. We have soup made with vegetables."

"But there must be strictly no meat, you understand, for I am vegetarian and never eat the flesh of animals."

On hearing these words, the *camarero* takes a pace backwards. He looks and sounds as though someone has given him a hard punch in the stomach. With a sharp intake of breath, he stares open-mouthed at Cosmo for a moment, then, pulling himself together, nods his understanding and hurries away. Those at the next table, overhearing what has been said, stop talking and turn in their seats to stare at my weird companion.

In a short while, our bowls are filled to the brim with steaming *estufado* – a typical Andalusian dish consisting of cabbage, onion, beans, potato and – oh dear! – pieces of chicken and pork! Cosmo takes one look and throws up his hands in disgust and despair and turns to the man with the ladle.

"Look! There's meat in this! I told you! You promised!"

The waiter remains unruffled.

"Calm yourself, *señor*. I am a man of my word."

Then, leaning across, he proceeds to spoon the offending lumps of protein from Cosmo's plate and, with a flick of the wrist, deposits them back into the tureen.

Married life carries on quite happily for a year or two. Our beachfront neighbours make my wife and me very welcome.

Many, aware of my past errant ways, think it high time I settle down to family life, for I am no longer footloose and fancy free. Their friendliness and generosity are a bit overwhelming at times, though. By throwing wide hearth and home with the words "*mi casa es tu casa*" (my house is your house) they expect, in return, to be able to pop in to visit us whenever they choose. I think Catharine finds this lack of privacy a bit hard to take, for sometimes I return home to find a bewildered-looking wife sitting at the table, surrounded by half a dozen Spanish neighbours, all talking at once in a language she does not fully understand. Our son has no such problem. Being blond and bonny, he becomes everybody's darling. Due to the Spanish belief that babies must continually be nibbling at something sweet and sticky, he can usually be found sitting on our front doorstep, covered in flies, with a sugary cake or bun in each hand, growing fatter and fatter.

In some ways, living at my present address proves beneficial. Firstly, as the local authorities consider the rental value of the houses in the Calle de Don Gonzalo to be less than that of Casa Roy at San Nicolás, the *contribución urbana* (rates) are lower and, secondly, because the houses are connected to a mains supply, the two 500 litre storage tanks up on the flat roofs are filled with water via the reservoir in Almuñécar. Although the stock may have to last three days or more during dry spells, it is still much better than before. At San Nicolás, sloping roofs prevent the use of storage tanks, so those living on the estate have to rely on water being gravitationally fed down to their homes from the tower depository at the top of the hill. When that runs dry, so do the taps. It is easy to see why village houses are built with flat roofs. Not only do they afford a level surface for water tanks but, at the same time, as there are no gardens, this *terrado* or terrace provides somewhere to hang out washing to dry while gossiping with neighbours.

By 1975, my wife, pregnant once more, decides that, this time, she wants to be back home with her family for the birth of our second child, so flies back with me to England in the Spring, when she is delivered of another son, Peter, in June.

Six months later, on 20 November 1975, an event takes place that changes the way of life for Spain and its people forever. The Head of State, General Francisco Paulino Hermenegildo Teódulo Franco, *El Caudillo,* has really and truly died. I add the 'really and truly' because rumours of his demise have been circulating for the past year. His medical condition has been reported as being anything from *grave* to *muy grave* or even *gravísimo.* People ask themselves, and each other, whether the great man is really and truly dead, or is merely pretending to be, in order to find out how the nation will react to reports of his death. Is that why he has not been seen in public lately? Nobody can be sure of anything. When a news bulletin shows his frail figure on the television screen, everybody wonders whether the pictures are current or are they being shown archive material?

A joke going around at the time tells of Franco's body lying in state in a Madrid cathedral, with sad-looking chiefs of the Guardia Civil, police, government dignitaries and various other officials filing past the open coffin with bowed heads and tears in their eyes. Each mutters a few words as they pass.

"*Adiós,* my leader and mentor."

Suddenly, Franco sits up and glares at one and all.

"Why, where are you all going?"

13

1976

*In which politics are discussed in the barber's shop,
elections take place – and the result is announced.*

Returning from England to a new, Franco-less Spain in February
of the following year, 1976, I note the changes that have taken
place over the last decade as I drive along the N 340 coast road
from the airport to La Herradura. I know that, to the west,
Torremolinos, Marbella and Fuengirola have long lost any
'Spanishness' they once had, but now I am saddened to see that
parts of Málaga are going the same way. Some of the lovely old
houses on the outskirts of the city, with their green-tiled roofs,
ornate brickwork, beautiful wrought iron balustrades and
moulded shutters are being torn down. What a shame! Further
on, El Candado, Cala del Moral and Rincón de la Victoria now
have new banks, estate agents, shiny bars and restaurants lining the main streets. Torre del Mar has become an absolute eyesore. Multi-storied, concrete blocks of apartments loom upwards on each side of the road. I think back yearningly to the
first time I drove through this once pretty little village.

There has been no let-up on the Capistrano estates, which
continue to expand outwards and upwards into the hills to the
east of Nerja. Standing there, lined up, row upon row, the
houses remind me of a line in Pete Seeger's song, *Little Boxes*:
'*all made out of ticky-tacky and all looking just the same*'.

But the Costa del Sol is not the only Costa to suffer ugly
development. Other slices of the Mediterranean coastline are
being ripped apart and developed at the same frenetic rate. The

Costas Brava, Blanca, de la Luz, Dorada and del Azahar are all heading in the same direction, along with the Balearic and Canary Islands. It brings a sigh of relief and gasp of pleasure, then, when I finally round the high point of Cerro Gordo and look down on my beloved La Herradura. Viewed from this angle the bay has not much altered. Passing years may have added a few more private vehicles to the roads and brought one or two new bars and apartment blocks to the seafront, but these innovations have developed at such a slow pace that they seem to have sneaked almost furtively onto the scene. A bit like growing older, I suppose. Lines and wrinkles come about almost unnoticed to those that look in the mirror every day.

Although the seafront may have suffered a few modifications, life in the old part of the village goes on much as before. Mules still clip-clop their way over cobbles, strangers continue to be regarded with suspicion and, although butane gas is available, charcoal burners can still be seen of an evening, glowing like fireflies. However, when walking through the little narrow streets I notice one difference. The former geometric, angular, square silhouette of skyline has now become a mish-mash of aerials, sticking out in every direction. Television has arrived – in a big way. In 1960, only one per cent of Spaniards had TV. By 1970, the figure has jumped to ninety per cent. Any chance of catching a snippet of flamenco wafting out through an open window has gone for ever. Instead, come blaring, full-volume sounds of bull-fighting, sport, *Batman*, *Star Trek*, *Z Cars* and ancient American westerns starring actors like Roy Rogers or Tom Mix, all dubbed into Spanish. I feel sorry for the poor little caged birds that used to chirp away so cheerily. They now sit silently on their perches looking very sad.

But flamenco, the traditional music of Spain, still lives on – after a fashion. Holidaymakers would return home very disappointed if they were not been given the opportunity to sample a click-clack of castanets to the accompaniment of strumming guitar. They need their dose of 'flamingo'. And so, with this in mind, places of entertainment in the more touristy resorts give customers what they want. Flashily-costumed performers are engaged to give a cocktail of stamping feet, twisting, contorted bodies and ear-shattering, shrill notes, in the hope the audience will believe they are being served up the genuine stuff. Those that know the music better, myself included, cringe in horror.

This show-business sort of flamenco has escaped La Herradura – so far. There are not enough non-Spanish around to make it worthwhile. As yet, the majority of visitors are still *granadinos* who can tell the real thing when they hear it and are unlikely to tolerate 'touristy' stuff.

Flamenco, in its true form, comes across as something very personal. It is said that the music comes from the Orient – part Jewish, part Moorish – even part Gregorian. Wherever it originated, it is now very much associated with this southerly part of Spain – and with Roma in particular.

A friend of mine, a German living in a restored and renovated ex-Guardia Civil building on the Cerro Gordo, invites me to a party where, he promises, there will be true flamenco. The real thing, he says.

"Zey kom down from Granada, Roy. Zere will be none of zis 'turística' shit, I tell you."

At 2 a.m. a beaten-up van pulls up in front of the German's house and out jump five mahogany-skinned characters decked out in the theatrical sort of costume expected of flamenco types. The two men wear loose, white, open-necked shirts and tight black trousers and three women have on wide, springy, low-cut, multi-coloured dresses. Each has circles of gold hanging from the earlobes. As they make their way towards a prepared little wooden stage, one of the men sidles across to me.

"Hiya, Roy! What you doin' 'ere then?"

I am astounded to see before me somebody I knew in England.

"Jingles!"

"Shush! Keep yer voice down, Roy. Don't let on who I am, will yer? They'll want their money back!"

Jingles may not be a true Romany, but looks every inch the part. He is reckoned, even by the Spanish, to be a very fine *guitarrista*.

One local man, employed as gardener at San Nicolás, can, quite often in the quiet of the day, be heard singing flamenco as he goes about his work. This thin, wasted-looking *cantaor* goes by the name of Manolo *El Ruso*, but why he has been dubbed 'the Russian' remains a mystery, for he has never gone far from the village. The sweet, up and down, rippling, heart-rending, notes have a mesmerising effect. People put aside whatever they are doing to lend an ear to this mournful *cante hondo*, or deep song – for this is the music of the poor South.

A few new bars have opened and closed in La Herradura over the years, but everybody's favourite, El Salón, carries on much as before. Apart from a new tiled floor, a huge TV and an added inside toilet, nothing much else has changed. The place seems to stand in a time-warp, the *clientèle* looking and acting just as they did when I first walked inside, all those years ago, accompanied by Pedro. Dominoes are being slapped down on tables in one corner of the room as earnestly and noisily as ever, while the same sort of characters stand at the bar, cigarette in hand, talking all at once in loud voices. Outside, in the Calle Real, 'pan' pipes can still be heard as the knife sharpener tours the streets. The only difference is that his pedal cycle has been replaced by a *moto* (motorbike).

Manolo, the proprietor of El Salón, now has his son, Juan, to assist him. This serious-faced boy stands behind the counter, smoothly and expertly dishing out *tapas* and pouring drinks. He and his young sister, María, have been helping out with the chores for a number of years. In the past, I have seen the girl giving her mother a hand in the kitchen while Juan collected and washed glasses. Now, though, Juan looks to be working full time. Aged 14, he should, by rights, still be at school, for the 1970 *Ley General de Educación* (Education Law) stipulates that children between the ages of 6 and 16 must receive full-time education. However, the law is not rigidly enforced in this part of Spain for the authorities realise that, in a country where unemployment stands at 50%, it does not make sense for children to stay at school until 16, if they can be useful at home. Most businesses tend to be family affairs and as soon as a child can help out, he or she is put to work. If the bar or restaurant succeeds, their future is assured. Besides, although schools are being constructed as fast as possible, there are simply not enough places to go around. All over Spain, children who turn up to school at the start of term are being told that there is no place for them: classes are full.

Fishing and sugar-cane growing, the two occupations by which villagers once made their living, are, by now, almost completely things of the past. Harvesting cane is no longer profitable and the only fishermen left are those too old, or not fit enough, to be employed on building sites. A few still make the five-kilometre journey out to Las Rocas to try their luck at 'hand-lining' but mostly, especially during the holiday periods, they take paying passengers with them. Outboard motors have taken the place of oars.

The goat routine has not changed at all. At midday, tattered, silent goatherds, loping along with an easy stride, continue to bring their gang of bell-tinkling, bleating goats along the beach road. Their daily programme seems to consist of being led to Punta de la Mona, where they munch away at whatever they like, including prized plants growing in prized gardens, then on to Cerro Gordo, where they do much the same. As they pass bars and restaurants, customers sitting at tables on terraces make sure to retreat inside, for the dust stirred up by fifty or so cloven hooves can be quite considerable. Besides, the smell of goats does nothing to improve the taste of *tapas*.

My first few days are spent at my abode in the Calle de Don Gonzalo, sweeping the rooms and shaking bedcovers free from sand. While I have been away it looks as though half of La Herradura's beach has blown under my front door, and it strikes me that living on the seafront might have its disadvantages as well as advantages. The sight of a layer covering just about everything in sight brings back memories of living above Pepe and Paco's carpentry workshop in Almuñécar, with sand replacing wood dust. After sprucing things up at home, I decide it is time to start on myself, so make my way to the barber's shop.

Ramón still maintains his monopoly when it comes to barbering. His salon remains the best place in town to catch up on football news or receive word of any scandalous behaviour in the neighbourhood. However, the death of Franco in November 1975 gives the little debating society that gathers each day a new topic. For the last 36 years the dictator's name has hardly ever been heard mentioned in public and, if then, only in a whisper. Now, he, and the future of the country, are starting to be discussed – albeit cautiously.

Pushing open the door of the salon, I see that nothing much has changed. None of those sitting sprawled around the edge of the room are there to take advantage of Ramón's services for, after a round of *¡Holas!* and *¡Buenos días!* from the assembly, I find myself ushered immediately to the familiar chrome and leather chair. A few snips of the scissors later, Ramón starts.

"Well, Roy, what do you think about it all, then?"

"About what?"

"Why, about General Franco, of course! He died last year, you know – in November."

Someone sitting over by the door speaks up. I cannot see who it is.

"How could Señor Roy know a thing like that? He was back in his own country at the time, wasn't he?"

I let it be known that news travels fast these days and that I did hear something of the sort back in England. It is my turn to ask a question.

"What's going to happen now, do you think?"

A tubby, bald-headed individual, seated on a sofa behind me, puts down a newspaper and looks at my reflection in the mirror.

"Well, for one thing, we now have a king back on the throne. You know, like you have a queen in England."

A wiry little man sitting next to him butts in. He has a high, piping voice.

"And now you'll see. When Spain last had a queen – Queen Isabela – our country ruled the world."

The chubby man sounds annoyed at being interrupted.

"Which Queen Isabela do you mean? There were two, you know."

The squeaker turns towards him.

"Well, I don't mean the one that couldn't leave the men alone, do I? She didn't do much for the country, did she?"

He refers to Isabela II, who, in 1833, at the age of three, found herself next in line for the throne. As her father, Fernando VII, died leaving no male heirs, her mother, María Cristina, proclaimed herself Regent and assumed power until her daughter reached an age when she could rightfully be crowned queen. However, Fernando's brother Carlos considered that he, too, had a claim to sovereignty and so instigated a war known as the 'Carlist Wars'. After a long and bitter struggle, which Carlos finally lost, Isabela was made Queen, still only thirteen.

The reference to 'not leaving men alone' comes from her reputation for being a nymphomaniac. Although Isabela's 23-year reign did not bring about any momentous changes, she is remembered for being the person responsible for forming a band of militia to combat widespread banditry: the Guardia Civil.

The scrawny speaker continues.

"No, I meant the other Isabela. The one that kicked out the Arabs. Ah, me! Spain had some muscle in those days."

This time he speaks of an age, 500 years ago, when a different Isabela, Isabela I of Castilla, shared the throne with her husband Fernando II of Aragón. Together, these two monarchs were responsible for bringing about the end of Muslim rule in Spain, when their combined forces took Granada in 1492. The resulting expulsion of the Moors from Europe had a tremendous celebratory impact on the rest of Europe, and I can see the event has not been forgotten. A report in the *Daily Telegraph*, dated 15 November 2003, claims that the passing centuries have not much changed Spanish attitudes towards the Arabs. Opinion polls show that North Africans are considered 'untrustworthy' and 'violent' and 71% of Spaniards say that, of all the foreigners they meet, Moroccans 'arouse the most animosity'. At the same time, they will strongly deny any intimation of descendancy from the Moors, even though the dark olive complexions and jet black hair of those living in the South (along with the fact that Muslims made up three quarters of the population in the 11th century) might suggest otherwise. 2 January is still (in 2003) recognized and fêted in Granada as the Día de la Toma ('handing over' day) – the date on which the Christian monarchs Fernando and Isabela were handed the keys to the city by the Moorish King Boabdil.

These two new Catholic rulers did, indeed, greatly increase Spain's power by bringing the country under united rule for the first time since Visigoth times. Firstly, they increased sovereign rule at home by reducing the power of the squabbling nobility and secondly, they expelled the Jews. Next, they financed Christopher Columbus' expedition to the Indies, made peace with the French and, by uniting forces with them, won several battles against Italy and managed to win Naples in the process. If all this were not enough, by marrying three of their children into the royal families of Portugal, England and Burgundy, and a fourth into the powerful Hapsburg family, they further increased Spanish influence throughout Europe. The man on the sofa might have been correct in thinking that Spain had 'muscle' at that period of its history.

Someone else joins in. I can just about see him in the mirror – a younger person, sitting flopped back in a broken armchair.

"And what about Doña Juana? She became another Queen of Spain."

This newcomer to the debate alludes to one of the aforementioned daughters of Isabela and Fernando. She married Felipe of Austria, one of the Hapsburgs. On Queen Isabela's death in 1504, the sovereignty of Castilla and part of Aragón (which constituted most of Spain) should have been inherited by her son, Juan, or grandson, Miguel. But, after their untimely deaths in 1497 and 1498 respectively, Juana found herself next in line to the throne when her husband, Felipe of Austria, also died, in 1506.

It is the turn of the chubby one again.

"Queen? Her? Juana la Loca? She's not much of an example. She didn't last long as queen. She was mad."

History tells us that the poor lady was indeed unhinged. The death of her husband Felipe caused her so much grief that she took his coffin with her on travels around Spain, taking out the decomposing body from time to time to see if the corpse had somehow miraculously come back to life again. Eventually, after carting the casket around for three years, she buried her beloved husband, or what was left of him, in the cemetery at Tordesillas and took up residence in a nearby palace. There she stayed for the next 46 years. By the end the first two years, it is reckoned that her mind lost track of events, so officials disinterred Felipe's remains and took his body to be laid at rest in the Royal Pantheon in Granada.

Although considered mad, Juana still retained the title Queen of Castilla and so posed quite a problem for the Spanish government of the day. In the end her son, Carlos V, had her declared mentally unfit to rule and took the crown for himself, leaving his mother to spend the rest of her days locked up at Tordesillas.

The young man in the armchair is not finished.

"Mad, eh? You say she was mad? Some say it was so but others were, and still are, not so sure."

Ramón breaks in here. He has been snipping away quietly for much too long.

"*Hombre!* She must have been. Would you keep the body of your dead wife with you for three years? It's bad enough having her around when she's alive!"

This brings a burst of laughter. When that and more talk about the mad, or not mad, queen finally comes to an end, the barber's eye catches mine.

"What's it like in your country, Roy, having a queen making all the decisions?"

Once again, the babble in the room dies down. They all want to hear what I have to say.

"She doesn't make decisions. Well, not important ones, anyway. The elected government does that."

A new speaker joins in – one whose voice I have not heard before. Again, I cannot quite see who it is, for the mirror image does not extend to that part of the room and I dare not turn my head for scissors are snapping too close to my ear. The unknown speaker has a fine accent, and is obviously not from these parts.

"But I understand your Queen Elisabeta to have great powers. Is she not head of your armed forces and your church?"

"Well, sort of."

"And does not your government have to seek her permission before introducing new laws?"

The man certainly knows his business. The others in the room listen attentively to my answer.

"You are correct in what you say, but it is only a traditional thing. Queen Elizabeth doesn't really interfere with decisions made by parliament. She just goes along with what they have decided. The same applies to the church and military." I chuckle.

"It's not like the old days. Can you imagine her leading our army to battle, sitting on her white horse?"

This idea brings more laughter to the salon. All the while this banter has been going on, Ramón has been clipping away. His expression shows him to be a little peeved at being left out of things and, as his scissors continue to click open and shut at a faster and faster rate, I start to wonder how much hair I will have left by the end of it all.

I can well understand why these people are interested in our way of going about things in England, for the rôle of the royal family interests them greatly. Six years before his demise, Franco had promised to restore the monarchy by installing Alfonso XIII's grandson, Juan Carlos, to the throne. Throughout his 36-year rule the dictator maintained that he supported the royal family and that his successor as Head of State would be one of their family. Initially, the thought of an inexperienced person such as Juan Carlos, aged only 37, taking over from a seasoned old hand like Franco, left many Spaniards fearing the worst. They had already seen the result when, two years previously, in December 1973, Franco's trusted friend, Admiral Luis Carrero Blanco, had been handed the premiership so that he might help the young prince when the time came. Six months later, Basque terrorists killed the admiral with a car bomb. Next, Franco named a lawyer, Carlos Arias Navarro, to become Carrero's successor. This rather uncharismatic man found himself in a hornet's nest of violence and civil unrest. Trying to calm things down, he promised a change to the system, but nobody held out much hope that he would be able to do much.

With this in mind, while Ramón, at last finished with his barbering, gives me a final brush down, I turn to the gathering.

"What do you think of Arias?"

Most of the men nod their agreement to the answer.

"Arias? He doesn't give a shit for us and we don't give a shit for him!"

Another calls out,

"That's right! We want to elect our own leader – not have someone like that in charge! We certainly don't want Arias. Why, you don't know where you stand with a man like that. At least with *El Caudillo* you knew where you were."

A fresh voice cuts through the clamour. It belongs to a bespectacled youth, a newcomer to the salon.

"Yes, for sure. You knew where you were with the General all right – up the creek without a paddle!"

His remark brings an instant hush to the room. There is no laughter this time – not even a titter. The assemblage does not find what he says at all funny. One or two remove cigarettes from their lips, chuck the ends on the floor, grind them underfoot, push open the hairdresser's door and hurry off without so much as an *adiós*. Most of those remaining glance down at their shoes for a moment, then look sheepishly and nervously at one another. Even Ramón seems lost for words. He turns and starts sweeping the floor. To the sound of scraping feet and loosened chair springs, the little gang of men breaks up and silently shuffles outside, leaving only the man wielding the broom and myself. It is easy to see that the spirit of General Franco lives on. He may have gone but, as yet, has certainly not been forgotten.

The next six months bring only turmoil and unease in Spain. Instead of introducing or, at least, considering democracy, Prime Minister Arias merely outlines a series of limited reforms, which do nothing to satisfy the demonstrators who have taken to the streets in many parts of the country, demanding a complete change, including autonomy. In the town of Vitoria, five people are killed when police open fire into a crowd of protesters. After 36 years of being told what they can and cannot do by a very dictatorial regime, the people are keen to form their own political parties and start to make decisions for themselves. In May, in an attempt to quell the growing unrest, Arias eventually manages to pass a bill through parliament (the Cortes) which allows the public to hold meetings and demonstrations without the risk of being shot. He finds it no easy matter, though, for the old die-hard Francoists in the assembly, who want Spanish affairs to remain as they were, do their utmost to block legislation and render the bill ineffective.

In July 1976 Arias resigns. He can see nothing but further conflict ahead with both his own ministers and Juan Carlos. Nobody much cares. As a replacement, the King opts for Adolfo Suárez, a good-looking man of 43 who has spent most of his working life serving Franco. At this, people who hoped for change begin to worry. With a man chosen by Franco as king, along with another of his supporters as Prime Minister, they can see the country slipping back into its old dictatorship ways. But they are wrong. Suárez and Juan Carlos combine forces to bring about a bill which allows for a new two-chamber parliamentary system. Despite, once again, strong opposition from the Francoist-filled Cortes, parliament endorses the reform.

Early the following year, 1977, a new cabinet of young Ministers votes out most of the old Francoists, legalises trade unions and allows for the setting up of political parties – including, almost unbelievably, a Spanish Communist Party! Only a few years before, the mere mention of the word 'communist' would have meant trouble. Francoism has certainly come to an end, once and for all.

The effect of such tremendous changes, culminating in an election set for 15 June, bursts upon La Herradura and Almuñécar like a bombshell. These will be the first free elections held in the country since 1920. The prospect rouses everybody, as if from a long siesta. Almost overnight, the villagers throw themselves into a burst of frantic activity. Scrawled slogans appear on the sides of buildings, urging support for this party or that, only to be plastered over during the night by posters of a different political persuasion. These, in turn, are either torn down or covered by some new notice. Foreign home-owners become a little apprehensive as the election draws nearer and we see an increase in hammer-and-sickle slogans, accompanied by the letters 'PCE'. We are well aware that, the year before, in neighbouring Portugal, a new Socialist constitution with a commitment to Socialism had threatened to confiscate private property.

When the first of these Communist symbols appears on the wall of one of the side streets in Almuñécar, the sight so alarms villagers that some refuse to walk past. They simply turn around and head the other way, not daring to get too close to such a profanity. They have been so used to a regime where a person thought to be, in any way, associated with a hammer and sickle sign could look forward to a visit from Franco's *Brigada de Investigación Social*, or Secret Police.

The Al Quirós crowd voice concern. What will happen here in Spain now? The general consensus of opinion seems to be that voters in this part of the country will plump for a 'safe' party. They want no trouble. Many of the older Spaniards I speak to still have vivid recollections of the bloody Civil War and are determined to cast their vote for anything or anyone promising peaceful transition from dictatorship to democracy. They are in no mood for hotheads.

John has his own ideas.

"Don't make judgements from what you see or hear down here, mun. Folk in these parts have never had it so good, what with the tourists and all, but it's very different for a lot of the poor buggers a few miles inland. They don't forget the time when they didn't have enough to eat. Not so long ago, they were literally starving. Did you know, Roy mun, that even today, average earnings in most of Andalusia are half of what they get in other parts of the country?" I admit that I did not.

"Take doctors, for instance. In Jaén – and that's only up the road – there are only 80 doctors for every 100,000 people, while in Madrid there are around 250. That's the sort of thing that gets up people's noses and that's the sort of propaganda the 'Commies' use to get votes. That and the fact that most of the land is owned by the idle, rich, absentee landlords who pay low wages to workers when they need them and don't give a toss for them afterwards."

He stops to wet his whistle.

"Oh, yes, mun. They've a hard time of it in this part of Spain all right, and Suárez knows it. He knows that if there's any trouble in store for him, it'll come from down here in Andalusia."

Of course, just about everybody in town, including the Americans, has his own views about the forthcoming elections. How will Spaniards choose to cast their vote after 36 years of dictatorship, we all ask? For those of us from countries used to democracy, the procedure comes as nothing new, but to the local people the whole idea of voting for a particular political party comes across as something very bewildering. I must admit that the number of different posters, changing day to day, has me confused at times too.

Suárez, although very popular, neither belongs to, nor has, a political party of his own. He solves the problem, in November 1976, by cleverly setting up the *Partido Popular* – a Centralist party that he hopes will attract both the votes of those that favour the old dictatorship and, at the same time, appeal to the ones who do not. At the beginning of the election campaign, posters show his smiling face, urging people to support his party. A little later, after mopping up a few minor political groups, the *Partido Popular* changes its name to the *Centro Democrático*. Up go more posters, now urging people to elect this new party of his. Two months nearer the election, in March, having roped in even more opposition parties, the *Centro Democrático* alters its name yet again. This time it calls itself the UCD, or *Unión del Centro Democrático* and, once more, slogans of different design and colour are pasted onto walls to take the place of the other two. No wonder the villagers are baffled. As well as those of UCD, handbills are given out and placards put up seeking support for the PSOE or *Partido Socialista Obrero Español*, the AP or the *Alianza Popular* (which later also joins Suárez's Popular Party) and the PCE or *Partido Comunista de España*. Most bills are stuck or half-stuck over the tops of the ones underneath, and, as none is completely visible, it is difficult to make out any of them properly. The mish-mash of paper hangs half an inch thick on some surfaces. When the weight becomes too much, the whole lot ends up a sorry mess on the ground. Printers must be having a field day. All the while, other opportunists are nightly running amok, armed with brushes and paint, scrawling, in large letters, the words *Andalucía Autónoma.*

As the date for the election draws nearer, the blurb for the PSOE seems to remain on walls longer than the others, so I guess it is gaining most support in this part of the country.

One day, while enjoying a glass of beer in the bar El Salón, I ask my builder friend, Fernando, whom he intends to vote for.

He appears surprised at such a silly question.

"For the Workers' Party of course. What else?"

I ask his reason for choosing the PSOE.

"Because I am a worker, naturally. Besides, all my friends are doing just that. We like the look of Felipe González. He's from

Seville, you know. As an Andalusian he'll make sure we in the south get a thick slice of the cake."

From what I have seen of his pictures in the newspapers, this young lawyer – even younger than Suárez – looks the part. Handsome and self-assured, he starts to steal the limelight from Arias.

Although the popularity of the PSOE party begins to increase as the election date nears, it does not win the election. The end result, on 15 June, gives Suárez's UCD 165 of the 350 seats in the Lower House, representing 34% of the total. González's PSOE comes a close second, with 121 seats, making their percentage 29%. The Communists manage to scrape together only 20 seats and the Alianza Popular a mere 16.

So, with the elections over, everybody sits back to wait and see what will happen now that two youngish, good-looking men are in the saddle: Juan Carlos as King and Adolfo Suárez as Head of Government. Since a middle-of-the road party has been voted into power, the transition from dictatorship to democracy has come about fairly smoothly. Posters gradually peel away from walls, television goes back to showing animated cartoons, newspapers print any scandal they can dig up, especially if it concerns any of the new ministers, and talk in Ramón's barber's shop returns to arguments about various football teams. However, not all slogans disappear. The painted signs demanding autonomy for Andalusia not only remain, but increase in number. Even today, in 2003, fading lettering can still be seen painted on rock faces beside the N 340 coastal road.

14

1977

*In which my friend John shows a different side to his
nature when he meets with Al*

Foreign property owners in Spain are delighted with the election result. Fears of a Communist, or even ultra left-wing, victory are laid to rest. Franco's death may also account for the increased number of visitors to the Mediterranean coastline in the summer of 1977. The fact that a military dictatorship has finally ended may have persuaded many to holiday in Spain for the first time, for many associated Franco with Fascism and this word brought to mind memories of Hitler and World War II. In point of fact, Franco regarded himself more as a saviour of Spain than a Fascist. Unlike Mussolini, he did not send Spanish soldiers to help Germany during World War II and, when he met Hitler in 1940, he refused permission for German troops to move through Spain to capture Gibraltar.

The flood of tourists ensures that beach bars, restaurants, hotels, shops and estate agents in the major resorts do better business than ever in 1977. Fortunately, sandwiched as it is between a bustling Almuñécar to the east and an even livelier Nerja to the west, La Herradura, which still has limited accommodation, avoids attention from 'package-deal' merchants, who continue to scout for hotels that can cater for planeloads of holidaymakers.

This lack of expansion does not much matter to the people of the village, for *granadinos* commandeer all available 'digs' at holiday times. Even out of season, many come down to the coast on Friday evenings and return home again on Sunday. This has been the custom since long before foreigners arrived. Quite a few restaurants, especially those on the seafront, open up to accommodate these week-end visitors but most close at the end of the summer and re-open only for another short-lived burst of activity at Easter. However, they nearly all throw wide their doors permanently in 1977 to take advantage of the sudden, almost overnight, introduction of fruit machines. Throughout the Franco era, any form of gambling, apart from the national lottery, has been outlawed but now games of chance are once again legalised and the clunk, clunk and occasional tinkle of these newly installed 'one-armed bandits' goes on all day and well into the night. Coins are fed into them by 'hooked' villagers, who just cannot leave them alone. Many play until they have squandered money they can ill afford to lose. In the bigger resorts nearer the airport, casinos and bingo halls are being built.

The N 340 coast road has been vastly improved. JCBs have replaced picks and shovels and these, along with liberal supplies of dynamite, have been used to blast and cut away whole sections of hillsides. The débris is then loaded onto giant lorries and carted away to use as in-fill somewhere else. This straightening out of bends, bridging and adding safety barriers makes the drive to and from the airport at Málaga much safer and faster. At least an hour has been saved in journey time. As well as this, rumours are circulating that tunnelling through the Cuesta del Marchante will soon become a reality, thus eliminating the need to make the long, twisting drive around the Cerro Gordo. The idea of burrowing through 500 metres of solid rock leaves many villagers shaking their heads in disbelief. However, the improvement to the road, combined with the prospect of this new tunnel, encourages more people to move to the La Herradura area. Those living in houses on the estate of San Antonio now outnumber those of San Nicolás and others have bought, and settled into, blocks of flats fronting the beach. When a line of new development starts on the stretch of land between my house and the sea, I decide it is time to sell. Anything high-rise built in front of my property would ruin any sea view I might have and, at the same time, cast a shadow over everything. No longer could I sit on my bedroom balcony and bask in warm sunshine. It does not take long to find a buyer. As soon as word gets around that my house is on the market, a builder from Granada approaches me and offers one million pesetas (£5000). I shake his hand and the deal is clinched. Once the paper-work is finished and the money handed over I bid a sad farewell to my beach house. Almost immediately, the building is demolished and four apartments go up in its place.

With my new-gained wealth I buy a single-storey, bungalow-style property standing on a plot behind Casa Pedro, back at San Nicolás. I refer to it as Casa Roy III. Pedro himself built it with the intention of living there in the summer months so that his main residence, with larger accommodation, could be rented out to holidaymakers and so supplement his income. My Norwegian friend learned the hard way how wise it is to

San Nicolás, showing my first and third houses

257

keep things simple when it comes to house construction. Because the water supply serving San Nicolás is 'hard', pipes tend to 'fur up' with calcium deposits over a period of time and have to be replaced. This new home of mine has all such pipes fitted to the exterior of the walls, both inside and outside, running in a straight line from the *calentador* (water heater) to and through the kitchen and then on to the shower and toilet. Because of this, plumbing problems can be put right without having to knock holes. Simply disconnect the section causing the blockage and replace. The layout of the property suits me fine. It has everything I need: one large living-cum-dining room with a huge fireplace at one end, two bedrooms, shower room, kitchen and toilet, all on one level. Its position, too, is ideal. Tucked away at the edge of the estate, overlooking a field of olive and almond trees, the location of Casa Roy III means that I do not have to contend with nosy or chatty neighbours.

By now, the days when all foreigners recognise each other by sight are all but gone. The little gang of us surviving from what we call 'the old days' clings together in desperation. We do not approve of these changes taking place and make a point of meeting up at some bar or other to group together in a sort of exclusive old boys' (and girls') club. Cocooned in our nest of nostalgia, we speak of the old La Herradura and Almuñécar we once knew. New arrivals are treated with disdain. If one of these alien upstarts happens innocently to interrupt our meetings with a comment of their own, we look down our noses at them. If we bother to reply at all, it is to put them in their place.

"Huh! You don't say! Well, I remember when..." or, "You should have seen it when..."

In retrospect, these episodes remind me very much of my army days when new recruits were treated in much the same way by the 'old soldiers' of the regiment. At times, I feel like following their example and shouting, "Get some in!" (referring to service time) to these new settlers.

By this time, the majority of the foreign contingent – that is, hippies, draft-dodgers and 'beach bums' – have moved on.

Sharp rises in the cost of living have put an end to the heady days when a person could live quite comfortably on a few pounds a week and, besides, the new, more affluent types moving into the area have put paid to the former carefree, happy-go-lucky atmosphere. Draft-dodgers are the last to go. Although the war in Vietnam finished officially in 1975, when the South Vietnamese surrendered after the fall of Saigon, many young Americans stay away from the US until the newly inaugurated President Jimmy Carter announces an amnesty to draft-dodgers in 1977. Slowly at first, then all at once, their absence becomes noticeable. Like old soldiers (which they most certainly were not) they just seem to fade away. I do not remember any of their number giving farewell parties or even saying goodbye. John the Plumber does his best to hurry them along and makes the most of any opportunity to pick off and antagonise stragglers. I remember an incident in The Bicycle Place when we happen to come across one of these imminent decampers. John makes sure to dig his dagger home while he has the chance.

"Finished yer studies then, mun? Doing a bunk, now, are we?"

The young American drinking at the bar does not reply. He knows enough about the plumber to want no trouble.

John leans on his elbow and turns his broken-nose in my direction.

"I bet you a dime to a dollar that this Yankee boy's off to Yankee-land pretty soon, Roy mun. Home to his 'maw' and 'paw'. Isn't it amazing how these boys have all finished their studies at the same time?"

He twists the other way again.

"Wouldn't be anything to do with the end of the war in 'Nam, would it, mun? Or the fact that Carter's letting you off the hook and all that, would it, mun?"

The young man has had enough. He quickly downs his beer and leaves.

But John does not always get away with this line of talk. I learn that new scars added to his already beaten-up face have been put there by members of a visiting American football team who took objection to his non-stop whistling of 'I'm a Yankee Doodle Dandy'.

Although the plumber's sarcastic, antagonistic attitude to Americans has not much changed over the years, I shall never forget one bizarre episode which shows him in an entirely different light.

On this particular evening, he, Felix and I are in La Ventura enjoying a quiet drink together when a blond-headed individual, dressed in blue denim trousers and check shirt, pushes his way in through the swing doors and takes a seat on the nearest barstool. Taking a packet of cigarettes from his top pocket, he lights up and leans forward, forearms on the counter. The stranger intrigues us. No word of greeting has been offered, nor notice taken of anyone else in the room. The man seems to be living in a world of his own. After a moment or two of silent rubbernecking, John asks Felix and me if we know the man. We do not. He does not seem to be one of the growing number of property purchasers moving into the area for these, mostly elderly, retired professional types have their own favoured haunts and steer clear of places like La Ventura. Anyway, their dress is usually a giveaway. Neatly pressed shorts, crisp shirts and, more often than not, socks under polished shoes or sandals. They are easy enough to spot. In an attempt to discover the stranger's nationality, we listen attentively as he raises his head to speak to the young Spaniard behind the bar.

"Oonah Servaysa."

There is no mistaking the accent. This is what John has been waiting for. He strikes home.

"He sounds like a bloody Yankee to me!"

To my surprise, the young man takes no notice. The usual reaction to John's loud Scouse accusation is not forthcoming. The three of us look at each other, mystified. Perhaps he is not a 'Yankee'. Perhaps he cannot understand. Perhaps he is deaf. Only after his drink has been placed in front of him and he has taken a long, slow sip, does our neighbour get down from his stool and make his way, in a leisurely fashion, along the bar to where we are sitting. Then, standing very much at ease, cigarette dangling from the corner of his mouth, clutching the beer glass in one hand and the thumb of the other hooked into the belt-loop of his jeans, he looks us each up and down in turn. I have never, in my life, seen such startling, staring, pale blue eyes. Not very tall and rather puny in build, he puts me in mind of the film star James Dean. (This heart-throb of an actor, a symbol of teenage rebellion, killed in a car accident in 1955 at the early age of 24, is still looked upon as a cult hero for his rôles in the films *East of Eden*, *Rebel Without a Cause* and *Giant*.)

The similarity becomes further enhanced as the young man drawls, "Yow referrin' to me?"

A spaghetti western scenario presents itself. This is where the honky-tonk piano stops in mid-tune and we all reach for our six-shooters, I think to myself. Antonio, the young barkeeper, moves as far away from us as possible, while Felix, sitting nearest to the stranger, empties his glass in one gulp, gets up and hurries away without a word. (He tells us later that he felt a sudden, urgent need to use the toilet.) That leaves just the three of us: John, myself and the unruffled stranger. I keep my mouth shut. John has started all this: let him give an answer. For a few moments nothing happens at all. Then, to my surprise, John inquires, a little more politely this time,

"You're American, aren't you, mun?"

The way they both stay very still, staring into each other's faces, reminds me of a couple of chameleons ready to pounce. The man in the check shirt moves first. Without taking his eyes from John, he slowly and carefully shifts the hand holding the glass from waist level up to his lips and takes another long swig of beer. He then gives a little burp.

"What the heel's that got toe doe wit yow?"

Oh dear, I think, this is the end. Any moment now. Under normal circumstances, I might feel sorry for any unfortunate person, especially an American – and a not very big American, at that – who makes the mistake of speaking to John in this manner. But something about this slight young man's confident, unbothered behaviour makes me wonder if he needs my sympathy. He reminds me of someone I knew in my merchant navy days.

On a night ashore in Panama City, a beefy-looking Swede picked an argument with one of our ship's frail-looking Chinese cooks. The big man had been drinking heavily and was looking for trouble. At first, the inoffensive, quiet Chinaman did his best to ignore the other man and only acted when his persecutor took a swing at him. The action lasted only a few moments. In a flurry of hands and feet it was all over and ended with the unconscious Swede's being carried away by his shipmates. I learned that his opponent, if you can call him that, happened to have been a champion kick-boxer.

Whatever this man facing John may be a champion of, I do not know, but I think it might be wise to step in and try to loosen things up a bit. The idea of putting my hand on the young man's shoulder crosses my mind, but I think better of it.

"Look here, my friend, we don't want to appear nosy, but we know, or at least used to know, quite a few Americans living in these parts, and er, well, we sort of thought you might have had something to do with the war in Vietnam."

The expressionless pale blue eyes turn in my direction. I can read nothing in them at all. They look so completely dead and I begin to wonder if perhaps this baby-faced man has been on some sort of hard drug. Cocaine or heroin, perhaps? He opens his mouth as if to say something, closes it again, looks once more at John, who by this time appears more perplexed than ever, then back to me. As he does so, his vacant look gradually fades, to be replaced by one of anxiety. For a fleeting moment, I get the impression that he might be about to break into tears. Shivering, he glances up at the ceiling, gives a little whistle between his teeth and, finally, with a shake of the head, looks down to the floor. Another thought strikes me. Perhaps we are in the company of some loony. After taking a long, hard draw on his cigarette he looks up again.

" 'Nam. Yeah, reckon being in 'Nam did hev something toe

doe with me headin' this way."

Have I misheard?

"Being in Vietnam? You mean to say that you've been out there?"

His answer comes through a cloud of blue smoke.

"Spent three yeyas in the fuckin' place, man."

After a moment's pause, he carries on.

"Ah've come out heya to trah en track down mah brother. He wuz lucky enough toe get out the country in tahm. Been searchin' all along the fuckin' coast, but now ah heya nooz he's moved on toe Greece or some fuckin' place lahk that."

All the while, John sits there, mouth open, lost for words. He appears flabbergasted. If we have heard correctly, this extraordinary nutcase of a man standing in front of him has actually been to, and returned from, Vietnam. The first of his kind either of us has come across. With raised eyebrows and a broken-toothed smile, the plumber can only splutter, "Can I get you another beer, mun?"

A surprised Felix returns to find the blue-eyed, blond man, John and me sitting huddled together, chatting and drinking away, acting as though we have known each other all our lives. 'Mans' and 'muns' are coming forth in friendlier tones. The newcomer, who now appears perfectly normal, introduces himself as Al and goes on to give a description of his long lost brother, Thorn. We think back to all the Americans we have come across, but none of us, including a now much happier Antonio, can remember seeing the man described. During conversation I make the mistake of asking our new friend about his experiences in Vietnam. Almost instantly, the expression on his face changes. He seems to freeze. The former blank look returns.

"D' ya mind if we talk about somethin' else, man? Ah'm doing mah fuckin' best toe forget all that – not that ah ever will."

However, as time passes and drinks go down, Al adopts a more relaxed mood and does begin to tell us more about himself. We are given to understand that he was drafted into the U.S. forces in 1967, trained as a marine and sent to Vietnam, where he saw plenty of action – including being mixed up in the terrible Tet offensive of 1968.

Back in the States, he tried to settle down. Welcomed home as a hero, he was offered various jobs of work but, like many war veterans, discovered that his experiences in Vietnam had left him unable to stick at anything for very long. After a period of being hospitalised, in the hope that it might help, as he put it, 'git mah head together', he simply 'drifted'. His generous war pension provided enough funds for him to travel around but Al found he couldn't settle anywhere. In the end, after a disastrous short-lived marriage, he decided to come to Spain to find Thorn.

During the course of the evening, La Ventura begins to fill with its usual gang of regulars, many of whom, inquisitive as ever, come across to find out more about the newcomer sitting with us. We ask each of them in turn if they know anything of Al's brother, but have no luck. All the time, an attentive John continues to pamper the young American. Among other things, he makes sure the man's glass is topped up, with instructions that all charges be added to his bill. Those that know the sort of treatment the plumber normally dishes out to 'Yankees' look on in astonishment. Who is this man with the weird eyes, they ask?

When Judy makes an entrance, accompanied by a tubby Italian named Vittorio, John goes across and whispers something in the young lady's ear. The next thing I know, she has left her escort sitting by himself and smilingly comes trotting across the room to join our party, demanding to be made known to our new, good-looking companion. Unfortunately, Felix obliges before anyone else has a chance – with his usual lack of tact.

"Judy! I want you to mit our fren Al. He is American – but no like ze uder, how you say, draft dodgists. He is all alone and looking for nice girl like you."

It is quite obvious that Judy fancies this James Dean look-alike. Her eyes widen, their lids flutter and she puts on her sexiest pose, with her ample breasts almost tumbling out from her low-cut dress. Al, on the other hand, may find her attractive, but does not show it. Giving her a brief nod, he swivels round on his stool to face Felix. From the look on the American's face I see that his condition has taken a turn for the worse again. So does Felix, who realises that his reference to 'draft dodgists' has brought about the change. He looks as though he may need to use the toilet again.

"Listen, man, you're right. It's true ah ain't no fuckin' draft 'dodgist', as you call 'em, but ah tell you straight, man: if ah'd hed any fuckin' sense back in '67, ah surely would hev been, make no mistake."

Without warning, Al's glass crashes down onto the counter. Bunching his shoulders he bangs a clenched fist down onto his knees.

"Whada you cunts know about it, anyways – out heya away from it all?"

He shifts his attention away from a relieved-looking Felix and turns his blazing, searchlight eyes in my direction. He is breathing more heavily now.

"And you, Roy, hev you ever really had a fuckin' hard time in your whole goddam life?"

Thinking back to my guardsman days, I may well have been able to provide him with an example or two, but, in an effort to calm the man down, simply shake my head.

"Naw, ah guessed not. Y'all sit out heya in your cosy little hideout and think you know it all! You don't know shit!"

He moves on to John, who sits, head bowed studying Al's hands. The one holding the glass is shaking so much that beer is spilling onto his jeans.

"And you! You! The big tough guy with a loud mouth! Hev you ever killed anyone? Hev you? Lahk little kids and women?"

John moves his head from side to side, more in sympathy than in answer. For one alarming moment, I think he might be about to receive a slap in the face from the young American, who raises one of his hands, hesitates for a moment, then drops it back onto his lap.

By this time, a few new customers have entered La Ventura

and are sitting at tables dotted about the room. Al's raised voice catches their attention and some stare in our direction. Seeing John keeping company with an American, they anticipate fireworks. The current owner of La Ventura, a tall German named Hans, who took over the premises from Tommy and Jos a few years back, looks worried. He senses trouble ahead.

"Gentlemen. No discord, if you pliss."

Something in Hans' tone of voice or, maybe, his use of the word 'discord' triggers a reaction from Al. The angry, screwed-up expression leaves his face and, to everybody's astonishment, he bursts out laughing. No ordinary laugh. The shrill sound comes in a series of short bursts. After a moment or two, he suddenly stops in mid-laugh, places one of his unsteady hands on my shoulder and the other on John's and starts to rock backwards and forwards on his stool. John and I look at each other, not knowing what to do.

Judy, who seems to have lost her infatuation for the ex-marine, makes her way to the back of the little crowd that has gathered nearby. Catching my attention, she makes a 'round the twist' motion to the side of her head with her index finger. I guess quite a few other onlookers must think likewise. Some look embarrassed at the sight of this young man's distress and shuffle away to other parts of the room. John, on the other hand, shows no sign of nervousness or embarrassment. He just looks very concerned. Raising a large, veined hand up to his shoulder, he gently places it on top of the one already there.

"Take it easy, mun. It's all over now."

A couple of young Spaniards sitting at the bar stare in our direction. As they giggle and whisper amongst themselves, I overhear the word *loco* (mad) mentioned. So does John. His look of tenderness changes to one of anger. Hans, who hovers nearby, nervously polishing a very shiny glass, receives snarled instructions.

"Tell those bastards to shut their face or I'll be down there to shut it for them."

His message is relayed and translated for the benefit of the two youths who, after taking a closer look at John, with me by his side, quickly finish their drinks and depart.

Very shortly afterwards, I follow suit, leaving Al sitting in a sort of stupor, his narrow shoulders encircled by one of John's brawny arms. Felix seems hypnotised by events, unable to move. There does not seem much point in my staying. Besides, at 2 a.m. I am more than ready for bed.

The following morning, suffering a nasty hangover, I drowsily make my way back to Almuñécar, sit myself down on the terrace of the bar Al Quirós and make short work of two cups of coffee. Although most of the usual crowd turns up, there is no sign of John, Felix or Al. An hour's wait later, I track down Hans and ask him what happened after I left. He tells me that a very groggy American staggered out from his bar at around 4 a.m. propped up on each side by John and Felix.

"That man iss very sick in zee het. He need to be – how you say – in zee loonibin."

I never did like Hans and decide to give him something to think upon.

"I'll pass your suggestion on to Al or John when I next see them."

I continue my search, calling at some of the other bars in the hope of finding the plumber or the war veteran, but have no luck. Later in the day, I bump into a droopy, red-eyed Felix, who tells me that the two of them left Almuñécar that morning on the 10 a.m. bus, heading for Málaga. After leaving La Ventura earlier that morning, the three of them had stumbled their way to the Hostal Victoria, collected Al's belongings and then moved on to John's place where they picked up his bag of tools. Then, on to the bar near the bus stop, which stays open all night.

"Why are they going to Málaga?"

Felix shrugs.

"The American say he look for his brusser and John say he go to keep 'im company."

His voice drops to a whisper.

"But I tink I know what ze crazy guy is looking for."

"Tell me."

He tells me.

"Drugs."

As far as I know, never more is John the Plumber's craggy, asymmetrical, scarred face seen in Almuñécar – at least, not by me or any of the others who know him. For years to come, when meeting at Al Quirós or La Ventura, one of the first questions asked is whether anyone has news of John. It all becomes a little like the English custom of bringing up the weather.

"Nice day today, isn't it? Any news of John?"

What happened after the bus journey to Málaga? And why Málaga, anyway? John's almost overnight disappearance from the face of the earth remains a mystery. Perhaps Felix is right about Al. The crazy American may well have been involved in the drug trade and John may have unwittingly become caught up in something nasty. Knowing him as I do, I feel certain he would not shy away from trouble if it came his way and might have found himself in deep water trying to protect his new friend. I shall never forget my good friend, and treasure the good times we shared. If he is still in the land of the living and reads this book, I wish him well. *¡Vaya con Diós*, mun!

One worrying bit of news comes to light some years later. When developers drain a deep, swampy area near Torremolinos, they find at its bottom two badly decomposed bodies, roped together, hands tied behind backs. They have been in the water for such a length of time that identification proves impossible. All they can determine is that they are both male – one tall and heavily built and the other much smaller.

15

The '80s

*In which rampant inflation hits hard, house accessories
make an appearance and property scams take place.*

By the '80s Felix has just about given up on his grumbling about
price rises. He finds it difficult to keep up. Inflation is rife and
nobody can be sure, almost from day to day, just how much anything – even everyday items such as bread, tobacco or booze –
will cost. I remember a cartoon of the day showing an old lady
asking the man behind the counter at an *estanco*, "and how
much is a twelve peseta postage stamp today?"

Partly due to its low starting point, Spain's economy has
grown at a faster rate than any other country in Europe, bringing about a sharp rise in the cost of living. Those like myself,
who came to Spain in the '60s looking for somewhere cheap to
live, find it hard to take on board the rocketing prices. Newcomers might find tariffs reasonable, but we 'old-timers' cannot forget how things were in 'the good old days'. To us, it seems
bizarre that the cost of a glass of beer in 1980 is more than a
three-course meal in 1966. This rampant escalation in prices
hits hardest those who live, or try to live, on a fixed income.
Many find it impossible to make ends meet and are forced to
sell up, lock, stock and barrel, and return to their own countries
– if they can. I feel particularly sorry for those who moved to
Spain from places like Kenya.

When, in 1964, this former British colony gained independence, many white residents fled the country to escape the
ensuing campaign of violence perpetrated by the Kikuyu (and

later the Mau Mau). Finding that this part of Spain offered fine weather and levies which suited their pockets, quite a few of these homeless, disgruntled white Kenyans came to settle locally. Having bought, built or rented a villa, they found it quite possible to carry on the sort of life they were accustomed to in Africa. A maid could be hired to do the cooking, cleaning, washing, waiting at table, baby-sitting etc. for 1000 pesetas (£6) a month or 12 pesetas (7 pence) per hour, while a gardener charged about the same. It suited many of the large, impoverished Spanish families, trying desperately to make ends meet, to farm out a few of their daughters. For one thing, it meant fewer mouths to feed. Gerald Brenan, who went to live in the Alpujarras in the 1920s, tells us in his book *South from Granada* that he hired a live-in servant, María, for the princely sum of one peseta a day. Ten years later, Laurie Lee, writing in *As I Walked Out One Midsummer Morning*, found that girls were still paid only the equivalent of a few pounds a year to see to all household chores. Their duties included, as he puts it, 'keeping the men from the brothels'!

I am one of the luckier ones. Between 1966 and the '80s, rents sent from my house in Twickenham have gone up, so my higher income just about allows me to absorb the rise in the Spanish cost of living. Still, I cannot exactly afford to live a 'life of Riley' and have to spend with care. Food is cheap enough as long as it is bought 'in season'. At certain times of the year, market shelves are piled high with luscious, sweet strawberries (*fresas*), cherries (*cerezas*), avocado pears (*aguacates*), oranges (*naranjas*) and so on. Then is the time to buy. The same applies to vegetables. A portent of what will soon be available can usually be determined by the *tapas* on offer. When handfuls of fresh beans, both green and broad, (*judías verdes* and *habas*) are tossed on to the counter of bars like El Salón, it suggests that the same harvest will soon be in the shops and inexpensive to buy. Fish prices depend on the weather. A prolonged windy or stormy spell keeps smaller boats from putting to sea, so whatever is caught by the larger vessels can prove expensive. At other times, it can be the reverse. Calm weather can result in *sardinas* and *boquerones* being netted in tens of thousands, bringing about a glut and making them very cheap. In the early '60s, not long before I arrived, a freak of nature delivered shoal upon shoal of little fish to the bay of La Herradura. As more and more tried to squeeze their way into the limited space, many were pushed onto the beach where they were scooped up to use as fertiliser on the sugar cane fields.

My Spanish diet keeps me in good health. I am not a food faddist, but the Costa del Sol's fine, sunny weather tempts me to eat plenty of salad and fruit. Who has appetite for a mixed grill on a baking hot day? Stodgy stews, pies and fry-ups are dishes for the colder, damper climates of northern Europe. A further saving to my pocket is helped along by the absence of large heating bills. In a sub-tropical climate where the temperature maintains an average of 18 degrees Centigrade, keeping warm is not much of a problem, although it can feel a bit chilly after sunset in winter. At these times, a portable gas fire may then be necessary for those without fireplaces. The electricity supply is metered, the cost depending, of course, on the amount consumed.

By the early '80s, more and more people are deciding to improve their lifestyle by having a swimming pool added to their estate. With certain favoured parts of the beach becoming a little crowded at holiday periods, many prefer to stay at home and cool off in private. What better than to get up in the morning, step out through the French windows and take a pre-breakfast dip? Or sit out on the patio, gin and tonic in hand, watching the kids splash about? Besides, a pool is a sound investment, adding value to the property. Before long, it comes to the point where many prospective homebuyers will not consider buying, or even viewing, a villa that does not have a pool. As a status symbol, it is a 'must', for 'drinks around the pool' parties are as fashionable as 'drinks on the terrace' parties.

The idea of owning a pool, therefore, seems terrific in theory and teams of specialist builders are waiting in the wings, only

My Spanish diet keeps me in good health

too happy to satisfy the wishes of those that can afford it. By now, the preliminary excavation work is made much easier and speedier by the use of mechanical diggers. Once a crater of the right dimensions has been scooped out from the hard ground, a double wall of bricks is laid around its edge. Then, a mortar mix, reinforced with iron bars running both vertically and diagonally, is poured between the gap. When everything has set hard, surfaces are given a finishing coat of fine cement, known as *griffi*, and finally, the inside of the pool is covered with tiles of choice. The end result looks terrific, glistening there in the hot sunshine, and proud owners cannot wait to have their first swim. It needs only to be filled with water.

It might appear then, considering all the benefits it brings, that a pool would be a great asset. Unfortunately, many find this is not the case. Most properties built away from the village are not connected to mains water and have to rely on a supply piped from nearby reservoirs. As most of these are open to the air, the combination of light and heat quickly encourages the growth of algae, and so, by the time the green-tinted liquid arrives at the swimming pool, spores have already developed and, if left, soon start to stink and attract mosquitoes. The most common solution is to add some sort of chemical, such as sodium hypochlorite or, more commonly, chlorine.

One elderly neighbour of mine at San Nicolás throws a party to christen her sparkling new swimming pool. To be on the safe side when it comes to putting paid to harmful bacteria, she tips a rather larger-than-necessary amount of chlorine into the water. The celebrations start well enough, but, after a while, those who have decided to take advantage of the virgin pool begin to show concern when their carefully cultivated suntans turn milky-white. Showering does not help. The lady's guests return home with dry, white hair, bloodshot eyes and bleached skin.

I once play chess with a man who, having just had a pool installed, finds it impossible to concentrate on the game. His eyes are constantly moving away from the board and turning in the direction of the pool and every time he notices a leaf or insect fall into the water, he has to get up from the table, rush across and scoop out whatever it is with a fine-meshed net.

By 1980, a more powerful electricity supply does, at least, allow for a pump and filter to be fitted. When I arrived in 1966, both La Herradura and Almuñécar had a voltage of 125 and an ampage of between five and seven and, because of this, few electrical appliances could be used. A one-bar fire would blow the fuse and even plugging in an electric drill dimmed the lights.

But although the addition of a pump and filter to the pool helps to clean the water, it brings its own problems. I lose track of the number of times my door has been opened to someone who wants me to help them track down someone who can either repair a defunct pump or supply a new one. My decision to lend a hand depends on the weather. Calm, windless days are reserved for fishing.

In the end, although a swimming pool might seem desirable at the time, many people fill them in. They become disenchanted with the time and money they require.

The more I watch people try to cope with problems and how they worry when things go wrong, the more fully I realise how important it is to keep things simple. Thoreau's *Walden* comes to mind and so does something written by George Orwell: 'Why should people constantly want more, when it would do them more good to better appreciate what they already have?'

I already have a splendid swimming pool at my disposal, larger than anyone else's. Entirely free from chemicals, it costs me nothing in water bills, needs no cleaning and gives no problems with pump or filter. What better than the Mediterranean?

The building boom of the '80s brings with it other innovations. Some residents are persuaded they should take advantage of the free source of energy shining down from above. Solar panels will give them a constant supply of hot water, thus eliminating the need to buy, and struggle with, heavy gas bottles. Before long, ugly, shiny, shimmering glass boxes are seen jutting out from roofs and balconies of villas and apartments. The sun's rays do the trick, all right – only too well! Unfortunately, the initial installations, carried out by inexperienced electricians and plumbers, lead to water becoming so heated that it bursts its container and sends a boiling cascade down over everything, cracking tiles and even bringing down ceilings. Later, better installed solar panels, fitted with thermostats and overflow pipes, do function properly for a while, but any slight damage to one of the fragile elements inside the glass leads to further knocks at my front door. Then, it is off to Málaga or Granada again in the hope of finding someone who can carry out repairs. Sometimes, this proves impossible. Quite frequently, after hunting high and low, we end up being told that the correct component can be obtained only in Madrid or, if not there, perhaps from Sweden! I still see plenty of broken glass panels gathering dust, hanging from the tops of buildings.

With a sharp rise in criminal activities, burglar alarms, too, start to be seen on the walls of many new houses, for break-ins are becoming commonplace. Hooked on drugs, young desperadoes will do anything to get hold of enough money to buy the next 'fix'. Soon after the death of General Franco in 1975, Spain's Socialist administration, to everyone's surprise, legalised the consumption of narcotics. This soon led to 'hard' opiates like cocaine and heroin becoming commonplace, especially along the Costas. By 1980, the sale and distribution of such material had become big business, especially in places like Torremolinos and Marbella, where criminals are known to live. Gangs, competing for control of this lucrative business, soon started fighting each other. Al Capone would have had a field day. One young local man, the son of a good friend of mine, ended up being found shot full of holes on La Herradura beach.

One of Bob Dylan's songs, popular in the '60s, has a line: '*The times they are a-changin*'. His words could certainly apply to this part of Spain. The shiny-hatted brigade, with rifles slung over their shoulders, pistols on hip and sometimes submachine gun in hand, no longer rule the roost. In Franco's day, they could more or less do as they please, but now, in 1980, they have to be careful. The old fort on the beach in La Herradura still acts as barracks, but the Guardia Civil's activities seem to be more concerned with traffic duties than watching out for criminal activity. If the dreaded Secret Police or *Brigada de Investigación Social* still listens to people's conversation in bars, nobody seems to care or take notice, for politics are discussed quite openly. Being caught and sentenced to six years in jail for possessing hashish is no longer a fear, for 'grass', imported from North Africa, can be smoked quite openly now. Ten years on, by 1990, 4 million Spaniards admit to smoking the occasional 'joint' and 1.5 million, one in twenty of the adult population, partake regularly. At the same time, in the same year, a survey shows that heroin addicts account for two out of every thousand of the adult population: a figure twice that of Holland, a country reckoned to have the worst problem in Europe.

As well as drug dealers, other devious types are moving into the area, intent upon finding a way to squeeze as many pesetas as possible from the pockets of gullible homeowners. Before long, the aforementioned pool installers, solar panel salesmen and burglar-alarm consultants are joined by those offering a range of different services, including insurance and financial advice, property maintenance and management (should you want to let), textured wall treatment (paint application that supposedly lasts for ever) and re-wiring specialists (who will remove electric cables from inside the brickwork and put them back encased in a metal conduit). Added to their number, and by far the worst, are the property 'scammers'. There are incidents of properties, rented on a long-term basis, being stripped of furniture and fittings and, worse still, of even being 'sold' while their owners are absent. You must remember that most property seekers coming to Spain have no knowledge of the language, the law or how to go about things. These poor people are ideal victims for the unscrupulous. Imagine the scene: an elderly, retired husband and wife, sitting having a drink on the *paseo*, 'just happen' to bump into a couple who 'just happen' to be thinking of selling their villa. What a lucky coincidence! After being invited for drinks, the newcomers look over their new acquaintances's home, approve of what they see, agree a price and, with a firm handshake, clinch the deal. Leave the paperwork to us, advise the vendors, we know the routine. They certainly do! A ten per cent deposit is handed over, for which, of course, a 'proper' receipt is given.

If that is all the money the husband and wife end up losing, they can count themselves lucky, for they could have forfeited much more. I have known of owners returning to their Spanish home after a long absence, to find it occupied by complete strangers who think they have bought it. To top it all, some rented houses have been sold and let to three or four different people at a time – and then stripped of furniture!

The early '80s also give rise to an increasing number of 'time-share' companies setting up business on the Costas. Their advertising blurb is very persuasive, pointing out that forking out a lump sum of money for a holiday home, occupied only for a month or two in the year, does not make financial sense. Surely it is far wiser to buy solely for the period of intended use? Costs, of course, depend on the time of the year. The scheme works well at first, for many Northern Europeans, wanting to escape their country's cold climate, see logic in buying somewhere in the sun for a month in the winter, when prices are reasonable. 'In season' periods – that is Easter and summer – are, of course, more expensive, but, if the purchaser chooses to rent out the property at these popular times of the year, a good return can be made on capital investment. Once the contract has been signed, purchasers are given a title deed which allows them to occupy or let the apartment for the agreed period, in perpetuity. An added clause, in small print, states that they will, of course, be liable for their share of the general upkeep of the block. When all the months of the year for each of the apartments have been sold, the developers transfer the maintenance side of things to a different company and, before long, time-share owners receive large bills for repairs, cleaning, management, etc., accompanied by a letter pointing out that if payments are not made, their apartment will be forfeited in lieu. As the sum demanded keeps rising and the condition of the apartments deteriorates, most owners eventually stop paying and end up losing their holiday homes. Not all companies run their affairs this way. There are many, I am sure, that operate quite legitimately and give value for money.

My brother happens to be one of these time-share purchasers. In 1980, while on holiday in Torremolinos, he parts with £4,000 and, by doing so, buys the right to use an apartment annually during the month of January. He later discovers that the cost of air tickets to Málaga, taxi to the address, buying food, replacing equipment either broken or taken by the previous occupant, as well as forking out a maintenance charge, adds up to more than the cost of an all-in holiday, for the same month, in a first-class hotel.

It is still pretty difficult to walk anywhere in any of the major resorts without being accosted by time-share touts who hand out leaflets promising a free gift or free food to those willing to visit some new project. Once there, selling methods are so highly charged that many holidaymakers leave the building committed to paying out a large sum of money.

Some, like myself, take advantage of these free offerings. We play the the sales teams at their own game. I quite often scoff a free lunch or dinner, then, when it comes to listening to a lecture on how wonderful time-share can be, let it be known that I already own a property in La Herradura. On hearing this, the disgruntled salesperson shows me the door.

Other companies use other tactics. Some go so far as to fly prospective clients from England on an all-expenses-paid weekend to somewhere like Torremolinos, in the hope of getting them to sign on the dotted line. As a means of journeying to Málaga gratis, I have availed myself of this generous offer on a number of occasions – but people like myself are spotted at once. Single, youngish and able to speak Spanish, I stick out like a sore thumb amongst the other passengers on the 'inspection flight'. They are nearly all retired, elderly couples on their first trips abroad.

On one particular flight, a man of generous proportions squeezes himself into the seat next to mine. He has a heavy gold chain hanging round his neck and, as his chubby face breaks into a professional-looking smile, I notice several gold teeth to match. Thrusting out a fleshy hand, he greets me with,

"Howdee, there! Bill's the name. Put it there, Roy! Got that right, ain't I?"

Bill turns out to be one of the two Texans employed as salesmen. During the flight I tell him that I already own a house in Spain and have no intention of buying another. I do not see any point in pretending otherwise. They can hardly chuck me off the plane. The American does not appear to mind my frankness.

"Gee, Roy, as a mattah of fact, ah guessed straight off you was a freeloader. We get that all the time, y'know. Just one thing though, pal. If any of these other folk ask your opinion, ah'd be much obliged if you could see yo' way clear to tell 'em you like it out in sunny Espanya."

I tell him the truth.

"I'll tell them the way I feel, Bill. As it happens, I do like it out in sunny Espanya."

Bill and his partner, Sam, are good at their job. That first evening, they collect our little party from the hotel, take us for a Spanish meal, which includes copious amounts of wine, then on to a very 'touristy' flamenco show, where everyone claps hands to a different rhythm while singing ¡Viva España! Next day, after a guided tour of the apartments, we are given a splendid buffet lunch, then, after a short siesta, afternoon tea and cakes. Later, at dinner, we find ourselves split into two separate groups, with a Texan sitting at the head of each table. After we have finished eating, Bill, who presides over our party, suddenly announces,

"Kin ah hev your attention for a moment, folks?"

All eyes turn in his direction. I can see that he is doing his best to look embarrassed.

"Ah'm afraid ah got bad news."

His opening words bring worried expressions to faces of many in our party of fifteen. Muttering starts. What can he mean? Has the plane been delayed? Have the Basque terrorists blown up the airport?

"Yessir. Y'all know me. Ah'm normally a man of mah word but…" and here he hesitates just long enough for his audience to catch their breath.

"But, ah'm afraid some you folk are goin' to be unlucky. Ah know I said there was ten apartments comin' up soon, but ah've jist larned that my pal Sam, over there at the other table, has sold seven of them."

He holds up his fat hands in front of him as if to ward off our disappointment.

"Gee, ah'm sorry, folks. Ah don't know what more I kin say to y'all."

The woman sitting next to me turns to her husband.

"You hear that, George! I told you! We've got to act fast! They'll all be gone!"

I have a suspicious feeling that Sam has repeated the same act with his flock at the other table for, by the time the group leaves the following morning, all ten apartments have been sold. From the hotel, I am going to make my way to the bus station in Málaga and catch the bus to La Herradura. The others will head for the airport and back to England. Before parting company, Bill gives me a final golden smile.

"No hard feelin's, pal. We all gotta make a livin'. See y' around."

Nothing much has changed. Only today, 4 July 2003, I read in a local Spanish newspaper that people are still paying deposits and signing legally binding agreements for something they do not really want. After suffering a 'prolonged period of boring "spiel",' the article reports, 'sometimes lasting as long as five hours, the brainwashed customer puts his name to anything, just to get away.'

It goes on to say that the young son of one couple is given a 'free gift' of a 'play-station'. After many hours of high-powered sales talk, they decide they have had enough and want to leave. They are warned that if they do not stay until the end, the 'free gift' will be taken away, so, in order to stop their son screaming, they sign. Another potential sucker, this time an old lady, is not allowed to use the toilet until she too makes her mark on an agreement to buy a machine that will allegedly cure osteoarthritis.

Almuñécar had one estate agent when I arrived in 1966. By 1980 it has four – and all doing good business. They handle not only new properties being built, but also have on their books a constant supply of homes belonging to those wishing to return to their own countries, for many find that their move to Spain has been a mistake. English people miss their family, friends and neighbours, *The Archers*, soaps on TV, a pint or two at the local pub, cricket, the football team they have supported all their life, and, among a long list of other things, even the wet weather! I understand the way they feel. To break away from a familiar lifestyle at the age of 65 and come to live in a country where the food, language and way of life are completely different, is no easy matter. Unfortunately, many of these homesick newcomers seek solace by joining other expatriates at drinks parties. With cheap booze, beautiful sunsets and balmy weather on offer, they find sitting out on a terrace overlooking the bay of an evening, knocking back a couple of large measures of *Larios* gin and tonic, very consoling.

A doctor friend of mine tells me that quite a number of his patients in the Granada clinic where he works are non-Spanish suffering from cirrhosis of the liver. He sympathises with these, mostly elderly, people who find themselves hospitalised in a ward where just about everyone else speaks in a tongue they cannot understand. The TV, radio and announcements are likewise incomprehensible and, if assistance of any kind is required, they find it a problem to make their wishes known to the nursing staff. This isolated, cut-off feeling is further aggravated by the fact that, while native invalids in neighbouring beds are constantly being visited by members of family or friends, they, as foreigners, lie there all alone, looking and feeling pretty forlorn.

Many find it wiser to return to their own countries if they fall ill. For those who can speak Spanish, however, medical care in Spain represents no problem. I myself have frequently driven up to the hospital in Granada, to take my place on a bench outside a designated room, wait in line to see a doctor and receive treatment on the spot.

Once, being in a hurry, I decide to pay a visit to a private clinic in Nerja. There, having given details of my name, age, nationality etc. to a pretty receptionist, I am ushered into a plush-looking room where, behind a large desk, sits a smartly dressed young man. He does not waste time.

"*Buenos días, señor,* do we speak in English or Spanish?"

"What's the difference?"

"Well, *señor,* the consultation will be more expensive in English."

The doctor goes on to explain his reasoning. To learn the English language, he says, cost him money and therefore he has a right to demand higher fees. We speak in Spanish.

Not so long ago, I drove up to Granada to find out what had happened to an English friend, Mike, who had gone to the clinic the week before complaining of pains in a leg. It turned out that, after a thorough examination, he had been diagnosed as having deep vein thrombosis and had been given a bed in a ward shared with five others. On giving his name at reception, I was shown to a large, brightly painted room and found my friend tucking into a splendid lunch, consisting of soup, lamb chops with three different vegetables, cake, cheese and fruit. He stayed two weeks, putting on weight, improving his Spanish and catching up on his reading. On his return to La Herradura, he let it be known that the whole experience had been 'a bit of a holiday'.

16

1980 and Beyond

In which I ask,
Where have all the old times gone,
when me and my mates could share
A drink or two without no fuss
and still have time to spare?
Nobody had white marks on their wrists,
for watches were obsolete.
We didn't live to a schedule
or have appointments to keep.

With Spain now democratised, liberated and common-market-ed, the way of life I knew in the '60s is long gone. To start with, nearly all my old friends have either moved away or passed away. My good friend El Mudo passed away in 1990. The parish church could not cope with the number of people at his funeral and many had to stand outside. He is sadly missed. Jean, the proprietor of the St. Tropez in Almuñécar, also died but his bar on the *paseo* stays open, managed by his wife. Donald moved from his house at San Nicolás and headed for the hills to join the escapees in the Alpujarras. I hear news, from time to time, that he is involved with some new building project or other. Another of the former trio, Juan, has also departed from La Herradura and now lives in Granada. The third member of the team responsible for building the estates at San Juan and San Nicolás, Antonio, quit the development business and took up painting (canvases, that is). He moved to Marbella some while ago but died of cancer in the late '90s. María, his sister, whom I drove to England in the Land Rover with Rosalind, is married to a Dutchman, Luis, and together they run a very successful marine shop, *Windsurfing La Herradura*. For a number of years the bay became a favourite spot for windsurfing. A couple of the 'crafters', seeing a potential for business as the number of holidaymakers increased year by year, opened shops in Almuñécar. One, an Englishman, sold hand-made leather items and the other, an American, dealt in jewellery. They traded successfully for a number of years but, now, unfortunately, at the time of writing, both are dead. Judy, the girl with the loose-fitting shirt, ends up going to Italy with the chubby Italian, Vittorio. They want to start an art gallery in Venice. Tan and Cindy, the English couple who opened and closed the bar El Cantador in Almuñécar, stay living locally long enough for Cindy to be delivered of a daughter, Fabian, at a hospital in Motril (almost coinciding with my son's birth in Granada). By the '80s, Felix says he, too, has had enough. He can't stand the changes taking place and feels that the adventure of living somewhere 'different' has ended.

"Zey are all ze same, now, Roy. Ze English sheet, ze German sheet, ze French sheet. Zey all build sheety leetle houses and drink zere *vinos tintos* on zere sheety terrace." I know what he means.

To my surprise, Felix doesn't head for the Alpujarras but decides to go back to Belgium, where, he reckons, his expertise in flamenco playing will stand him in good stead. On his last day in Almuñécar, I and a few others of the 'old' crowd accompany him to the brand-new bus station. As a farewell gesture, he rids himself of the last of his pesetas by buying a round of drinks in the very modern-looking waiting room *cafetería*. As we sit there in the bright sunshine, eyes screwed up against the dazzling glare reflected from the new, shiny aluminium tables, a sad-looking Felix gives a big sigh.

"Well, my frens, we haf seen ze best days, I tink."

He gives us all a hug and writes down an address in Brussels.

"Pliss to write, my frens. Gif me news of John."

Bodega Francisco

As well as familiar faces, some of the familiar places have vanished, too. The Hole in the Wall, The Bird Place, The Bicycle Place, the original Cafetería Al Quirós have either been pulled down or transformed into something else. (A new Cafetería Al Quirós stands in place of the old one.) The narrow, twisting streets of Almuñécar, with cobbles now replaced by slippery paving stones, have smart bars, restaurants, gift shops and boutiques on each side. Some bar owners have the intelligence not to modernise. One, the Bodega Francisco, situated in the Calle Real and run by Francisco and his wife, Carmen de los Ángeles, has large wooden barrels stacked up against the wall, each having the type of wine contained therein chalked on the outside. Another, Antonio's 'El Choco', in the Plaza de la Rosa, with dusty, mummified fish hanging from the ceiling, also stays much the same. In both establishments, the decision not to alter the décor or change the character of the place, proves profitable, for the 'traditional' feel attracts plenty of tourists. The Hotel Mediterráneo, where Laurie Lee worked in 1936 and then returned to again in 1951, has been demolished and in its place are three beach bars – El Bar Rincón del Mar, Bar Jaime and Bar La Pelillera Pipote. A plaque is supposed to mark the spot where the hotel once stood but I have never been able to find it. The rounded building once known as the Hotel Sexi still exists as a structure but no longer functions as a hotel. It has been turned into private accommodation and now bears the name 'Seximar'. In 1987 the Parque Ornitológico, called the Loro Sexi, was opened. It is now home to 1500 birds representing 120 different species, including parrots, cockatoos, swans, ducks and ostriches. I am pleased to report that the building at the bottom of Avenida de Europa, which I once described as 'flamboyant,' is still standing. The Palacete de la Najarra has been brought back to its former glory and now acts as a Tourist Office.

La Tartana, the inn at the bottom of San Nicolás, has had a chequered history. Several different owners have tried to make a success of the place but, as it is positioned away from the village and on the other side of the N 340, most attempts have failed. Holidaymakers do not want to travel far from the beach area and with only six bedrooms the hotel cannot accommodate many motorists. Those, like myself, who know what a charming place it is, do call in for a drink or two now and then, and resident home-owners who live on the estate above use the premises as a sort of private club. In the '90s, La Tartana becomes known for having a very rude lady proprietor who, at the drop of a hat, might take a sudden dislike to someone and decide to throw everybody off the premises. At other times she and her partner might start an argument, leading to both of them shouting, swearing, raving or even fighting each other. One evening, during this couple's term of management, I take a friend of mine there, warning him what to expect. As we walk up the hill towards the entrance patio, a bar-stool flies out from an upstairs window and smashes to pieces a few yards in front of us. My friend stops dead in his tracks and looks round at me, startled. He sees what I mean.

La Tartana's notoriety did not do it any harm, though. For quite a while people came from far and wide to see the 'show' and were most disappointed if nothing happened.

Property prices in the south of Spain, still cheap by English standards, are rising fast and, because of this, villas or apartments with easy access to the coast are seen as a good investment. The value of a small house, like the one I bought at San Nicolás in 1966 for £1800, would be valued at £40,000 in 1980 and twice that by 1990. Land values in the cities are rocketing, too. Between 1984 and 1988, they increase by 434% in Barcelona and 360% in Madrid. Anywhere offering potential profit (and that includes just about everywhere on the coast) is being exploited. From all over the world the property speculators and developers come, like '49ers from the old Californian goldrush days, keen to stake a claim in the building bonanza of new hotels, apartments, housing estates, casinos, leisure centres, marinas or anything else that might produce dividends. Instead of 'banjos on their knees' these get-rich-quick merchants bring large bundles of pesetas. Rumours start to circulate. Is it Mafia money? Arab oil money? Money from the former USSR? Most believe it to be 'black money' (*dinero negro*) – that is, illegally earned from some racket or other. But who cares? As long as the person on the receiving end gets paid in full, he asks no questions and the authorities show no interest.

Land with sea views is snapped up first and properties thereon purchased (usually for a song) and knocked down to make way for new development. It often turns out that quite a few of the men working on the construction sites are fishermen who once occupied the houses now reduced to heaps of rubble for, with fishing no longer profitable, they have no further need to live near the sea. They and their families are at first happy to relocate, for with money received for their beachfront homes they can move into an apartment equipped with power points in every room, modern plumbing and mains drainage. But it is not long before many regret the move. Gone are the days when friendly chats could be had with neighbours while hanging out the washing on the flat roof. Much the same happened in war-torn London after World War II. As an answer to the housing shortage, the government built high-rise flats to rehouse homeless people. The idea sounded good in theory, but councils soon found that their tenants missed the backyard, over-the-fence natter with neighbours. In both cases, it demonstrates that a rise in the standard of living does not always mean an improvement in the quality of life.

Once on the market, properties looking out over the Mediterranean sell first, for home-seekers prefer to buy something with windows and balconies facing the sea, and for this they will pay top money. With that in mind, companies begin their building project by erecting blocks of multi-storied apartments a hundred metres or so back from the beach and selling them with an assurance that nothing will be built to spoil the glorious, uninterrupted view. Later, though, once the first row has been sold, a second wave goes up directly in front. This underhand practice applies to clusters of houses, as well. Once they see what is happening, many homeowners live in fear that some future development will not only destroy their outlook but, at the same time, devalue their property. There seems to be no form of redress. Angry residents, who know they've been tricked, can complain until they are blue in the face, but to no avail.

Although territory nearer to Málaga and the airport continues to bear the brunt, the rape of village and countryside is gradually spreading its way eastwards towards La Herradura. However, as yet, high-rise seems to have escaped the centre of Nerja. Perhaps the powers-that-be in Málaga have taken note of what has happened elsewhere in their province, especially in Torre del Mar, and do not want Nerja to go the same way. Development on the outskirts of town is inevitably taking place, but anything new being built near the Balcón de Europa is low-rise, so those sitting at tables nearby are still able to escape the long shadows and bask in warm sunshine.

In 'my' village of La Herradura, greedy developers have their eyes focused on the few remaining open spaces that exist among the sugar-cane fields fronting the beach. The old part of the village continues to remain pretty much intact, although building is going on all around it. There seems to be no such

Development on Cerro Gordo – green changing to white

thing as building regulations. The two curves of the horseshoe that jut out into the sea are gradually changing their colour from green to white as properties replace vegetation. One of these headlands, the Cerro Gordo, is home to a rare species of *cabra montés* or *ibex* (wild mountain goat) and I have always been led to believe that, because of this, the wild, rugged part is classed as *zona verde* or green belt, safe from development. But, somehow, authorisation has been given for the trees and bushes to be cut down to make space for hundreds of square, box-like little houses, stuck one on top of the other, looking from a distance like one huge cemetery or *columbario*.

In order to keep the purchase price to a minimum, most new buildings are built with cheap materials. The apartments on the beach, put up in the '70s and '80s, are already a horrible eyesore, with crumbling walls and flaking paintwork. The horseshoe's magic spell, if not yet broken, is showing serious signs of rust.

Marina del Este

La Herradura is not alone. To my mind, the whole of the Spanish Mediterranean coastline is being pulled apart piece by piece, with much of its natural, rugged beauty being destroyed. But, having seen and known how things used to be, and witnessing the transformation, perhaps I am biased.

A marina, the Puerto Deportivo Marina del Este, has been built on the Almuñécar side of Punta de la Mona and a new diving school, Centro Internacional de Buceo, has been established on the beach of La Herradura. With people in wetsuits swimming under the sea and jet-skis skimming noisily over the surface, fishing with *panera* is no longer worthwhile at certain times of the year. The fish have the sense to find somewhere quieter.

But some things remain much the same. The two-peseta glass of beer or wine I knew in the '60s may now cost fifty times that but the ration of *tapas* served with each drink is as copious and delectable as ever. El Salón is now being managed by Juan, the serious-faced boy who helped his father behind the bar in the '70s. He has children of his own, ready to step into his shoes.

Not much has altered at the barber's shop, although an older and greyer Ramón has competition from a new, very handsome-looking hairdresser, Julio, who calls himself a hair stylist and offers the latest fashion in haircuts.

Certain more 'up-market' tourist resorts become a crooks' refuge – Marbella in particular. In 1978, because of disagreement over Gibraltar, the Spanish authorities refuse to extradite British wrongdoers, declaring that, as these people have committed no offence in Spain, they are welcome to stay and spend their time and, more particularly, their loot – ill-gotten or otherwise. Because of its reputation as a safe haven for criminals, the Costa del Sol soon attracts all sorts of villains and, before long, becomes known as 'the Costa del Crime'. In the mid-'80s, some of these law-breakers push their luck too far. Unable to resist an opportunity to make easy money, they foolishly decide to muscle in on the flourishing trade in narcotics – namely, cocaine and heroin. The drugs business has moved up a step from the small-time affairs of the '60s and '70s, when impoverished young people, desperate to make a few extra pesetas, took the 'hippie trail' to Morocco, bought small amounts of marijuana from local touts and smuggled it back into Spain to sell for profit.

On discovering that these ungrateful overseas miscreants, to whom sanctuary has been given, are now involving themselves in unlawful activities, the Spanish authorities show their displeasure by re-introducing extradition. As a consequence, some of those who took part in the famous Security Express Robbery at Heathrow Airport on Easter Monday 1983, are deported. In 1989, Freddie Foreman is sent back to England to receive a sentence of nine years in prison for handling stolen money and, soon afterwards, another member of the gang, Ronnie Knight, is jailed for seven years.

It used to be said that travelling 'broadens the mind' and those that practise it do so in order to 'get away from it all'. This may have been true once, but most of those I meet coming to this part of Spain in the '80s do not want their minds broadened and have no intention of 'getting away from it all'. Quite the opposite, they seek the company of others like themselves who speak their sort of language and eat their sort of food. The Spanish government does all that it can to accommodate these people for, as tourists and residents, they are the ones who spend money. Travellers, on the other hand, are cold-shouldered, being considered an impoverished lot, usually passing through the country on their way to somewhere else.

An old folk song I used to sing has in it the lines:

'Goodbye to the days of the rover,
For there's nowhere to go and there's nowhere to stay;
The traveller's time is over.'

In the early '80s, I decide to escape the new band of tourists and residents for a while and become a traveller myself, before it is too late. My last fifteen years in Spain have been spent on, or near, the coast and I know very little of other parts of the country. I set off on my first walk from Granada to Madrid, accompanied by an American doctor of clinical psychology, Bob Smith. By simply drawing a straight line on a map and keeping to it as much as possible, we come across many little towns and villages not yet spoiled by tourism. Our adventures and, more often than not, misadventures, are related in my book *North from Granada* (The Oleander Press, 2002). The experience is so rewarding that we set off again the following year – only this time starting at Spain's northern border, San Sebastián. The walking bug is hard to shake off. Trekking through parts of Spain off the beaten track opens my eyes to the fact that the way of life I knew in the '60s does still exist in most regions. Many little *pueblos* have cobbled streets, *parrillas* are still used for cooking and mules have not been made redundant. Prices for meals and overnight stops are much lower than on the coast, too.

Later on, our travels take us east from Lisbon, passing through central Portugal and finally, we trek across eastern Spain, inland from Valencia. Each journey covers a distance of approximately five hundred kilometres and, on each occasion, we are given sanctuary in Madrid by a hospitable lady friend, Ann Swanson, who has a holiday home at San Nicolás, La Herradura. Pedro would have loved the name she has given her house. The words on the wall outside read CASA BLANCA!

From mules to motorways, 1966–2000